MW00986700

唐詩三百首

300 Tang poems
translated by
Innes Herdan

FAR EAST BOOK COMPANY

THE THREE HUNDRED TANG POEMS

TRANSLATED
BY
INNES HERDAN
ILLUSTRATED
BY
CHIANG YEE

Published by
The Far East Book Co., Ltd.
www.fareast.com.tw

North America Distributor
Elite Culture Educational Co.
www.eliteculture.com

ISBN 978-957-612-471-6

出版弁言

為了向全世界展現中國詩歌之美，我們出版此書。
能夠使異文化的人領略唐詩之麗，我們不遑多讓。

有唐集古典詩歌精粹於一朝。無論是五言還是七言，無論是古體詩、律詩、絕句抑或樂府，文采薈萃，百花齊放。而豐富的題材益顯出色，有寫實主義與浪漫主義，也有田園詩風與山水詩派；有邊塞詩作的雄壯慷慨，也有抒情寫景的俊朗雅致；有揚厲奇險之風，也有悲憤時局、懷國憂民之作；有淡泊平實的語言，也有瑰麗刻畫的文字。眾詩家們才氣縱橫，從初唐的陳子昂，盛唐的王維、孟浩然、李白、杜甫，到中唐的韓愈、柳宗元、白居易，晚唐的杜牧、李商隱等，名家輩出，震古鑠今，不可勝數。唐代的詩歌極致，實是中國文學的璀璨遺產。

鑑於發揚中國文化，躋身世界文化交流之職志，我們特地費時數年翻譯出版「英譯唐詩三百首」。此書譯者 Innes Herdan 擁有牛津大學英國文學榮譽學位，並且曾於中國武漢大學進修，充分的中文知識令其盡可能保存唐詩的原貌，而其英國文學的素養則使書中的譯文盡可能優美。此外，亦蒙哥倫比亞大學中文系榮譽教授蔣彝先生親繪國畫四十幅共襄盛舉。書中漢字音譯部分均採用漢語拼音。

唐詩寶藏浩瀚似海，值得欣賞領略。期以本書與崇尚中國文學、愛好詩歌文采的您一同分享。

「英譯唐詩三百首」，是我們的責任，更是我們的榮耀。

遠東圖書公司
千禧年謹獻

CONTENTS

Written for Music

Written for Music

Section 3. Five-character 'regulated' verse

Section 4. Seven-character 'regulated' verse

Written for Music

INTRODUCTION

By Chiang Yee

Chinese poetry has been known to the Western world at least since the late sixteenth century, when French and Italian Jesuit missionaries arrived in China. We are told that these Jesuits were excellent scholars who acquired a considerable knowledge of the Chinese language. They helped Chinese scholars to translate a number of European works of science and philosophy into Chinese, and a number of Chinese classics, including poetry, into Latin. The translation of Chinese prose into Latin presents considerable difficulties, but these are slight compared with the difficulties of translating Chinese poetry. Nevertheless, the little that was achieved by the Jesuits in this latter field was pioneer work of real value and importance.

It must be stressed that while it is not impracticable to translate, for instance, an historical narrative, a literary essay, or even a philosophical treatise, from any language into any other, even though precise verbal equivalents may be lacking, the translation of poetry requires not only the finding of foreign words to convey straightforward meaning but also words and rhythms which will release subtleties of feeling and emotion that in the original are bound up with the sound, the etymological echoes, the contemporary or immemorial usages, even the look, of the words or characters. Indeed it is plain that the poetry of one language is never completely realizable in another language.

For anyone who can read, for instance, French or German or English it will always be preferable to read a poem in the original language rather than in a translation however good. But at least French, German and English are all alphabetic languages, using the same 26 letters. Moreover European languages often borrow — or more precisely, appropriate — words and expressions from one another, incorporating them into their own tongue. So, within these languages, it is feasible for a skillful translator to produce a translation capable of conveying a considerable part of the poetic quality of the original and one which is in itself worthy of consideration on its own merits as poetry.

It is true, however, that the most notable examples of translations which are universally acclaimed as poems in their own right, such as Fitzgerald's *Omar Khayyam* or Ezra Pound's *Cathay*, are also much criticized by scholars as being inexact equivalents of the originals they purport to translate. But this fact only makes clear the inherent difficulties. A translation which *is* itself poetry inevitably contains something of the personal spirit of the translator. To the scholar, even the faintest trace of a translator's personality stains the purity of the original. To the perhaps less scholarly lover of poetry, a translation which is a poem will always seem more valuable than what he regards as pedestrian transliteration. The differences of opinion resulting from this problem can never be resolved.

Chinese is not an alphabetic language and the translation of it into any Western language presents unique obstacles. The grammar of Chinese is very simple. There are no articles, no gender, no case, no tenses, and (in poetry) few pronouns or prepositions. Readers of Chinese poetry in translation should remember these peculiarities of Chinese in order to understand what may seem peculiarities in translations.

In view of the extreme difficulty of translating Chinese poetry it is surprising how many volumes of such translations, into English, French, German and numerous other languages, are to be found in the great libraries of the world. Starting with the sixteenth century Latin examples, the number of new translations will be found to increase with passage of time, until the selections and new versions published in the present century heavily outnumber all those published in earlier times. Translated Chinese poetry appears to have a wide appeal; but there remains the puzzling fact that the same poem appears so different in various translations as to leave no doubt that the real equivalence of the Chinese characters has still not been found. The way of endeavour is still very much open.

In China there are a great many anthologies of poetry, but three are outstanding: *The Book of Songs*, *The Songs of Chu* and *Three Hundred Tang Poems*. These three collections illustrate the development of Chinese poetry from the earliest times to the full flowering of the Tang period (A.D. 618-906). *The Book of Songs*, owing to its social and historical as well as its literary importance, early attracted the attention of Western scholars who learned Chinese. The first complete translation of it into English was made by James Legge in 1890; he called it *The Book of Odes*. B. Karlgren made another translation and Arthur Waley a third, under the more accurate title of *The Book of Songs*. The book comprises three hundred and five popular songs dating from the 12th to the 5th centuries B. C. or even earlier. Nothing is known of the author or authors, and the poems do not conform to any of the established patterns of Chinese poetry as that is known today. Moreover, because the pronunciation of Chinese has changed in the intervening centuries, one can be misled into thinking that these ancient songs have no rhyme or meter when in fact the rhyme scheme is perfectly regular (alternate lines) and the lines are of even length (four characters) with very few exceptions. As a rule there are four lines to a stanza, and two, three, or four stanzas to a complete song. Confucius was long reputed to have been responsible for the compilation of *The Book of Songs* but many contemporary scholars doubt this. All three hundred and five songs were drawn from the region north of the Yellow River and a smaller area immediately to the south of it, this being the area administered by the Kings of the House of Zhou in Confucius's time. The songs are typical products of north China — original, simple, plain expressions of human moods.

By the 4th century B.C. China's boundaries had expanded to include the vast area of the Yangtze river valley, where the strong State of Chu became even stronger. This region is very fertile and the life of the inhabitants was more highly developed than that of the northern people. They produced their own type of song, a representative collection of which was compiled under the name of *Chu Ci* or *The Songs of Chu*. Only isolated items from this collection were translated until as recently as 1961, when Professor David Hawkes made the first complete rendering under the title of *Songs from the South*. These poems are not limited, like those in *The Book of Songs* to four characters to the line, some have as many as eleven or thirteen; an even number is the rule. They represent a real development.

After the third century B.C. the various States of China were repeatedly annexed by whichever was militarily the strongest among them. The first Chinese Empire was formed under the House of Qin and extended over a wider area than any of the preceding agglomerations of States. The Qin dynasty was succeeded by the Han dynasty (206 B.C.—219 A.D.), whose territory was pushed far to the south-east and south-west. By the time the Tang dynasty, which was founded in A.D. 618, had fully established itself, China covered roughly the same large area as it does today.

Something like a thousand years separated *The Book of Songs* and *The Songs from the South* from the literature of Tang. During this long period Chinese literature, and especially poetry, did not stand still. The two old anthologies continued to be read, re-read, interpreted and imitated, but there were also always poets who attempted new and more complex forms. In the Han period the employment of five characters to the line was found to be a more rewarding measure, permitting a smoother and more melodious effect and the evocation of subtler human feelings. The rhyme still fell on alternate lines—second, fourth, sixth and so on—but there was no standard number of lines to the poem nor was the old tonal pattern insisted upon. Some Han poems have seven characters to the line. By the beginning of the seventh century a few clearly-defined poetic forms had crystallized: four or eight lines to a poem, each line having five or seven characters; a great range of diction; extreme subtlety of tonal arrangement.

The Tang period is the golden age of Chinese poetry. All subsequent Chinese poetry derives its forms from the creations of this time. The Tang poets explored with the zeal of pioneers all the possibilities of arranging five-character and seven-character lines beautifully and rhythmically. Thus the translation of the complete *Three Hundred Tang Poems* anthology, which includes the most representative, and some of the most beautiful, Chinese poems, is of immense value to those who wish to acquire a general idea of what Chinese poetry really is.

The number of known Tang poets runs into thousands; their output was enormous, and almost every great poet's work was published in one way or another. Yet for almost another thousand years no one seems to have felt the necessity for a selection for common use from this vast field. It was not until the 18th century that an anonymous scholar who signed himself Heng-tang-tui-shi, the Retiring Scholar of the Fragrant Pool, compiled the third standard anthology of Chinese poetry, the *Tang Shl Sun Bai Shou* or *Three Hundred Tang Poems*. Of course there were not lacking critics to complain that the anthology omitted many great poems, but no anthologist escapes this complaint. Readers in general accepted the book, and it has been reprinted in countless editions for two hundred years. Schools have used it all over China, and scholars generally know a great deal of it by heart. However imperfect it may be, it contains representative poems by seventy-seven of the greatest Tang poets.

A fair number of these poems have been separately translated into English and other languages, but it is high time the *whole* anthology was translated. Western readers need a more complete picture of the Chinese world, as well as its poetry, of over a thousand years ago. The makers of existing translations have furnished good reasons for not treating the entire collection; but the fact that some of the poems are very much more difficult to translate than others does not shake my conviction that someone should attempt all of them, for the entire book affords a deeper insight into the life of the people than is obtainable from selected poems.

The present translator, Mrs. Innes Herdan, has worked on the *Three Hundred Tang Poems* for several years, and has striven to make her translations as close to the originals as possible, despite the difficulty of finding equivalent expressions in two such totally different languages as Chinese and English. She holds an honours degree in English Literature from Oxford University, and in 1937 she spent a year at the National Wuhan University of China. Thus she possesses two of the essential qualifications for a poetry translator: her knowledge of Chinese enables her to be faithful to the text, and her study of English literature helps her to bring out the beauty of the original in her own language. I am delighted that she has made the effort to carry through this work and so fill a gap that has existed for a long time in the study of Chinese literature.

Nine of the twenty-seven poets in the anthology: Wang Wei, Zhang Jiuling, Meng Haoran, Li Bai, Du Fu, Li Shangyin, Bai Juyi, Du Mu and Liu Zongyuan, are read more than the others by the Chinese themselves. Of these, four: Wang Wei, Li Bai, Du Fu and Bai Juyi are widely known in translation in many lands outside China. Though some of the English translations of Li Bai are good, no one in my view has yet succeeded in conveying the qualities in which Li Bai excelled—the spontaneous movement and flow of his rhythm and his inspired manipulation of language. For this reason Li Bai's greatness as a poet—and he is one of the greatest Chinese poets, if not the greatest of all—is not yet manifest to readers dependent upon translation. His feeling for nature and for life differ from Wang Wei's, for he was an unconventional, romantic, even 'Bohemian' figure, who never held an official post, while Wang Wei knew public life to the full, comparing it with his withdrawal from the world of affairs upon his retirement.

Du Fu possessed neither Li Bai's unrulable romantic nature, nor Wang Wei's reticence. He was a careful hard-working scholar who tasted all the bitterness of life in war and peace. His poems reveal a deep understanding of human life and suffering, reflecting not only his own experience but that of human beings in general. All Chinese history has alternated between wars and periods of stability, and Du Fu's work has touched the hearts of successive generations right up to the present.

The outstanding quality of Bai Juyi's poetry lies in the use of popular expressions which can be easily understood by simple people as well as by the learned. His choice of words and their arrangement seem effortless and easy, though not quite so forceful as Li Bai's. Bai Juyi had what must be considered a successful life, though he felt dissatisfied at times. He was born too late to know the three poets Wang Wei, Li Bai and Du Fu, but the work of all three influenced him.

One cannot do justice to these great poets in a sentence or two. Each shows some differences in conception, imagery and expression which the careful reader will discover for himself: I think the present translator has had considerable success in preserving and reproducing these differences.

The natural conditions and geographical position of the land in which the Chinese live, shaping their way of life from the beginning, have inevitably left their mark on their poetry. In the valley of the Yellow River, where the earliest group lived, the soil is largely loess—a fine sand blown over from the Gebi desert. Plants grow well there provided there is sufficient rainfall, but sufficient rain by no means always falls, and the five or six months from May to October can be very hot and dry. Rain after drought was, and is, a joy to everyone in the land, and the poets expressed their joy in it in verse. Rain is seldom a subject for poetry in England, but it appears frequently in this anthology, more often in fact than any other natural phenomenon.

The moon too, whose waxing and waning form the basis of the Chinese lunar calendar, is closely associated with Chinese life. It is an important symbol of home life (the full moon), of separation (a waning moon), and of contemplation. It is not easy to contemplate under the sun! The changes of the moon inspire poets to sing of 'reunion' or 'distant longing'. In China's Tang period, communication and transport from one place to another were not easy; every Chinese was a home-bird under the Confucian family system. And each was attached to his home life above everything else. If some member of the family had to leave home, it was his chief desire to return again as soon as he could. Examples of this feeling are certainly not lacking in this anthololgy.

It is curious that the compiler of these poems included the work of only one poetess, and of her work only one poem (p.782), for there were many women writers in the Tang period. But there are numerous expressions in the book of women's agony through enforced separation or ill-treatment, of the loneliness of existence inside and outside imperial palaces, and of 'failure in love' though they all were written by men. Under the Confucian regulations for life, there were many restrictions on men and women, and much suffering resulted. Nothing shows these social ills more clearly than the poetry.

Though China has a very long sea-coast, the Chinese people on the whole have never been seafarers, possibly because their early civilization originated inland, round the central Yellow River rather than along the sea-coast. The wonder and cruelty of the sea have never attracted the Chinese people, no doubt because they concentrated on agriculture and husbandry. There is no seascape in Chinese art, no sea poetry, no sea stories. Unlike the ancient Greeks, the Chinese live on a great land mass, in a temperate zone, and have never experienced the need to cross the sea and make war on neighbouring countries. War, too, has never been glorified in Chinese writings; we have no 'Happy Warriors'. Genghis Khan was sung by the English poet Coleridge but not by the Chinese. China has all too often experienced wars in her long history, but her people, tillers of the soil from time immemorial, and bound by the Confucian principles of a closely-knit family system, have never had a good word to say for those who caused the break-up of family life and the disruption of agriculture. There are many poems *about* war in this anthology, but none in *praise* of it.

Again, although immortals and spirits and their mysterious dwellings appear in these pages, there is no single poem recording the ecstasies of mystical contemplation, as there is in the work of Persian and Indian poets, nor any comparable with the English religious lyrics. China has never had an established state religion, for Confucianism is not a religion in the strict sense of the word and Confucius has never been worshipped as a God. Many forms of religion have had their footing in China at various times, and the Chinese have put their faith in one or the other or in several at once. We do not quarrel over religious dogmas, and there has never been a religious war in China. The human aspect of things remains the most important to the Chinese poet. He sings of the inevitable in life, of the calm wisdom of living in the moment, of the pangs of parting and separation, of human affection and love. On these themes the Tang poets have left us many masterpieces.

Translator's Preface

In the modern translation of Chinese verse, Ezra Pound, we must admit, opened up a new vista. His versions of poems by Li Bai, published in 1915, in the collection *Cathay*, brought the feeling of Tang China so close to our senses that we felt all that life with a new immediacy. But Pound could not read Chinese. He based his work on the notes of Ernest Fenellosa and the 'decipherings' of two other Japanese scholars, and with a poet's liberty, forsook both words and sense when he saw fit. This is one way of translation.

In making my version of this great anthology of Tang poetry, I have followed the other school of thought in trying to keep as close to the originals as it is possible to do in a language so utterly different. I resisted the temptation to expand the lines in order to clarify the meaning, or to change an eastern for a western metaphor, simile, or image, and I looked for ways of reproducing technically some elements at least of the Chinese manner of writing as well as the matter. As an earnest of this attempt, the Chinese text of each poem has been printed together with the English version so that English students of Chinese, and indeed Chinese students of English, can read the two side by side and form their own judgement. It is another way of entering the Chinese world and sharing the Chinese imagination.

A word first about the arrangement of the book. The division into six sections is according to metrical form, and within each section the poets and their work appear to have been arranged more or less chronologically. This is how the eighteenth century Chinese scholar, Heng-tang-tui-shi, sorted his material and although one could think of other ways of grouping it, more in conformity with western practice: by authors, for instance, or subject matter, I have preferred to follow his plan.

The six groups exemplify the six types of prosody practised

by poets of the Tang period. The core of the collection is in the two central sections, the 5-character and 7-character *lü shi* or 'regulated' verse. Each poem is composed of 8 lines, with either 5 or 7 characters to a line. At the time when these poets were writing, the 4 tones on which the Chinese language is based had, for the purposes of poetry, been divided into 2 groups: the *ping* or 'level' tone and *ze* or 'deflected' tone, and the characters were classified under these two groups. Elaborate tonal patterns were devised for the *lü shi* in which the *ping* and *ze* tones alternated and harmonised with one another in definite arrangements. One of the great skills was to manipulate thought and feeling within the rigid patterns without loss of spontaneity.

Parallel with the regularity of tones was one of meaning.

> Blue hills rearing over the north wall;
> White water swirling to the east of the city.

Two adjectives of colour qualifying two opposing elements of nature, a static verb opposite a verb of motion, two adjectives of direction qualifying two 'building' nouns: this kind of verbal balance or duality was obligatory in the *lü shi* and seems to be deeply rooted in the language itself and in the Chinese way of thought so that one can imagine it came naturally to the poet. The very units of language, the characters, are formed of two parts, the radical and phonetic, the one indicating meaning and the other sound. The linguistic expressions are often double-sided in the same way: for example, the colloquial expression for 'thing' is *dongxi*, 'east-west', and for 'landscape', *shanshui*, 'mountain-river'. Still more fundamental is the ancient Chinese philosophy based on the complementary elements *yin* and *yang*, the female and male principles. Not just 'Jack shall have Jill' but a complete system under which all the elements in the universe were subsumed, and only when these elements maintained a balance did human affairs prosper. Thus the development of this involved poetic form with its elaborate system of balanced elements evidently responds to something basic in the Chinese mind.

In content, very many of the *lü shi* are 'occasional' poems: a friend is leaving for a distant appointment; the poet calls on an acquaintance, finds him out and 'leaves a poem'; he has visited some beauty spot and makes a record of his impressions, and so on. The thought may be quite a small one but the expression is perfect.

The poems in the first two sections of the book, the 5-character and 7-character *gu shi* or 'old style' verse, are less demanding. This was the form developed before the Tang period, less rigid in metre and poetic convention, and since the length was not limited to a set number of lines, with room enough to develop an idea or to tell a tale (such as Bai Juyi's famous *Guitar Song*, p.212) The last two sections, of 5-character and 7-character 'cut-shorts', so called because the sense is to be carried on in the reader's imagination after the brief poem of 4 lines ends, could be thought of as epigrams. But epigrams in rather a different way from those in the West, with more emphasis on compression and elegance of expression and less on the neatness of thought. They are like exquisite miniature landscapes or portraits; word pictures.

At the end of each section except the third is a little group of poems called *yue fu*. They were properly songs: poems composed by these poets to old-established airs, and with rather different metrical rules. The difference cannot be conveyed in translation, but it is well to realize the close link between verse and music in China. The earliest surviving collection of verse, the *Shi Jing*, recommended by Confucius for the education of a gentleman, was in fact a book of songs of which the tunes were known long ago. So was the next important body of verse, the *Chu Ci* or *Songs from the South*, less stark and more sensuous, we are told. And when a Chinese reads poetry aloud, which he does to himself as well as to his friends, he intones rather than reads it.

> I hold you in my thoughts this autumn night
> While I stroll in the cool air and chant poetry.

writes Wei Yingwu (p. 594). Indeed the Chinese words for 'recite' *yong* (詠，咏) and *yin* (吟) mean literally 'hum' or 'chant'. To a westerner the musical side is unfortunately missing. We look at the characters and, beautiful though they are, to us they do not sing. Like the young shepherd whom Keats addresses on the Grecian urn, they must

> Pipe to the spirit ditties of no tone.

Now to the method of translation in more detail.

The effect on the ear of the 5 or 7 monosyllables in a line of Chinese poetry is not easy to reproduce in a western, syllabic language. The best method is perhaps to replace the number of characters by a similar number of stressed syllables: this was Arthur Waley's discovery with his 'sprung rhythm'. In fact, as Professor A. C. Graham pointed out in his fine introductory essay to *Poems of the Late Tang* (Penguin, 1965), for the most part a Chinese poem almost translates itself in this way, each character going over into the stressed word in English. I do not think it greatly matters that we are obliged to link these stressed words with unimportant connectives: prepositions, articles, pronouns and so on, for in our natural speech they are so little emphasised that here they do not much interfere with the bare statement of the original.

> (At) dusk (I) come down (the) green mountain

does not greatly differ in brevity of effect from its Chinese equivalent

Mu cong bi shan xia.

What I have aimed at then is to choose the short, non-Latinate English words wherever possible and to restrict the 'grammar words' to essentials, while keeping the same number of stresses in English as there are characters in Chinese.

Chinese verse almost invariably uses end-stopped lines, another feature which contributes to its impressionist character: the words are strung together without links and the lines follow one another like an addition sum. They are like

Big pearls, little pearls, falling on a jade plate

as Bai Juyi wrote of the guitar player's notes. Readers of translations from the Chinese are aware that the lines are self-contained, but it is less often realised that there are stresses and pauses within the lines: usually after the second character in a 5-word line

In middle age/I grew to love the Way,
Growing old/I live by the South mountain.

or after the second and fourth characters

Faint wind/through the fine grass/on the shore,
High mast/and lonely boat/in the night.

In a 7-word line, the pause comes after the fourth character, or after the second and fourth. There are other variations but these are the most common. I have tried, as far as possible, to bring out this rhythm, and have given a rough indication of it by the arrangement of the lines on the page, breaking them where the pause might come. As a bi-product, the look of the page with its long narrow poem helps to suggest the original with its characters running vertically downwards and which, as written by the poet with brush and ink, like an abstract scroll painting, are pleasing in themselves. Paradoxically, for reasons of space, the Chinese text in this volume is not printed in the traditional way but reads horizontally, from left to right, more like a western poem.

Lastly the question of rhyme. Because the great majority of translators have used free verse, it is sometimes supposed that there is no rhyme in Chinese poetry. However, this has always been an important factor. There is no blank verse to be found in Chinese, and free verse has only appeared since the 1920s in imitation of western styles; in Tang times there were strict rules for rhyming. Some early translators, such as Herbert Giles, attempted rhymed versions, and a few more recently as well, but very few came over the hurdle successfully. It is significant that Waley has published only one rhymed translation, *Immeasurable pain* by Li Houzhu, the last Emperor of Southern Tang, and this was a special lyric form (*ci*), with lines of unequal length, more amenable than the regular *shi* form of this collection.

> Immeasurable pain!
> My dreaming soul last night was king again.
> As in past days
> I wandered through the Palace of Delight,
> And in my dream
> Down grassy garden-ways
> Glided my chariot, smoother than a summer stream:
> There was moonlight,
> The trees were blossoming,
> And a faint wind softened the air of night,

For it was spring.

The rhymes here drop easily into place without contorting the expression or forcing the sense, but some of the brevity and poignancy have been lost all the same. To bring in rhyme and keep consistently close to the Chinese wording is hardly possible, but I have tried to hint at it in places by devices like assonance, or by alternating 'strong' and 'weak' endings to the lines, which supply something that the ear expects and are not too hard to come by.

I have added footnotes only where the sense would not be clear without them. The great mass of place-names, for instance, I have not thought necessary to identify unless they held some special significance. Chinese poets, passionate lovers of their own country, and each attached in particular to those regions which were familiar to him, would have a whole range of associations for these names which is missing with us. At best, we can appreciate the sound of them. Additional notes, for the reader or student who would like to understand the poems on a deeper level, are to be found at the back, together with some very brief outlines of the poets' lives.

My special thanks are due to Lanoy Badock who as a literary scholar patiently read and mildly criticised my English versions. Also to Alan White, former Director of Methuen, whose correspondence with me on the problems of poetry translation and the qualities of Chinese poetry in particular, through a whole summer, were an inspiration. Some of his concrete suggestions were very helpful too. Two Chinese scholars, Professor L.S. Yang of Harvard, U.S.A. and Dr. H.C. Chang of Cambridge, England, gave me invaluable information and opinions on points of translation and historical allusions, for which I warmly thank them. My particular gratitude is reserved for Chiang Yee, professor Emeritus at Columbia University, New York, who steadily encouraged me through the several years I spent on this work, is enlightening my readers with his able Introduction, and has enlivened the whole book with his many, delightful illustrations.

I am grateful also to Mr. George Pu of the Far East Book Company for exercising much patience over the preparation for press, and also for agreeing to print the Chinese text, which I consider a most valuable part of the book. My friend, Ling Su-hua, checked this for me in proof, and I thank her too.

Innes Herdan
London, 1972.

SECTION 1

Five-character 'Old Style' verse

DESCENDING ZHONGNAN MOUNTAIN AND MEETING HUSI THE HERMIT WHO ENTERTAINS ME WITH WINE

Li Bai

At dusk
　　I come down the green mountain;
The mountain moon
　　travels along with me.
Looking back
　　over the path I followed —
Blue, blue the mist
　　across the middle hills.

You lead me by the hand
　　towards your cottage;
A young lad
　　opens the wicket gate:
Green of the bamboos
　　invades the dim pathway,
Blue wistaria
　　touches my clothes as I pass.

Happily I cry —
　　"Here is somewhere to rest!"
Delicious wine
　　passes from hand to hand.
Long we chant
　　the "Wind in the pines" song:
The stars are almost set
　　when our singing ends.
My head swims but you are light of heart,
And we have no quarrel with the world.

Looking back
   over the path I followed—
Blue, blue the mist
   across the middle hills.
   卻顧所來徑，蒼蒼橫翠微。

下終南山過斛斯山人宿置酒

李 白

暮從碧山下，山月隨人歸；
卻顧所來徑，蒼蒼橫翠微。
相攜及田家，童稚開荊扉；
綠竹入幽徑，青蘿拂行衣。
歡言得所憩，美酒聊共揮。
長歌吟松風，曲盡河星稀。
我醉君復樂；陶然共忘機。

DRINKING ALONE UNDER THE MOON

Li Bai

Among the flowers, with a whole pot of wine,
— A solitary drinker with no companions —
I raise my cup to invite the bright moon:
It throws my shadow
    and makes us a party of three.

But moon
    understands nothing of drinking,
And shadow
    only follows me aimlessly.
For the time
    shadow and moon are my fellows,
Seizing happiness
    while the Spring lasts.
I sing:
    the moon sails lingeringly,
I dance:
    my shadow twirls and bobs about.
As long as I'm sober, we all frolic together;
When I'm drunk, we scatter and part.
Let us seal for ever
    this passionless friendship —
Meet again
    by the far-off River of Stars!

I raise my cup to invite the
bright moon.
舉杯邀明月

月 下 獨 酌

李 白

花間一壺酒，獨酌無相親。
舉杯邀明月，對影成三人。
月既不解飲，影徒隨我身。
暫伴月將影，行樂須及春。
我歌月徘徊，我舞影零亂。
醒時同交歡，醉後各分散。
永結無情遊，相期邈雲漢。

SPRING THOUGHTS
Li Bai

In Yan, the grass is
    like green silk threads;
In Qin, the mulberry
    droops its tender boughs,
And while you plan
    the home-coming day
My heart
    is already breaking.
O the spring wind is a stranger —
What business has it to
    enter my gauze bed-curtain?

Yan and *Qin* are the names of ancient States, corresponding to present-day Hebei and Shanxi. The husband was evidently fighting on the north-east Border; the wife living far to the west, where spring was already well advanced.

春　思

李　白

燕草如碧絲，秦桑低綠枝；
當君懷歸日，是妾斷腸時。
春風不相識，何事入羅幃。

GAZING AT MOUNT TAI

Du Fu

Oh how shall I describe Tai mountain?
Over Qi and Lu, greenness without end!
Nature endowed it with a mysterious beauty,
On the one face sunlight and the other shadow.
It shakes my heart when the great clouds rise rolling,
If I strain my eyes I can see birds returning to roost.
When I have clambered to the very summit
I shall see all the other hills, so small, in one glance.

When I have clambered to the very summit
I shall see all the other hills, so small, in one glance.
會當凌絕頂，一覽眾山小。

望　嶽

杜　甫

岱宗夫如何？齊魯青未了。
造化鍾神秀，陰陽割昏曉。
盪胸生層雲，絕眥入歸鳥。
會當凌絕頂，一覽眾山小。

FOR MR. WEI, A RETIRED SCHOLAR

Du Fu

In human life, friends so rarely meet —
Their motion like the morning and evening stars.
This night — how wonderful a night,
When we share the same candle-light!
How long can youth and strength remain?
We are turning grey already at the temples.
We discover half our friends have died —
The shock sickens us inwardly.

We little guessed it would be twenty years
Before I came again into your hall.
When last we parted
    you were still unmarried:
Look at you now with this row of boys and girls
Who merrily pay me respect —
    their father's friend,
And ask me where I come from.

Long before the questioning has ended
The children spread a feast for me, with wine:
Spring leeks gathered in the night rain,
Freshly steamed rice sprinkled with millet.
You plead —
    "Another meeting may be hard:
Down with ten cupfuls in a single bumper!"
Ten cups even cannot make me drunk:
I glow with the sense of our old affection.
Tomorrow a mountain will divide us,
Our separate futures
    engulfed by the world's affairs.

贈衛八處士

杜　甫

人生不相見，動如參與商；
今夕復何夕，共此燈燭光。
少壯能幾時，鬢髮各已蒼。
訪舊半為鬼，驚呼熱中腸。
焉知二十載，重上君子堂。
昔別君未婚，兒女忽成行！
怡然敬父執，問我「來何方」？
問答乃未已，兒女羅酒漿。
夜雨剪春韭，新炊間黃粱。
主稱「會面難」，一舉累十觴；
十觴亦不醉，感子故意長。
明日隔山岳，世事兩茫茫！

THE BEAUTY

Du Fu

She is a young woman of matchless beauty
Living unnoticed in a lonely valley.
The daughter of a good family, she says,
But ruined now, with woods and weeds for company.
When battle-havoc raged in the Guan Zhong,
All her brothers met their death there:
What availed their high official rank?
She could not even gather their bodies for burial.
It's the world's way to despise the luckless;
Fortune is like a flickering candle-flame.

Her husband is a fickle, callous fellow
And his new love beautiful as jade.
Even dusk-closing flowers follow their nature;
Mandarin ducks never roost apart.
But he only notices his new love's smile —
How should he hear his old love's weeping?
Spring water runs clear in the hills
But away from the hills it turns muddy.

When her little maid returns from selling her pearls
They pull down creepers to mend the cottage thatch.
She plucks a flower, but not to wear in her hair,
And gathers cypress in armfuls.
Her sky-blue sleeves are thin for the cold air;
In the twilight, she still stands beside the tall bamboos.

天寒翠袖薄日暮倚脩竹
嗚乎竹也

Her sky-blue sleeves are thin for the cold air;
In the twilight, she still stands beside the tall bamboos.
天寒翠袖薄，日暮倚修竹。

佳　人

杜　甫

絕代有佳人，幽居在空谷。
自云良家子，零落依草木。
關中昔喪亂，兄弟遭殺戮。
官高何足論？不得收骨肉。
世情惡衰歇，萬事隨轉燭。
夫婿輕薄兒，新人美如玉；
合昏尚知時，鴛鴦不獨宿。
但見新人笑，那聞舊人哭？
在山泉水清，出山泉水濁。
侍婢賣珠迴，牽蘿補茅屋。
摘花不插髮，采柏動盈掬。
天寒翠袖薄，日暮倚修竹。

DREAMING OF LI BAI

Du Fu

(I)

Of death-partings
    it is better not to speak —
Even life-partings
    are an endless sorrow.
South of the Yangtze is a land of fever-swamps
And you, the exile, send me no news.
But, old friend, you came to me in a dream
To prove you knew of my longing for you.
Though you're caught now in a net
And how have you freed your wings?
I fear it was not your habitual ghost —
The road between
    is so immeasurably long.
When your shade set out
    the maple woods showed green;
As it turned away
    the mountain pass was in darkness.
The setting moon
    shone full on my cottage rafters;
I half believe
    it still lights up your face...

The River is deep and the waves wide —
Don't let a water dragon get you!

夢 李 白

杜 甫

死別已吞聲，生別常惻惻。
江南瘴癘地，逐客無消息。
故人入我夢，明我長相憶。
君今在羅網，何以有羽翼？
恐非平生魂，路遠不可測。
魂來楓林青，魂返關塞黑。
落月滿屋梁，猶疑照顏色。
水深波浪闊，無使蛟龍得。

(II)

Drifting clouds sail by all day
But the wanderer hasn't been back for a long while.
Three nights I kept dreaming of you;
From my close affection
    I understood your thoughts.
You seemed to say, your return was always hampered,
Ruefully complained, the coming was not easy,
Rivers and lakes full of wind and waves —
You feared the oars of your boat
    would be swept away.

You went away then, scratching your white head,
As if defeated of your whole life's purpose.
Official 'caps' and carriages fill the Capital,
You alone feel bitter and dejected.
Who says, Heaven's net has wide meshes?
Growing old, your body is tangled in them.
A thousand and ten thousand years' fame —
A cold and useless thing
    when we are dead!

Rivers and lakes full of wind and waves —
You feared the oars of your boat
   would be swept away.
   江湖多風波，舟楫恐失墜。

其 二

杜 甫

浮雲終日行，遊子久不至；
三夜頻夢君，親情見君意。
告歸常局促，苦道來不易。
江湖多風波，舟楫恐失墜。
出門搔白首，若負平生志。
冠蓋滿京華，斯人獨顦顇。
孰云網恢恢，將老身反累。
千秋萬歲名，寂寞身後事。

FAREWELL

Wang Wei

Dismounting from my horse
    to drink some wine with you,
I asked you —
    "Where are you going?"
You replied —
    that your heart's desires were ungranted,
You were going back to rest on South Mountain.
Then you went —
    I put no more questions,
The white clouds floated endlessly by...

送　別

王　維

下馬飲君酒，問君何所之？
君言：「不得意，歸臥南山陲。」
但去莫復問，白雲無盡時。

TAKING LEAVE OF QIWU QIAN WHO HAS FAILED THE OFFICIAL EXAMINATION AND IS RETURNING TO HIS VILLAGE

Wang Wei

There were no hermits in the golden ages:
The brilliant and gifted all appeared at Court.
Following the call, guest of East Mountain,
You might not stay, gathering country simples.
Far you journeyed, to the Gold Horse gate —
Who could say you had not tried to serve?
By the Yangtze and Huai
    you will spent the Cold Food Festival[1],
At the Capital and Luoyang
    they stitched your spring clothes.
I prepared wine for you on the Chang'an road —
The friend so close to my heart is leaving me!
Now you shall float away in your cassia boat,
Soon will be tapping on your thorn-wood door;
Far trees will bid the traveller welcome,
A lone city glitters in the sunset.
You may lament —
    "My plans proved unacceptable,"
But do not say,
    there are few to understand you.

---

1. Jie Zhitui, a scholar and statesman of Zhou dynasty, had lost interest in politics and retired to the mountains. Duke Wen tried unsuccessfully to recall him and eventually ordered the mountain to be set on fire. Jie was burnt to death. In his remorse the Duke ordered the people to commemorate the dead man by lighting no fires on the anniversary of his death, and by eating only cold food on that day, a custom which was preserved for centuries.

送綦毋潛落第還鄉

王 維

聖代無隱者，英靈盡來歸。

遂令東山客，不得顧采薇。

既至金門遠，孰云吾道非。

江淮度寒食，京洛縫春衣。

置酒長安道，同心與我違。

行當浮桂棹，未幾拂荊扉。

遠樹帶行客，孤城當落暉。

「吾謀適不用」，勿謂知音稀。

GREEN GULLY

Wang Wei

If I want to reach Yellow Flower river
I always follow Green Gully stream;
It coils through the mountains
    with ten thousand turnings,
Hurrying along
    it barely covers a hundred *li*.
What a clamour it makes among the jumbled rocks!
Deep in the pinewoods
    how quiet and still it seems.
Adrift with water-chestnuts, lightly swaying,
Translucently it mirrors reeds and rushes...
    My heart is free and at peace,
    As tranquil as this clear stream.
    Let me stay on some great rock
    And trail my fishing-hook for ever!

What a clamour it makes among the jumbled rocks!
Deep in the pinewoods
    how quiet and still it seems.
    聲喧亂石中，色靜深松裡。

青　谿

王　維

言入黃花川，每逐青谿水；
隨山將萬轉，趣途無百里。
聲喧亂石中，色靜深松裡。
漾漾汎菱荇，澄澄映葭葦。
我心素以閑，清川澹如此。
請留盤石上，垂釣將已矣。

FARMERS BY THE RIVER WEI

Wang Wei

Slanting rays light the villages
    in the sunset,
Along the lanes, cattle and sheep return.
An old peasant is thinking of the herd-boy;
Leaning on his staff,
    he waits by the wicket-gate.
Pheasants squawk, wheat is coming into ear,
Silkworms sleep, mulberry leaves are few.
Farmers with shouldered hoes pass by;
When they meet their talk flows endlessly.
How enviable this calm unhurried life!
Despondently I sing the 'Shiwei' song.[1]

1. *Shiwei* is the title of a song in the classic *Book of Songs* which includes the line 'Why don't you go home?'

渭 川 田 家

王 維

斜光照墟落，窮巷牛羊歸。
野老念牧童，倚杖候柴扉。
雉雊麥苗秀，蠶眠桑葉稀。
田夫荷鋤至，相見語依依。
即此羨閒逸，悵然歌式微。

SONG OF XI SHI

Wang Wei

A lovely face
    is treasured by all under Heaven:
Could Xi Shi remain long in lowliness?
One morning, just a girl by Yue stream —
That evening, a favourite in the Palace of Wu.
In her penniless days,
    who distinguished her from the throng?
When honours came,
    the whole region noticed her rarity.
She sent for servants
    to powder and rouge her cheeks,
Would not even fasten
    her fine silk dresses.
Her Lord's devotion increased her haughtiness.
The King's blind love knew no right or wrong.
Girls who had washed yarn with her in the old days
Could not accompany her in the royal chariot.
Meekly she would plead with her neighbours' daughters:
"How can frowning help
    without beauty?"

When Yue and Wu Kingdoms were rivals, Xi Shi, a beautiful country girl, was discovered by a Yue minister washing clothes by a stream, and was sent to the King of Wu to distract him from affairs of State. He became so infatuated with her that the government was weakened, and his Kingdom eventually fell to Yue. It is believed that Xi Shi suffered from a heart disease, and people said that when she frowned with pain, she looked more appealing than ever.

西 施 詠

王 維

艷色天下重，西施寧久微？
朝為越溪女，暮作吳宮妃，
賤日豈殊眾？貴來方悟稀。
邀人傅脂粉，不自著羅衣。
君寵益驕態，君憐無是非。
當時浣紗伴，莫得同車歸。
持謝鄰家子，效顰安可希。

ON CLIMBING ORCHID MOUNTAIN IN AUTUMN —
A POEM FOR ZHANG THE FIFTH

Meng Haoran

Up the north peak, lost in white clouds,
The hermit is happy in his solitude.
To visit him I try the steep ascent —
My heart lifts with the wild-geese
    winging out of sight.
Poignant feeling rises with the dusk,
Vigour surges with the clear autumn.
At times I watch the homing villagers
Tramping over the sands
    to wait at the ferry-head.
On the far horizon
    the trees look tiny as grass;
Down in the river
    an islet resembles the moon.
When could we climb up here with our wine
And grow tipsy celebrating the autumn festival?

To visit him I try the steep ascent —
My heart lifts with the wild-geese
   winging out of sight.
   相望試登高，心隨雁飛滅。

秋登蘭山寄張五

孟浩然

北山白雲裡，隱者自怡悅。
相望試登高，心隨雁飛滅。
愁因薄暮起，興是清秋發。
時見歸村人，沙行渡頭歇。
天邊樹若薺，江畔洲如月。
何當載酒來，共醉重陽節。

IN THE SOUTH PAVILION ON A SUMMER DAY, THINKING OF XIN THE ELDER

Meng Haoran

Sunlight on the hill
    suddenly drops to the west,
The moon in the pond
    climbs slowly out of the east.
Loosening my hair
    to enjoy the evening cool,
With window wide
    I rest in airy quietness.
The breeze carries a scent
    from the lotuses,
Dew drips off the bamboos
    with a clear plash.
I should like to take up my lute
    and play
But there's none here
    to care for my music:
In such a mood
    I pine for you, old friend.
As the night deepens
    memories trouble my dreams.

山光忽西落

池月漸東上

Sunlight on the hill
    suddenly drops to the west,
The moon in the pond
    climbs slowly out of the east.
山光忽西落，池月漸東上。

夏日南亭懷辛大

孟　浩　然

山光忽西落，池月漸東上。
散髮乘夕涼，開軒臥閒敞。
荷風送香氣，竹露滴清響。
欲取鳴琴彈，恨無知音賞，
感此懷故人，中宵勞夢想。

ON STAYING AT MY TUTOR'S MOUNTAIN RETREAT AND WAITING IN VAIN FOR MY FRIEND DING

Meng Haoran

Evening rays
    have passed the western peaks —
In a cluster of valleys
    it is suddenly dark.
Moon over the pines
    brings the cool of night,
Wind and stream fill my ears
    with clear sound.

Returning woodcutters
    are almost gone,
In the mist, birds are just
    settling to roost;
You promised
    to come to me tonight —
I am waiting with a lute
    on the path of vines.

宿業師山房待丁大不至

孟 浩 然

夕陽度西嶺，群壑倏已暝；
松月生夜涼，風泉滿清聽。
樵人歸欲盡，烟鳥棲初定。
之子期宿來，孤琴候蘿徑。

ENJOYING THE MOONLIGHT WITH MY COUSIN IN THE SOUTH STUDY AND THINKING OF MY FRIEND MR. CUI, DEPUTY-GOVERNOR OF SHANYIN

Wang Changling

I was resting idly in the South study.
Through the open curtains
    the moon was just rising.
The clear brilliance lay quietly on water and tree,
Drifted glittering through my window casement...
How many times can she have waxed and waned?
Under her pure light past has changed to present.
My good friend
    beside the untroubled river,
Will gravely hum the songs of Yue
    on such a night.
How can we bridge the thousand miles between us?
A light breeze may blow you the scent
    of my orchids and pollia.

同從弟南齋翫月憶山陰崔少府

王　昌　齡

高臥南齋時，開帷月初吐。
清輝淡水木，演漾在窗戶。
苒苒幾盈虛？澄澄變今古。
美人清江畔，是夜越吟苦。
千里其如何？微風吹蘭杜。

AFTER FAILING TO FIND A HERMIT
FRIEND ON WEST MOUNTAIN
Qiu Wei

To your lone hut on the mountain top
Was a good ten miles' climb.
I tapped on the door — no servant boy.
Peeped inside — only your table and bench.
Riding in your mountain litter,
    I wonder?
Or else you may be fishing
    the autumn streams:
On these uneven ways
    we missed each other.
In vain I tried my best
    to pay you respect.
There is only the colour of the grass
    fresh from rain,
And the sough of pines at dusk
    beside your window —
Sight and sound
    fit for utter calm,
Adept for soothing
    mind and ear.
Although between us
    no thoughts passed,
I almost comprehend
    your pure philosophy.
My exaltation passed,
I descend the mountain —
Why need I await your coming?

Sight and sound
 fit for utter calm,
Adept for soothing
 mind and ear.
及茲契幽絕，自足蕩心耳。

尋西山隱者不遇

邱　為

絕頂一茅茨，直上三十里。
叩關無僮僕，窺室惟案几。
若非巾柴車，應是釣秋水？
差池不相見，黽勉空仰止。
草色新雨中，松聲晚窗裡。
及茲契幽絕，自足蕩心耳。
雖無賓主意，頗得清淨理。
興盡方下山，何必待之子。

SPRING BOATING ON RUOYE STREAM

Qiwu Qian

With nothing to disturb my quiet thought,
I'll float now wherever chance carries me.
A twilight wind blows my boat along;
By flower banks I enter the stream's mouth.
Till the edge of night I sail,
    to a creek in the West;
I can see the Southern Dipper
    beyond the nearest hills.
Mist sweeps in eddies over the deep pool
And a moon hangs low behind the woods.
The cares of life are like a flood without bounds —
I wish I could just be an old man
    with a fishing rod.

此身閱漫碼芯特半里彭壽

The cares of life are like a flood without bounds —
I wish I could just be an old man
 with a fishing rod.
生事且瀰漫，願為持竿叟。

春泛若耶溪

綦毋潛

幽意無斷絕，此去隨所偶。
晚風吹行舟，花路入溪口；
際夜轉西壑，隔山望南斗；
潭烟飛溶溶，林月低向後。
生事且瀰漫，願為持竿叟。

RESTING AT WANG CHANGLING'S RETREAT

Chang Jian

The limpid stream
    is deep byond sounding;
Over your secret retreat
    only a single cloud.
A slender moon
    shows between the pines.
Its clear radiance
    is all for you!
It traces the shapes of flowers
    on your thatched hut
And in your herb-garden lights
    the devious patterns of the moss.
I too shall take leave of the world and depart
To join phoenix and crane on West Mountain.

宿王昌齡隱居

常　建

清谿深不測，隱處惟孤雲；
松際露微月，清光猶為君。
茅亭宿花影，藥院滋苔紋。
余亦謝時去，西山鸞鶴群。

CLIMBING THE PAGODA AT CI'EN MONASTERY
WITH GAO SHI AND XUE JU

Cen Shen

The pagoda seems to spring out of the earth,
High and lonely, it soars to Heaven's palaces.
Climbing it we leave the world behind,
Stone steps coil into empty space.
Its height dominates this blessed land,
Awesome, dignified, like the work of spirits.
Its four roof-corners hinder the white sun,
Its seven storeys touch the blue of space.
Peering down, we mark the highest birds;
Leaning over, hear the wind's alarm.
Mountain ranges rear like sea-horses,
As if hastening in homage to the east.
Green locust-trees line the Imperial highway,
The palaces and mansions — how marvellously wrought!
The colours of autumn appear out of the west —
Misty blue fills the Guanzhong.
The Five Imperial Tombs on the northern plain
Ages old, vague grey shapes.

Here I can apprehend the Doctrine of Purity,
The Law of Causes is what I ever venerate.
I vow to hang up my official cap —
To perceive the Way is gain beyond measure.

Climbing it we leave the world behind,
Stone steps coil into empty space.
　登臨出世界，磴道盤虛空。

與高適薛據登慈恩寺浮圖

岑參

塔勢如湧出，孤高聳天宮。
登臨出世界，磴道盤虛空。
突兀壓神州，崢嶸如鬼工。
四角礙白日，七層摩蒼穹。
下窺指高鳥，俯聽聞驚風。
連山若波濤，奔湊似朝東。
青槐夾馳道，宮館何玲瓏？
秋色從西來，蒼然滿關中；
五陵北原上，萬古青濛濛。
淨理了可悟，勝因夙所宗。
誓將掛冠去，覺道資無窮。

ADDRESSED TO MY OFFICIALS AND SUBORDINATES
AFTER THE RETREAT OF THE REBELS

Yuan Jie

In former times when all was at peace,
For twenty years I lived among hills and woods;
A spring used to bubble up near my courtyard,
Deep ravines fell away before my gate.
The land tax was collected at fixed times
And one could sleep in quiet until the sun was high.
Suddenly I was caught in the unrest of the age,
For many years served under war banners.
Since I came here as governor of the region
Mountain bandits are on the move again.
But our little town is too small for them to ravage,
Our citizens quite pitiful in their poverty.
That's why they have sacked the neighbouring region —
Only this district is left unmolested.
Those envoys, appointed by imperial mandate,
Are they any different from the brigands?
Only look at the tax-collectors —
Burning up the people like fire under a cauldron.
Can someone cut short human lives
And yet become a good official of the time?
My own desire is to have done with office,
To take a bamboo pole and push off my boat,
Make my home where fish and grain are plentiful
And spend my old age by lake and riverside.

賊退示官吏

元 結

昔年逢太平，山林二十年。
泉源在庭戶，洞壑當門前。
井稅有常期，日晏猶得眠。
忽然遭世變，數歲親戎旃。
今來典斯郡，山夷又紛然。
城小賊不屠，人貧傷可憐！
是以陷鄰境，此州獨得全。
使臣將王命，豈不如賊焉？
令彼徵斂者，迫之如火煎。
誰能絕人命，以作時世賢？
思欲委符節，引竿自刺船，
將家就魚麥，歸老江湖邊。

ENTERTAINING SCHOLARS IN MY OFFICIAL RESIDENCE ON A RAINY DAY

Wei Yingwu

Guards on watch with ranks of bright halberds,
Fresh fragrance hovers in the guest rooms.
While wind and rain drive over the sea
We take our ease in this cool garden house.
Ailments and vexations soon melt away
As honoured guests crowd my hall again.
Although it shames me to own these lavish quarters
When I cannot see to the comfort of the common people,
Good sense will silence wagging tongues;
The broad-minded will ignore appearances.
Fresh fish and meats are forbidden now
But fruit and vegetables can be sampled in abundance.
Come, let us drink a cup of wine
And listen to a recital of poetry.
A joyful spirit makes the body light,
As if we whirled upward on the wind!

Wu State was famed for its literary men,
And what a band of scholars here today!
All acknowledge the honour of our province —
Who would claim it rests only on wealth and taxes?

郡齋雨中與諸文士燕集

韋 應 物

兵衛森畫戟，燕寢凝清香。
海上風雨至，逍遙池閣涼。
煩痾近消散，嘉賓復滿堂。
自慚居處崇，未覩斯民康。
理會是非遣，性達形迹忘。
鮮肥屬時禁，蔬果幸見嘗。
俯飲一杯酒，仰聆金玉章。
神歡體自輕，意欲凌風翔。
吳中盛文史，群彥今汪洋。
方知大藩地，豈曰財賦強。

ON SETTING OUT ON THE YANGTZE — FOR THE SECRETARY, MR. YUAN

Wei Yingwu

Sad, sad the parting from my loved friend —
Gliding on, we pass into the mists;
They are rowing me back to Luoyang...
Dying bells sound
  from the woods of Guangling.

Early this morning
  came our separation —
Where shall we find each other again?
Human affairs
  are like a boat in the waves
Carried away on the current —
  who can stay it?

今朝此地別何處
還期相遇菊花舜

Early this morning
    came our separation —
When shall we find each other again?
今朝此為別，何處還相遇？

初發揚子寄元大校書

韋 應 物

悽悽去親愛，泛泛入烟霧。
歸棹洛陽人，殘鐘廣陵樹。
今朝此為別，何處還相遇？
世事波上舟，沿洄安得住。

FOR THE MOUNTAIN HERMIT OF QUANJIAO

Wei Yingwu

Feeling cold today in my city office
I suddenly thought of the hermit on the mountain —
Gathering thorn twigs in the dry bed of a torrent,
Returning then to cook on the bare stones...

I should like to carry up a gourdful of wine
To cheer you there on this evening of rain and wind,
But fallen leaves have covered the empty hillside —
How could I discover the track of your feet?

寄全椒山中道士

韋　應　物

今朝郡齋冷，忽念山中客。
澗底束荊薪，歸來煮白石。
欲持一瓢酒，遠慰風雨夕；
落葉滿空山，何處尋行迹。

ON MEETING FENG ZHU AT CHANG'AN

Wei Yingwu

My guest came from the East country,
His gown still wet
    with the rains of Baling.
I asked him —
    "What have you come for?"
"To buy an axe
    for cutting wood in the hills!"

Stealthily now
    flower-buds burst,
Young fledgling swallows
    tumble and swoop:
Another spring is here
    since we parted,
But the hair on our temples
    is streaked with white.

長安遇馮著

韋　應　物

客從東方來，衣上灞陵雨。
問客何為來？采山因買斧。
冥冥花正開，颺颺燕新乳。
昨別今已春，鬢絲生幾縷。

ANCHORING AT XUYI IN THE EVENING

Wei Yingwu

We dropped sail to enter Linhuai,
Moored the boat by a desolate landing-stage.
Hao! Hao! — wind whips the waves;
Dim, dim — day drowns in dusk.

People have all gone home, hills and walls darken;
Geese fly down to islets white with reeds.
Alone in the night, I am thinking of Qin Pass —
A sleepless traveller, listening to a temple bell.

潮平風起波冒天
日沉夕蔣彝

Hao! Hao! — wind whips the waves;
Dim, dim — day drowns in dusk.
浩浩風起波，冥冥日沉夕。

夕次盱眙縣

韋應物

落帆逗淮鎮，停舫臨孤驛。
浩浩風起波，冥冥日沉夕。
人歸山郭暗，雁下蘆洲白。
獨夜憶秦關，聽鐘未眠客。

ON THE EASTERN OUTSKIRTS

Wei Yingwu

Cramped in my office
    all year through,
I left the city
    to squander the bright sunshine.
Willows waft
    a kindly spring wind,
Blue hills
    smooth away my cares.
I take my rest in leafy woodlands,
Come and go by the green mountain torrent.
A fine rain veils
    the sweet-smelling fields.
Where was that wood-dove crooning?
A heart that loves solitude
    is often baulked,
Official business
    keeps one hustling.
When my public duty is over
    I shall build a hut here —
Try to live
    like Tao Yuanming.[1]

---

1. Tao Yuanming was a pastoral poet of the 4th century, prototype of the scholar who retires from office, to live the simple life and write poetry.

東　郊

韋　應　物

吏舍跼終年，出郊曠清曙。
楊柳散和風，青山澹吾慮。
依叢適自憩，緣澗還復去。
微雨靄芳原，春鳩鳴何處？
樂幽心屢止，遵事跡猶遽，
終罷斯結廬，慕陶直可庶。

SAYING GOODBYE TO MY DAUGHTER, WHO IS TO MARRY INTO THE YANG FAMILY

Wei Yingwu

For many days you looked so woebegone —
You are going on a far, far journey:
Today you are setting out to be married.
The Great River beats against your frail boat.
You and your sister were early left motherless —
I tried to rear you with special tenderness and love.
The little one was mothered by the elder;
Leaving each other, you can't help crying,
And to see it makes my own heart ache.
But it's your duty to go — I dare not hold you.
From early girlhood you lacked a mother's guidance:
The mother-in-law business causes me anxiety!
I'm entrusting you to the care of a good family.
They will be kind and just — no reason for complaint.
Modesty and thrift are what you should cultivate;
What need is there for dowry and servants?
A wife's part is filial respect and obedience;
Your manner and conduct must follow the right examples.
Early this morning we had to separate:
How many autumns till I see you again?
In our daily life I can almost master my feelings;
Now, suddenly moved, I can hardly control them.
Coming home, seeing your little sister,
The tears stream down and fall on the strings of my cap!

送楊氏女

韋應物

永日方慼慼，出行復悠悠。
女子今有行，大江泝輕舟。
爾輩苦無恃，撫念益慈柔。
幼為長所育，兩別泣不休。
對此結中腸，義往難復留。
自小闕內訓，事姑貽我憂。
賴茲託令門，仁卹庶無尤！
貧儉誠所尚，資從豈待周。
孝恭遵婦道，容止順其猷。
別離在今晨，見爾當何秋！
居閒始自遣，臨感忽難收；
歸來視幼女，零淚緣纓流。

AN EARLY MORNING VISIT TO THE BUDDHIST PRIEST CHAO TO READ THE CHAN SCRIPTURES

Liu Zongyuan

Drawing water from the well,
    I rinse my cold teeth,
I brush the dust from my clothes
    and purify my mind;
Calmly I turn the leaves of a Buddhist sutra
And recite as I stroll out of the east study.

The true Way has not been accepted —
False tracks are what the world follows.
Buddha's teaching promises joy after Nirvana:
How can I master with it my habitual nature?

Here in the quiet of the priest's courtyard,
The green of the moss blends with the dense bamboos;
As the sun breaks through the strands of damp mist
It bathes the blue pines as if with oil.

Such freshness! — hard to express in words...
Enlightened, satisfied,
    my heart is at peace.

晨詣超師院讀禪經

柳 宗 元

汲井漱寒齒，清心拂塵服，
閒持貝葉書，步出東齋讀。
真源了無取，妄跡世所逐。
遺言冀可冥，繕性何由熟？
道人庭宇靜，苔色連深竹。
日出霧露餘，青松如膏沐。
澹然離言說，悟悅心自足。

LIVING BY A MOUNTAIN TORRENT

Liu Zongyuan

I was long cramped
    by official girdle and hatpin
Till happily I was banished
    to these southern wilds;
Idleness gives me
    farmers' plots for neighbour —
Chance has made me a guest
    of hills and woods.

At dawn the ploughmen
    split the dewy turf,
At dusk the boat-poles plash
    along a pebbly stream:
I come and go
    without meeting a soul —
I sing and sing
    to the blue skies of Chu!

溪　　居

柳　宗　元

久為簪組束，幸此南夷謫。
閒依農圃鄰，偶似山林客。
曉耕翻露草，夜榜響谿石，
來往不逢人，長歌楚天碧。

COMPLAINT

Zhang Jiuling

(I)

A lone swan flies in over the sea,
— Not deigning to glance at pond or pool —
With sidelong glance at a pair of kingfishers
Perched among the three Pearl trees.
"High, high on the crest of those precious trees,
Are they not fearful of a golden shot?
Gaudy plumage will draw the finger of envy,
Too high a climb invite the malice of spirits.
But I who roam the far wastes of the sky —
What should the fowler want with me?"

感　遇

張　九　齡

孤鴻海上來，池潢不敢顧。
側見雙翠鳥，巢在三珠樹。
矯矯珍木巔，得無金丸懼？
美服患人指，高明逼神惡；
今我游冥冥，弋者何所慕？

(II)

In Spring the leaves of orchid grow profusely,
Cassia blooms in autumn bright and pure;
Happily they enjoy their living nature,
Naturally help to make the season fair.
Who knows the heart of the forest hermit?
He hears of the flowers and comes to take his joy.
Plant and tree have their own ways;
Why should they seek to be plucked by ladies?

其 二

張 九 齡

蘭葉春葳蕤，桂華秋皎潔。
欣欣此生意，自爾為佳節。
誰知林棲者，聞風坐相悅。
草木有本心，何求美人折！

(III)

The lover of quiet withdraws to lie in solitude,
A pure hermit cleansed of his heavy cares,
Entrusting his thoughts to a high-flying bird
To carry them to his distant Sovereign.
Day and night I ponder fruitlessly,
For who will recognise the truth of my being?
The high-flier and the hermit are worlds apart,
So what consolation is there for my loyalty?

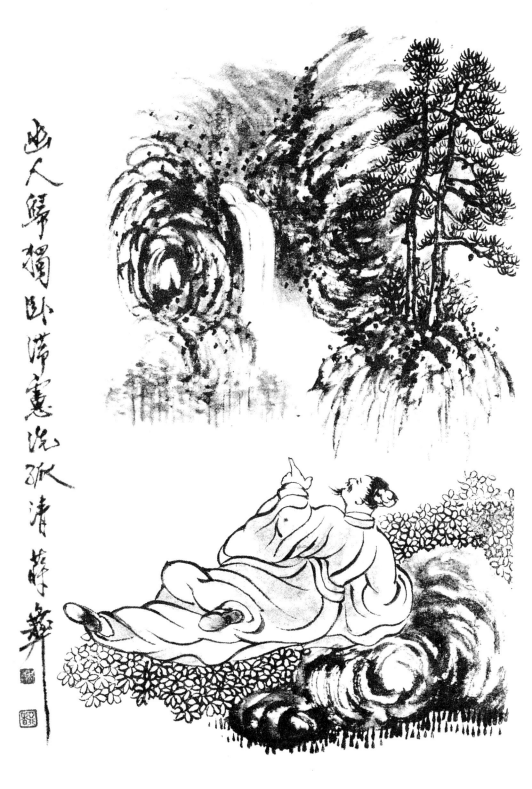

幽人歸獨臥滿壑泣孤清　蔣蕲舞

The lover of quiet withdraws to lie in solitude,
A pure hermit cleansed of his heavy cares.
幽人歸獨臥，滯慮洗孤清。

其　三

張　九　齡

幽人歸獨臥，滯慮洗孤清；
持此謝高鳥，因之傳遠情。
日夕懷空意，人誰感至精？
飛沉理自隔，何所慰吾誠？

(IV)

South of the Yangtze are the red oranges,
All winter through the groves remain green:
Is it that the soil is warmer there?
Rather it is their cold-enduring nature.
Worthy to set before our honoured guests —
A pity they are left so deeply hidden!
Our fate revolves and we must take what comes;
Life moves on — we cannot seek for reasons.
People talk of planting peach and plum —
Surely this tree will grow shady too?

These four poems were written by Zhang Jiuling after he had fallen from favour and lost his position. In the first and second he pictures himself in retirement as a solitary swan or a plant which does not "seek to be plucked by ladies," i.e. by the Premier. In the third and fourth he regrets that the Emperor no longer appreciates his services.

其　四

張　九　齡

江南有丹橘，經冬猶綠林；
豈伊地氣暖，自有歲寒心。
可以薦嘉客，奈何阻重深！
運命惟所遇，循環不可尋。
徒言樹桃李，此木豈無陰。

POEMS WRITTEN FOR MUSIC

GOING UP TO THE FRONTIER

Wang Changling

Cicadas chirp in the empty mulberry groves
Along the Xiaoguan road at the eighth moon.
From one pass we file into another;
Everywhere, yellowed grass and sedge.

Wanderers from You and Bing since ancient days
Grew old with the desert sand and died.
Better not to imitate those roving gallants,
Bragging about the prowess of their black-maned ponies!

樂　府

塞　上　曲

王　昌　齡

蟬鳴空桑林，八月蕭關道。
出塞復入塞，處處黃蘆草。
從來幽并客，皆共塵沙老；
莫學游俠兒，矜誇紫騮好。

RETURNING FROM THE FRONTIER

Wang Changling

We watered our horses crossing the autumn river.
Cold was the water, and the wind like a knife!
The sun had not quite set
    over the level sands;
In the gathering darkness
    we could see Lintao.

There were battles ages ago by the Great Wall;
All declared with what high hearts they went:
Yellow dust
    is all that remains of the past,
And white bones
    spilt among weeds and thistles.

塞 下 曲

王 昌 齡

飲馬渡秋水，水寒風似刀。
平沙日未沒，黯黯見臨洮。
昔日長城戰，咸言意氣高。
黃塵足今古，白骨亂蓬蒿。

THE BORDERLAND MOON

Li Bai

A clear moon rising over Tian Shan
Glides into a boundless sea of cloud;
Steady wind
    from the far, far distance
Howls across the Yumen pass.
The Sons of Han descend the Baideng road,
Tartars peer into the Kokonor;
Since the old days
    this was a battleground
From which no living man ever returned.

Guards keep gazing towards the frontier town,
Many a face bitter with thoughts of home.
This very night,
    in the upper chambers
Their women moan and sigh and cannot rest

關 山 月

李 白

明月出天山，蒼茫雲海間；
長風幾萬里，吹度玉門關。
漢下白登道，胡窺青海灣。
由來征戰地，不見有人還！
戍客望邊邑，思歸多苦顏。
高樓當此夜，歎息未應閒。

ZIYE'S AUTUMN SONG

Li Bai

A thin strip of moon
    over Chang'an,
From a thousand homes
    the sound of beating clothes;
Autumn wind
    blows without ceasing.
Their thoughts are all
    at Yumen pass:
"When will the Tartars be thrown back
And our husbands return from the distant battlefield?"

子 夜 秋 歌

李 白

長安一片月，萬戶擣衣聲。
秋風吹不盡，總是玉關情，
何日平胡虜，良人罷遠征。

BALLAD OF CHANGGAN

Li Bai

When my hair just began to cover my forehead
And I played with the flowers I picked outside our gate,
You'd come riding to me on your bamboo horse;
Round and round the well we pelted each other with green plums.
So we both lived in Changgan village,
Both young, both trustful and innocent.
In my fourteenth year I became your wife —
So bashful I seldom smiled at you,
But hung my head and turned to a dark corner:
You called me a thousand times but I wouldn't turn to you.
At fifteen I began to straighten my brows;
We vowed to be true till we were dust and ashes.
You meant to keep faith like the lover by the bridge-post:[1]
Why should I ever climb the Looking-for-husband tower?[2]
I was sixteen when you left on a long journey,
To Qutang where rapids crash upon the rocks of Yanyu.
In the fifth month those rapids are impassable,
Even monkeys howl piteously on the heights...
Before my door are the tracks of your parting feet,
And the green moss creeps over them one by one;
The moss grows so thick I cannot sweep it away.
Leaves are falling already in the autumn wind.
The yellow butterflies of October
Flutter in pairs over the grass of the west garden.

長 干 行

李 白

妾髮初覆額，折花門前劇。
郎騎竹馬來，遶床弄青梅。
同居長干里，兩小無嫌猜。
十四為君婦，羞顏未嘗開。
低頭向暗壁，千喚不一回。
十五始展眉，願同塵與灰。
常存抱柱信，豈上望夫臺。
十六君遠行，瞿塘灩澦堆。
五月不可觸，猿聲天上哀。
門前遲行跡，一一生綠苔。
苔深不能掃，落葉秋風早。
八月蝴蝶黃，雙飛西園草。

Feeling this change makes my heart ache;
As I sit and sorrow, my rosy face grows old.
One morning or evening you will return from San Ba —
I beg you, send me a letter first!
I will come to meet you, and not call it far —
Right up to Chang Feng Sha.

1. A young man of the 6th century B.C. called Wei Sheng had promised to meet a girl under a bridge. She was late in coming, but rather than break his tryst when the river began to rise, he clung to the bridgepost and was drowned.
2. A 'Looking-for-husband tower' is said to have existed in Zhong-zhou, Sichuan. The legend attached to it says that a young husband, though deeply in love with his wife, felt compelled to leave her and became a recluse. She had a tower built from the top of which she could gaze across to his mountain retreat.

感此傷妾心，坐愁紅顏老。
早晚下三巴，預將書報家，
相迎不道遠，直至長風沙。

THE CHASTE WIFE

Meng Jiao

On the wutong tree, phoenix and mate
    grow old together;
Duck and drake cleave to each other
    till death.
A chaste wife will gladly die with her husband,
Taking leave of life
    like drake and phoenix.
She will not break faith
    like the changeable sea waves:
A wife's heart is like the water
    in an old well.

烈　女　操

孟　郊

梧桐相待老，鴛鴦會雙死。
貞女貴殉夫，捨生亦如此。
波瀾誓不起，妾心古井水。

TO THE AIR 'THE WANDERER'

Meng Jiao

Thread in the hand of a loving mother
Is worked into the jacket
    of her wayward boy.
Firm and close she sets the stitches now
For she fears he will be slow, slow
    to return.

Who can say that the heart
    of an inch-long grass
Will repay the sunlight
    of full Spring?

慈母手中線
縫遊子身上衣

Thread in the hand of a loving mother
Is worked into the jacket
  of her wayward boy.
  慈母手中線，遊子身上衣。

遊子吟

孟郊

慈母手中線，遊子身上衣，
臨行密密縫，意恐遲遲歸。
誰言寸草心，報得三春暉。

SECTION 2

Seven-character 'Old Style' verse

Although the poems in this verse-form are predominantly in lines of 7 characters, the classification is a fairly loose one. Some lines of 2, 3, 4, 5, 6, or even 10 characters will be found among them.

ON CLIMBING YOUZHOU TOWER

Chen Zi'ang

Ahead I cannot see the ancient faces;
Behind I cannot see the coming ages.
I brood upon the endlessness of Nature,
Lonely and sick at heart, with falling tears.

登幽州臺歌

陳子昂

前不見古人， 後不見來者；
念天地之悠悠，獨愴然而涕下。

AN OLD THEME

Li Qi

Since boyhood, their task was distant fighting;
As youngsters, the heroes of You and Yan.
Bending low in the saddle
    they competed for mastery;
Those days, they held their lives light.
So ready to kill, none dared approach them,
Their beards bristling like quills of porcupine!
Through yellow clouds of harvest tore
    the white clouds of horses:
No going home till they repaid the Emperor's favour.

There's a little maid of Liaodong,
    fifteen years old,
Clever at playing the flute, knows how to dance and sing.
Today she piped on her shepherd's flute
    a 'leaving the frontier' tune —
She made my whole legion's tears
    flow like rain.

古　意

李　頎

男兒事長征，　　少小幽燕客，
賭勝馬蹄下，　　由來輕七尺；
殺人莫敢前，　　鬚如蝟毛磔。
黃雲隴底白雲飛，未得報恩不能歸。
遼東少婦年十五，慣彈琵琶解歌舞。
今為羌笛出塞聲，使我三軍淚如雨。

GOODBYE TO CHEN ZHANGFU

Li Qi

The fourth moon and the wind in the south,
    barley turning yellow;
Petals not fallen from the date trees,
    wutong leaves growing huge,
The green hills we left at dawn
    still seen in the dusk;
A horse's neigh on passing the gates
    reminding one of home.

How dignified is your bearing,
    my friend, Marquis Chen!
With your dragon beard and tiger brows,
    massive forehead too!
The learning of ten thousand volumes
    is stored in your belly —
You could not bear to lower your head
    among coarse rustics.

By the east gate you bought wine
    to drink with all of us;
To your gay spirit ten thousand affairs
    are like a wild-goose feather!
Dazed with wine, you hardly saw
    the white sun was sinking;
At times you watched a solitary cloud
    high in empty space.

送 陳 章 甫

李 頎

四月南風大麥黃，棗花未落桐葉長，
青山朝別暮還見，嘶馬出門思舊鄉。
陳侯立身何坦蕩，虬鬚虎眉仍大顙，
腹中貯書一萬卷，不肯低頭在草莽。
東門酤酒飲我曹，心輕萬事皆鴻毛，
醉臥不知白日暮，有時空望孤雲高！

The wave crests of the long river
    join with the darkening sky;
The ferryman has anchored his boat —
    none can get across.
The traveller from Zhengzhou[1] hasn't reached home.
The voyager at Luoyang vainly heaves a sigh![2]

I heard tell, in your woodland village
    you had many good friends:
Yesterday you lost your post —
    how will they greet you today?

1. Chen Zhangfu
2. Li Qi was in Luoyang at the time.

長河浪頭連天黑，津吏停舟渡不得，
鄭國遊人未及家，洛陽行子空歎息。
聞道故林相識多，罷官昨日今如何！

A LUTE SONG

Li Qi

Our host brings wine
    for merry-making tonight,
And bids the guest from Guangling
    play upon the lute.
Moonlight bathes the city walls,
    crows fly in mid-air;
Frost petrifies a thousand trees,
    wind pierces our gowns.
But the copper stove gleams bright,
    and candles add their glitter.
First he strikes up "Lu Water"
    then "The Princess of Chu":
As the first note trembles
    all else falls silent —
From the whole company not a word
    till the stars begin to pale...
The thousand miles to Qinghuai,
    I was sent by the Emperor's mandate:
On such a night I venture to speak of
    retiring to the mountains and clouds.

琴　歌

李　頎

主人有酒歡今夕，請奏鳴琴廣陵客，
月照城頭烏半飛，霜淒萬木風入衣。
銅鑪華燭燭增輝，初彈淥水後楚妃。
一聲已動物皆靜，四座無言星欲稀。
清淮奉使千餘里，敢告雲山從此始。

ON HEARING DONG TINGLAN PLAY THE 'SONG OF THE TARTAR PIPE', WRITTEN ALSO FOR THE GOVERNMENT CLERK, FANG.

Li Qi

Years ago, the Lady Cai
    composed an air on the Tartar pipe;
The whole was a melody of eighteen bars:
It made the Tartars weep until their tears
    wet the wayside grass,
And the Chinese envoy's heart ache
    when he saw his guest turn homeward.
Green now are those ancient battlefields,
    and the beacon fires cold,
The border wastes dreary and the white snow flying...

As you touch first the *shang* string, then the *jue* and *yu*,
Comes the rustle, rustle of tumbling autumn leaves —
Master Dong,
You are inspired!
From the dense pines, phantoms steal to listen,
Slow or fast, the notes answer your touch,
Fading first then again swelling
    like a sigh of passion,
Or on the bare hills, a hundred birds would scatter and return,
Or ten thousand leagues of floating cloud would lower, then
    drift away.

聽董大彈胡笳兼寄語弄房給事

李 頎

蔡女昔造胡笳聲，一彈一十有八拍。
胡人落淚沾邊草，漢使斷腸對歸客。
古戍蒼蒼烽火寒，大荒沉沉飛雪白。
先拂商弦後角羽，四郊秋葉驚摵摵。
董夫子，通神明，深松竊聽來妖精。
言遲更速皆應手，將往復旋如有情；
空山百鳥散還合，萬里浮雲陰且晴；

A bitter throbbing tells of a fledgling goose
    that has lost its flock at night;
Broken notes sound like a Tartar child,
    sobbing for its mother.
Streams still their ripples,
Birds cease their cries,
Wuzhu tribesmen remember their distant homes —
From the sand and dust of Tibet
    rises a bitter lament.
Suddenly the sad notes change — to gale and torrent;
A long wind strains the forest,
    rain dashes on tiles,
Cascades of spray fly hissing over tree-tops,
Wild deer bay as they run past this hall...

In Chang'an city, near the East wall of the Palace,
Between Phoenix Pool and the Gate of Blue Carvings,
Works a scholar who despises fame and profit:
Day and night he is waiting for you to come,
    bringing your lute.

嘶酸雛雁失群夜，斷絕胡兒戀母聲。
川為靜其波，　　鳥亦罷其鳴。
烏珠部落家鄉遠，邏娑沙塵哀怨生。
幽音變調忽飄洒，長風吹林雨墮瓦；
迸泉颯颯飛木末，野鹿呦呦走堂下。
長安城連東掖垣，鳳凰池對青瑣門。
高才脫略名與利，日夕望君抱琴至。

ON HEARING AN WANSHAN PLAY THE
TARTAR PIPE

Li Qi

Bamboo cut on South mountain formed this Tartar pipe —
An instrument that came first from Kuchah;
Transplanted to the Han lands,
    its tunes turn strangely pleading.
A Tartar from Liangzhou plays it for me now,
And my companions hearing it heave sigh on sigh;
Travellers from afar grow homesick and all shed tears.

Many people like to listen, but few appreciate it:
It is like the sound of a great wind moving freely in space,
Or aged cypress and withered mulberry rattling in a cold blast,
Or nine phoenix nestlings, squeaking and twittering together,
The howl of dragons mingled with the roar of tigers,
The voice of autumn in a hundred springs
    and ten thousand living things.

Suddenly the tune changes to the drum-song of Yuyang:
Yellow clouds hang dreary; the white sun is darkened.
Another change and we seem to hear 'Spring in the willows':
Banks of flowers in the Royal park glow before us afresh.
In the great hall this New Year's eve, bright candles are set;
Of grand wine, each has a goblet; for music, these songs.

聽安萬善吹觱篥歌

李 頎

南山截竹為觱篥，此樂本自龜茲出；
流轉漢地曲轉奇，涼州胡人為我吹。
傍鄰聞者多歎息，遠客思鄉皆淚垂！
世人解聽不解賞，長飆風中自來往。
枯桑老柏寒颼飀，九雛鳴鳳亂啾啾；
龍吟虎嘯一時發，萬籟百泉相與秋。
忽然更作漁陽摻，黃雲蕭條白日黯。
變調如聞楊柳春，上林繁花照眼新。
歲夜高堂列明燭，美酒一杯聲一曲。

RETURNING AT EVENING TO LUMEN

Meng Haoran

From a hill temple, bells sound;
    day turns to dusk.
At Yuliang ferry-head
    they are wrangling for a passage;
Some follow the sandy shore
    back to the river hamlets.
I too have climbed aboard,
    homing to Lumen.
On Lumen the moonshine
    will break through misty trees;
Soon I shall reach Pang Gong's
    hidden retreat:
A gate of rocks, a path through pines,
    utter stillness and peace,
Only the hermit is there,
    coming and going alone.

夜歸鹿門山歌

孟 浩 然

山寺鳴鐘晝已昏，漁梁渡頭爭渡喧。
人隨沙岸向江村，余亦乘舟歸鹿門。
鹿門月照開煙樹，忽到龐公棲隱處。
巖扉松逕長寂寥，唯有幽人自來去。

SONG OF LU MOUNTAIN, SENT TO THE MINISTER-IN-WAITING, LU XUZHOU

Li Bai

I am just a madman of Chu
With a crazy song, mocking Confucius.
Clasping in my hand a green jade staff,
I went at dawn from Yellow Crane Pagoda.
I shall seek the mountain spirits of the Five Peaks,
    not minding the distance:
All my life I have loved to wander on famous mountains.

Mount Lu the splendid climbs to the Wain stars,
Like a nine-fold screen embroidered with clouds.
Its shadow falls across the sparkling lake, a shimmer of
    emerald;
Its two peaks soar to where the Golden Gate swings wide.
The cascades of Sanshiliang hang like a silver river;
The waterfalls of Xianglu greet me from afar.
Twisted cliff and massed ranges lead to the blue deeps of
    the sky:
Their green shapes in rosy mist glisten in the sunrise.
Bird flight cannot reach the remote skies of Wu.
I have climbed the heights and with bold spirit survey earth
    and heaven —
How the Great River flows on and on never to return.
Mile on mile yellow clouds sail before the wind;
Nine ways the river foams, white as mountain snow.

廬山謠寄盧侍御虛舟

李　白

我本楚狂人，　　狂歌笑孔丘。
手持綠玉杖，　　朝別黃鶴樓；
五岳尋仙不辭遠，一生好入名山遊。
廬山秀出南斗旁，屏風九疊雲錦張，
影落明湖青黛光，金闕前開二峰長。
銀河倒掛三石梁，香爐瀑布遙相望。
迴崖沓障凌蒼蒼。翠影紅霞映朝日，
鳥飛不到吳天長。登高壯觀天地間，
大江茫茫去不還。黃雲萬里動風色，
白波九道流雪山。

How I love to sing of Lu mountain!
Lu mountain is the spring of my poetry.
A calm gaze at Stone Mirror purifies my heart.
I know the path trod by Xie,[1] lost under dark moss.
I have long swallowed the sacred pill and shed worldly
    passions,
Attuned my spirit and begun to understand the Way.
From afar I see immortal spirits in the many-coloured clouds,
Clasping hibiscus they approach the Celestial City above
    the Ninth Heaven.
I want to join Lu'ao[2] and stray through limitless space.

---

1. This Xie was Xie Lingyun (385-433), a mountaineer who invented special climbing shoes.
2. Lu'ao, a famous recluse of Qin dynasty (255-209 B.C.)

好為廬山謠，　　興因廬山發。
閒窺石鏡清我心，謝公行處蒼苔沒。
早服還丹無世情，琴心三疊道初成。
遙見仙人彩雲裡，手把芙蓉朝玉京，
先期汗漫九垓上，願接盧敖遊太清！

A DREAM OF WANDERING ON TIAN MU —
A SONG OF FAREWELL

Li Bai

Seafarers have tales of an eastern isle
Lost in the breakers and mist
    and hard to reach;
Yue people speak of Tian Mu[1] —
Glimpse it at times
    through dawn mist and cloud-wrack.

Tian Mu soars to heaven, massed against the sky;
It dwarfs the Five Mountains
    and towers over 'Scarlet Castle'.
'Terrace of Heaven' is thousand on thousand feet high —
Beside Tian Mu it seems to crumble away to the south-east.

Dreaming one night of the southlands
    Wu and Yue,
I flew across the 'Mirror Lake'
    under the moon.

The moonlight threw my shadow on the lake,
And travelled with me up to Shan stream
Where the dwelling of Master Xie[2] stands to this day.
The green waters glistened,
    shrill the monkeys cried!

1. All the scenery mentioned is in N. Zhejiang; Scarlet Castle and
Terrace of Heaven belong to the same mountain range as Tian Mu.
2. Xie Lingyun (385-433), see note to previous poem.

142

夢遊天姥吟留別

李 白

海客談瀛洲，　　煙濤微茫信難求，
越人語天姥，　　雲霓明滅或可覩。
天姥連天向天橫，勢拔五嶽掩赤城。
天台四萬八千丈，對此欲倒東南傾。
我欲因之夢吳越，一夜飛度鏡湖月。
湖月照我影，　　送我至剡溪。
謝公宿處今尚在，淥水蕩漾清猨啼。

Slipping on the sandals of Master Xie,
I climbed a mountain stair into the dark clouds.
Halfway, I saw the sunlight on the sea
And in the empty air heard heaven's cock.

By a thousand precipices, ten thousand gorges,
      the path meandered;
Beguiled by flowers I rested on a rock
      when suddenly darkness fell:
Bears roared, dragons howled,
      streams crashed from the heights!
Oh I feared the dense forest — the endless peaks
      filled me with terror!

Clouds on dark clouds assembled, threatening rain;
Waters tumbling, foaming, and the mist rising!
Lightning and thunderclap!
Hills and precipices split and crumbled,
The stone gates of the Immortals' cavern
Swung open with a crash!
Of Heaven's immensity I could see no end;
Sun and moon shone brilliantly
      on the gold and silver court.

Clad in the rainbow, riding the wind,
The deities of the clouds descend
      multitudinous...
Tigers play upon lutes, a phoenix draws their chariot.
Oh the immortals throng as thick as hemp stalks!

腳著謝公屐，　　身登青雲梯。

半壁見海日，　　空中聞天雞。

千巖萬壑路不定，迷花倚石忽已暝；

熊咆龍吟殷巖泉，慄深林兮驚層巔。

雲青青兮欲雨，　水澹澹兮生烟。

列缺霹靂。　　　丘巒奔摧，

洞天石扉，　　　訇然中開。

青冥浩蕩不見底，日月照耀金銀台。

霓為衣兮風為馬，雲之君兮紛紛而來下。

虎鼓瑟兮鸞迴車，仙之人兮列如麻。

Suddenly terror seized me —
    my spirit quaked,
Startled, I sprang awake with a long sigh.
All I saw now were pillow and mat:
Lost was my vision in the veils of sunrise.
This is the way too with human joys,
Passing away like the water flowing east since time began.
Now I must leave you and go — when to return?
I will free a white deer[1] to stray in the green hills
And ride again to visit Tian Mu.
How can I bow and stoop before the mighty?
Would it not cramp my soul?

1. *White deer* symbolizes long life. In Chinese legend, a white deer
   or stag would often accompany an Immortal, or carry him on its back.

忽魂悸以魄動，　　怳驚起而長嗟。

惟覺時之枕席，　　失向來之烟霞。

世間行樂亦如此，古來萬事東流水。

別君去兮何時還？且放白鹿青崖間。

須行即騎訪名山。安能摧眉折腰事權貴，

使我不得開心顏。

PARTING AT A JINLING WINE SHOP
Li Bai

A breeze blows the willow flowers
    filling the inn with their fragrance;
A girl from Wu is brewing wine —
    she begs the guests to taste.
Young men of Jinling
    have come to speed my going;
I have to leave — and cannot leave,
    we drain our cups together.
I pray you, try to ask the water
    flowing towards the East —
"Which will last the longer, you
    or our parting thoughts?"

金陵酒肆留別

李 白

風吹柳花滿店香，吳姬壓酒勸客嘗，
金陵子弟來相送，欲行不行各盡觴，
請君試問東流水，別意與之誰短長。

AT A FAREWELL BANQUET FOR SHU YUN, THE IMPERIAL LIBRARIAN, IN XIE TIAO'S PAVILION, XUANZHOU

Li Bai

It has left me and gone —
Yesterday is a day that cannot be drawn back!
Disturber of my heart —
Today is a day bleak and joyless.
Long winds from a great distance
    speed the autumn geese.
Before this scene, let us carouse
    in the high pavilion!

Your writings are like the work of Immortals
    on Peng Lai,
    in essence like the School of Jian'an,
In purity and freedom like the younger Xie's,
With power to exhilarate and lift the spirit
So that we yearn to mount the heavens and clasp
    the bright moon!
But draw a knife to cut the stream —
    the stream only flows the faster;
Raise a cup to quench your sorrow —
    sorrow grows heavier still.
Man's life in this world
    seldom matches his hopes:
Early tomorrow, with unkempt hair,
    I shall take to a small boat.

The School of Jian'an was a school of poets at the end of Han dynasty and flourishing in Wei dynasty of the Three Kingdoms (220-265). Jian'an was actually a reign title of the last Han Emperor, Xian Di.

宣州謝朓樓餞別校書叔雲

李 白

棄我去者，　　昨日之日不可留；
亂我心者，　　今日之日多煩憂。
長風萬里送秋雁，對此可以酣高樓。
蓬萊文章建安骨，中間小謝又清發，
俱懷逸興壯思飛，欲上青天攬明月。
抽刀斷水水更流，舉杯消愁愁更愁。
人生在世不稱意，明朝散髮弄扁舟。

'TROTTING-HORSE RIVER': A FAREWELL POEM FOR GENERAL FENG ON HIS LEADING OUT THE WESTERN EXPEDITION

Cen Shen

Do you not see how the Trotting-horse River
    races into the Sea of Snow,
And the level sands, yellow and endless, reach to the sky?
At Luntai in the ninth moon, wind bays all night.
Broken stones from the gullies, big as pint-pots,
Scooped up by the wind, tumble all about.
In the Xiongnu country, the grass withers
    but their horses are sleek and fat;
Away to the west, by Gold Mountain, smoke and dust billow.

A great general of the Han people
    is leading our troops westward!
Even at night he keeps his armour on.
The army marches at midnight, lances clanging,
Wind blows sharp as a knife, cutting the face.
Sweat and snow steam from the horses' coats;
Icicles form on the 'Five Flowers' and 'Chains of Cash'.[1]
When our challenge was written in camp,
    water froze on the ink-stone.

When the enemy horsemen hear of our coming
    they should lose heart
And not dare to engage us at close quarters,
    sword to sword.
At the west gate the staff officers await your announcement
    of victory.

1. Breeds of horse.

走馬川行奉送封大夫出師西征

岑 參

君不見走馬川行雪海邊，平沙莽莽黃入天。

輪台九月風夜吼，　　　　一川碎石大如斗，

隨風滿地石亂走。

匈奴草黃馬正肥，　　　　金山西見煙塵飛，

漢家大將西出師，　　　　將軍金甲夜不脫。

半夜軍行戈相撥，　　　　風頭如刀面如割。

馬毛帶雪汗氣蒸，　　　　五花連錢旋作冰，

幕中草檄硯水凝。

虜騎聞之應膽懾，　　　　料知短兵不敢接，

軍師西門佇獻捷。

SONG OF LUNTAI: PRESENTED TO GENERAL FENG, LEADER OF THE WESTERN EXPEDITION

Cen Shen

On Luntai city wall
    the night horns are blowing;
Northward over Luntai
    the Pleiades sink.
Last night a feathered despatch passed through Quli:
    "Chanyu the Tartar chief is west of Gold Mountain!"
From the watch-tower, peering to the west
    we can see smoke and dust
Where the forces of Han are camping
    north of Luntai.
You our Marshal, flanked with banners,
    will lead the expedition westward.
At first light the fifes shrill,
    the great army moves off.
On all sides, the boom of drums
    like the pounding of Snow Sea's waves,
From three armies a great roar
    seems to shake Mount Yin!
At the enemy border, the breath of war
    reaches into the clouds;
On the battlefield, grass roots will clamber
    over their white bones.
Wind tears across Dagger River,
    piling cloud on cloud;
On icy stones at Shakou
    the horses' hoofs slither.
A vice-premier in the Emperor's service must bear pain and
    hardship;

You have vowed to reward your country by quietening the
    border lands.
Who has not read the histories of old times?
Now we see your fame and merit surpassing the ancients.

輪臺歌奉送封大夫出師西征

岑 參

輪臺城頭夜吹角，輪臺城北旄頭落。
羽書昨夜過渠黎，單于已在金山西。
戍樓西望煙塵黑，漢兵屯在輪臺北。
上將擁旄西出征，平明吹笛大軍行。
四邊伐鼓雪海湧，三軍大呼陰山動。
虜塞兵氣連雲屯，戰場白骨纏草根。
劍河風急雲片闊，沙口石凍馬蹄脱。
亞相勤王甘苦辛，誓將報國靖邊塵！
古來青史誰不見？今見功名勝古人。

A SONG OF WHITE SNOW:
FAREWELL TO MR. WU, AN OFFICIAL
WHO IS RETURNING HOME

Cen Shen

A north wind snatches at the earth
    tearing the pale grass;
September in the Tartar clime
    brings the snow whirling
As if suddenly one night
    the spring wind would rise
And from a thousand and ten thousand pear trees
    scatter the blossom.
Flakes flutter through the screens and wet the gauze curtains;
Fox furs cannot warm us, nor the light brocade quilts.
Our General can hardly draw his horn-emblazoned bow;
The Border Commissioner freezes, even in his coat of mail.
A hundred feet of ice masks
    the mounds and hollows of the desert;
Mile after mile, dreary clouds hang dull and petrified.

The Commander sends for wine
    to toast our guest who is leaving,
To the music of Tartar lute, guitar and shepherd's pipe.
Wildly whirls the evening snow beyond the camp gates;
Wind pulls on the scarlet flag, frozen motionless.
At the east gate of Luntai I bid you farewell:
As you move away, snow blots the Tian Shan road.
At the hill's shoulder, in the turn of the road,
    I can see you no longer:
Only your horse's hoof prints remain
    in the snow.

白雪歌送武判官歸京

岑　參

北風捲地白草折，胡天八月即飛雪；
忽如一夜春風來，千樹萬樹梨花開。
散入珠簾濕羅幕，狐裘不暖錦衾薄。
將軍角弓不得控，都護鐵衣冷猶著。
瀚海闌干百丈冰，愁雲慘澹萬里凝。
中軍置酒飲歸客，胡琴琵琶與羌笛。
紛紛暮雪下轅門，風掣紅旗凍不翻。
輪臺東門送君去，去時雪滿天山路；
山迴路轉不見君，雪上空留馬行處。

LOOKING AT A HORSE PAINTING BY GENERAL CAO AT THE HOUSE OF THE RECORDER, WEI FENG

Du Fu

Since the birth of the dynasty, of those who painted saddle-
  horses,
Only the Prince of Jiangdu was reckoned a wonder,
Till General Cao won a name, in the last thirty years,
And men saw again the true yellow thoroughbreds.

When he drew the late Emperor's grey, 'Night-shiner,'
Thunder-claps rolled for ten days over Dragon Pool.
In the inner Treasury was a red cornelian bowl:
Court ladies passed an order to the maids of honour to fetch it.
The bowl presented, the General made obeisance and danced
  home elated.
Filmy silks and fine brocades were speedily showered on him;
Noble relatives and powerful families acquired samples of his
  painting:
For the first time they found their screens radiating brilliance.

In past years, Taizong had a curly-maned dun;
In our days, General Guo has a piebald called 'Lion':
Here in this freshly painted picture are the two horses together,
Making the connoisseur time and again sigh with admiration.
Both were war-chargers, each a match for ten thousand.
There on the white silk, winds and sand blow endlessly;
The seven other horses are splendidly painted too,
Colours blended like snow and sunset on a winter sky.

韋諷錄事宅觀曹將軍畫馬圖

杜 甫

國初已來畫鞍馬，神妙獨數江都王。
將軍得名三十載，人間又見真乘黃。
曾貌先帝照夜白，龍池十日飛霹靂。
內府殷紅瑪瑙盤，婕妤傳詔才人索。
盤賜將軍拜舞歸，輕紈細綺相追飛。
貴戚權門得筆跡，始覺屏障生光輝。
昔日太宗拳毛騧，近時郭家獅子花。
今之新圖有二馬，復令識者久歎嗟！
此皆騎戰一敵萬，縞素漠漠開風沙。
其餘七匹亦殊絕，迥若寒空雜霞雪。

Frosty hoofs trample between great catalpa trees,
Horse officials and grooms stand by in ranks.

How lovable these nine horses, vying with one another —
Their clear, brave glance, their dignified bearing!
I humbly ask, who has a mind keen enough to appreciate
    them?
Lately there is Wei Feng and before him Zhi Dun.
I remember of old the Imperial processions to
    the palace at Xinfeng,
How the kingfisher banners brushed the sky, streaming towards
    the east,
Rearing and prancing, peerless in form,
    thrice ten thousand horses,
Each strong in muscle and bone like those in this painting.
Since the day when precious gifts were offered to the spirit
    of the river,
Never again has a dragon been shot in the waters of the
    Yangtze.
Do you not see the burial mound by Jinsu mountain, in
    pines and cypresses,
The dragon horses gone and the birds crying on the wind?

King Mu of Zhou is said to have met the god of the Yellow river
and offered him treasure. Emperor Wu of Han shot a dragon while
sailing on the Yangtze river. Du Fu was thinking of the glories of
Xuanzong's reign, now vanished; the burial mound by Jinsu mountain
refers to this Emperor's tomb in Shanxi.

霜蹄蹴踏長楸間，　　馬官廝養森成列。
可憐九馬爭神駿，　　顧視清高氣深穩。
借問苦心愛者誰？　　後有韋諷前支遁。
憶昔巡幸新豐宮，　　翠華拂天來向東；
騰驤磊落三萬匹，　　皆與此圖筋骨同。
自從獻寶朝河宗，　　無復射蛟江水中。
君不見金粟堆前松柏裡，龍媒去盡鳥呼風。

INSCRIPTION FOR A PAINTING:
FOR GENERAL CAO BA

Du Fu

You, general, are descended from King Wu of Wei,
Though now a commoner of respectable family.
That heroic carver of kingdoms is no more!
But his writings and achievements are with us still.
In learning calligraphy, you first studied the style of Lady Wei,
Only regretted you could not excel Wang Xizhi.
You painted on and did not notice old age coming;
Riches and honour, you said, are like floating clouds.

In the years of Kaiyuan, you were often in audience with
    the Emperor,
By imperial favor, frequently ascended the Hall of Southern
    Fragrance.
In the Hall of Rising Mists, the portraits of worthy ministers
    had grown faint
You worked on them with your brush and drew out the living
    faces:
The virtuous ministers' heads were graced with high official
    hats,
The fierce generals' waists were fitted with great feathered
    arrows.
With the Duke of Bao and the Duke of E, the beards and hair
    seemed to bristle,
Their valiant mien suddenly sprightly, as if drunk with battle.

丹青引贈曹將軍霸

杜 甫

將軍魏武之子孫，於今為庶為清門，
英雄割據雖已矣，文采風流今尚存。
學書初學衛夫人，但恨無過王右軍。
丹青不知老將至，富貴於我如浮雲！
開元之中常引見，承恩數上南薰殿；
凌煙功臣少顏色，將軍下筆開生面。
良相頭上進賢冠，猛將腰間大羽箭；
褒公鄂公毛髮動，英姿颯爽來酣戰。

The late Emperor had a horse, a 'jade flower' piebald;
Painters numerous as the hills could not catch his likeness.
One day, this horse was led to the Red Terrace steps:
As he stood within the imperial gateway, a great wind
    seemed to blow.
The order was given you, General, to unroll a piece of white
    silk:
In deep thought, you worked out a fine composition,
In a little while a veritable dragon emerged from the Ninth Heaven;
With every stroke you showed all the painted horses of the
    past to be lifeless.
There was a 'jade flower' then above the royal couch:
Above the couch and below the steps they stood facing each
    other.
His Imperial Highness, blandly smiling, pressed gold on you,
Stable boys and Head Groom looked quite downcast.

Your disciple Han Gan long studied your fine technique;
He too had special skill with many kinds of horse,
But Gan could only paint the flesh, not the bone-structure:
The true spirit of these splendid beasts he allowed to escape.

You, General, so excellent in painting, catching the horses'
    spirit,
If you chance to meet a handsome scholar can draw him too
    to the life.
But here you are now, drifting in the disorder of war,
Sketching from time to time some common passer-by.
At poverty and changed fortune, the vulgar turn up their eyes;
In the whole earth, no well-born person so poor as you!
Only look at the glorious names from past history —
In the end, misery tied up their existence.

先帝御馬玉花驄，畫工如山貌不同。
是日牽來赤墀下，迥立閶闔生長風。
詔謂將軍拂絹素，意匠慘淡經營中。
斯須九重真龍出，一洗萬古凡馬空。
玉花卻在御榻上，榻上庭前屹相向；
至尊含笑催賜金，圉人太僕皆惆悵。
弟子韓幹早入室，亦能畫馬窮殊相。
幹惟畫肉不畫骨，忍使驊騮氣凋喪。
將軍善畫蓋有神，偶逢佳士亦寫真。
即今飄泊干戈際，屢貌尋常行路人。
途窮反遭俗眼白，世人未有如公貧！
但看古來盛名下，終日坎壈纏其身。

FOR HAN THE CENSOR

Du Fu

Today I am not happy — thinking of Yueyang;
My body longs to fly to you, but I lie sick in bed.
My charming friend, graceful as a girl, you are held by the
    waters of autumn;
You lave your feet in lake Dongting, gaze everywhere on
    wastes.
Geese fly in dark flocks, sun and moon glare white,
Green leaves of the maple crimson, frost falls from the air.

In Jade City a host of gods gather by the Pole star,
Some astride unicorns, others straddle phoenixes,
Hibiscus banners droop, under the mists and vapour:
Their reflection shimmers on the ripples of Xiao and Xiang.
Nectar intoxicates the dwellers in the Palace of Stars,
Though few of the winged immortals are by their side.
I seemed to hear Chi Song was among yesterday's throng,
But perhaps it was only Zhang Liang, statesman of Han times,
Who formerly helped Liu Bang to found a dynasty at
Chang'an —
His strategy still survives, but his spirit must be grieving!
Who am I, you say, to measure the fate of states?
In this troubled world, the fragrant maple tastes better
    than stale meats.
To be detained like the old historian in Zhounan is indeed
    cause for regret,
For where the South Pole star reigns, there should be long
    life and prosperity.
Yet why should my friend be held by the autumn waters
And not raised up, to make offering at the Jade Palace?

The poet sympathises with his friend Han, who appears to have lost his post at the Capital and has retired to the south. He envies the state of the Immortals who are free from care, but nevertheless expresses the hope that his friend will be able to return and serve at Court. A more detailed explanation is given in the Notes, p. 789.

寄 韓 諫 議

杜 甫

今我不樂思岳陽，身欲奮飛病在床！
美人娟娟隔秋水，濯足洞庭望八荒。
鴻飛冥冥日月白，青楓葉赤天雨霜。
玉京群帝集北斗，或騎麒麟翳鳳凰。
芙蓉旌旗煙霧落，影動倒景搖瀟湘。
星宮之君醉瓊漿，羽人稀少不在旁。
似聞昨者赤松子，恐是漢代韓張良。
昔隨劉氏定長安，帷幄未改神慘傷！
國家成敗吾豈敢，色難腥腐餐楓香。
周南留滯古所惜，南極老人應壽昌！
美人胡為隔秋水，焉得置之貢玉堂？

THE OLD CYPRESS TREES

Du Fu

Before the shrine of Zhuge Liang
    grows an aged cypress —
Trunk like green bronze, roots like rock:
Its hoary bark smoothed by rain
    is forty spans round;
Its sombre green pierces the clouds
    two thousand feet high.
When the clouds roll up, long mists
    reach to Wu Gorge;
When the moon rises, its cold whiteness
    touches Snow mountain.
Prince and Minister would meet here
    in days gone by
And the tree is still loved and honoured
    by the people.

I remember yesterday's road
    winding east of Brocade Pavilion,
And the obscure shrine that the First Ruler
    shares with his Marshal:
Gnarled and huge the ancient tree there on the plain;
Dim and forgotten the red and blue painted chamber, empty
    now.
Firm, firm squats the tree, gripping the soil,
Tall and solitary in the heights of heaven, baiting the rough
    winds.

古柏行

杜 甫

孔明廟前有老柏，柯如青銅根如石。
霜皮溜雨四十圍，黛色參天二千尺。
雲來氣接巫峽長，月出寒通雪山白。
君臣已與時際會，樹木猶為人愛惜。
憶昨路遶錦亭東，先主武侯同閟宮。
崔嵬枝幹郊原古，窈窕丹青戶牖空。
落落盤踞雖得地，冥冥孤高多烈風。

It draws support from some unearthly power,
Created sturdy and true, the merit of Nature.
A great mansion about to collapse
    would need timber like this,
But countless oxen with straining necks
    could hardly shift the weight.
Though it does not figure in learned writings,
    it still amazes people;
Though it has not refused the feller's axe,
    who could carry it away?
Its steadfast heart cannot escape
    the boring of tiny insects,
But its scented foliage still gives shelter
    to *luan* and phoenix.

Ambitious scholars and retired officials
    should not sigh and complain:
Since ancient days, the greater the timber,
    the harder to work.

Towards the end of his life, Du Fu came to live in Guizhou, Sichuan, formerly part of the Kingdom of Shu. The poem describes the temple there to Zhuge Liang, the great statesman and general, who helped to establish Liu Bei as the First Ruler of Shu. The cypress is reputed to have been planted by Zhuge himself. The second stanza refers to another shrine to this statesman, in Chengdu (known as 'Brocade city') where Liu Bei is also commemorated. Du Fu describes this again in his poem 'A Premier of Shu' (p.472) and 'Remembering the past' (p.488).

扶持自是神明力，正直原因造化功。
大廈如傾要樑棟，萬牛迴首邱山重，
不露文章世已驚，未辭剪伐誰能送？
苦心豈免容螻蟻，香葉終經宿鸞鳳。
志士幽人莫怨嗟，古來材大難為用！

ON SEEING A PUPIL OF LADY GONGSUN PERFORM THE SWORD DANCE

Du Fu

There was once a lovely woman, Lady Gongsun,
Whose performance of the Sword Dance amazed the whole
  world:
Onlookers massed as hills watched her with dizzy senses
As she made heaven and earth appear to plunge and soar.
Her sword flashed: it was like the nine falling suns
  shot by Yi the archer;
She leapt and you thought a crowd of gods bestrode a soaring
  dragon!
She advanced like a peal of thunder, with the rage of a
  gathering storm;
She ceased like rivers and seas frozen with glittering ice.
The red lips, the pearl-embroidered sleeves — all are turned
  to dust.
But the old lady had a pupil to carry on her good name:
A lovely girl of Linying, living at Bai Di,
Who performs this dance with marvellous skill and
  imagination.
She and I had much to speak about,
Recalling the old times and the old events with growing
  heartache.
The late Emperor, Xuanzong had eight thousand such
  women,
Yet Gongsun in the Sword Dance excelled them from the
  first.

觀公孫大娘弟子舞劍器行並序

杜 甫

昔有佳人公孫氏，一舞劍器動四方，
觀者如山色沮喪，天地為之久低昂，
㸌如羿射九日落，矯如群帝驂龍翔。
來如雷霆收震怒，罷如江海凝清光。
絳脣珠袖兩寂寞，晚有弟子傳芬芳。
臨潁美人在白帝，妙舞此曲神揚揚。
與余問答既有以，感時撫事增惋傷。
先帝侍女八千人，公孫劍器初第一。

Fifty years have passed now, like a flick of the hand;
Wind and dust, wave on wave, darkened the Imperial dwelling,
The players of the Pear Garden dispersed like mist:
A wintry sun lights the dwindling beauty of those sweet
    singers.
Trees already meet over the mound at Jinsu;
On the rocky walls of Qutang, grasses rattle in the wind...
At our feast tonight, when the urgent pipes and songs had
    ended,
At the height of our pleasure, sorrow struck
    as the moon rose in the east.
And I, an old man, knowing not where to go,
Must stumble up the rough mountain on blistered feet,
    ruing the pace.

五十年間似反掌，風塵澒洞昏王室。
梨園弟子散如煙，女樂餘姿映寒日。
金粟堆南木已拱，瞿塘石城草蕭瑟。
玳筵急管曲復終，樂極哀來月東出。
老夫不知其所往，足繭荒山轉愁疾。

TIPSY SONG ON STONE FISH LAKE[1]

Yuan Jie

Stone Fish lake
Is like Dongting
When the summer water is brimming
    and Jun hill green.
The hill is our beaker,
The water our wine-pool:
Tipplers, one by one, settle on the rocky islet.

Strong wind for days has formed great billows,
But they cannot daunt the men
    bringing up the wine boats.
Seated on Ba Qiu, I seize a long ladle
And pour drink on all sides
    to drive away care.

1. The lake gets its name from a fish-shaped rock which rises out of
   it. Jun hill is an island on Dongting lake, and Ba Qiu a hill in
   Hunan, similar in shape to the 'Stone Fish'.

石魚湖上醉歌

石魚湖，似洞庭，夏水欲滿君山青。
山為樽，水為沼，酒徒歷歷坐洲島。
長風連日作大浪，不能廢人運酒舫。
我持長瓢坐巴邱，酌飲四座以散愁。

MOUNTAIN ROCKS

Han Yu

A tiny path twisted between
    jags of mountain rock;
In the grey dusk, with bats darting,
    I reached the monastery.
I sat on the hall steps — fresh-smelling
    rain had just ceased;
The banana leaves were huge and buds bulged
    on the gardenias.
A monk told me there were good frescoes of the Buddha
    on their ancient walls:
He brought a lamp to light
    those rarely seen treasures.
He arranged my bed and shook out the mat,
    and put soup and rice before me —
Coarse food, still enough
    to satisfy my hunger.
Night deepened and I went tranquilly to rest,
    the sounds of insects ceased,
A clear moon rose over the mountain ridge
    and shone through my doorway.

At daybreak, I left alone,
    before the path became visible;
Ahead and behind, high and low,
    the damp mists thinned.
The rosy tints of the mountains and the green
    of the torrents scattered their brilliance.
Sometimes I saw huge pines and oaks,
    ten spans in girth.

Crossing swift streams, I stepped
    barefoot over boulders.
Water gurgled noisily, the wind
    puffed out my gown.
Human life spent like this
    would be joyful indeed!
Why must man be held in check,
    like a horse with a bit?
Well, you two or three fellows, my tried companions,
Shall we not return here in our old age?

山　石

韓　愈

山石犖确行徑微，黃昏到寺蝙蝠飛。

升堂坐階新雨足，芭蕉葉大梔子肥。

僧言古壁佛畫好，以火來照所見稀。

鋪床拂席置羹飯，疏糲亦足飽我饑。

夜深靜臥百蟲絕，清月出嶺光入扉。

天明獨去無道路，出入高下窮煙霏。

山紅澗碧紛爛縵，時見松櫪皆十圍。

當流赤足踏澗石，水聲激激風生衣。

人生如此自可樂，豈必局促為人鞿。

嗟哉吾黨二三子，安得至老不更歸？

PRESENTED TO ZHANG THE CLERK ON THE FIFTEENTH NIGHT OF THE EIGHTH MOON

Han Yu

Filmy clouds from the four quarters;
    Heaven has lost its stars;
A clean wind sweeps through space,
    moonlight flows in ripples.
On level sands and quiet waters
    sound and shadow cease.
I beg you, drink a cup of wine
    and sing a song to me.
The notes of your song are harsh,
    the words bitter indeed —
My tears run like rain
    before I have heard to the end.

"Where Dongting meets the sky
    and Jiuyi soars,
Dragon and crocodile rise and vanish,
    apes and racoons yelp.
Nine chances of dying to ten of life
    to reach this post,
In rooms so silent and still
    as if we had gone into hiding!
We are fearful of snakes when we rise from bed,
    of poison when we eat;
Air from the sea clammy and damp,
    Its odour rank and musty...

八月十五夜贈張功曹

韓　愈

纖雲四卷天無河，清風吹空月舒波，
沙平水息聲影絕，一杯相屬君當歌。
君歌聲酸辭且苦，不能聽終淚如雨！
「洞庭連天九疑高，蛟龍出沒猩鼯號。
十生九死到官所，幽居默默如藏逃。
下牀畏蛇食畏藥，海氣濕蟄薰腥臊。

Yesterday, by the District Office,
 they were beating the great drum:
A new Emperor had succeeded in the royal line
 and elevated loyal ministers.
Pardons travelled in a single day
 many hundreds of miles;
Criminals due for execution
 escaped the death sentence;
Those in exile are recalled,
 the banished ones return;
Evil and vice are washed away,
 the Court ranks purified.
The Governor proposed our names but
 the Chief Censor suppressed them:
We were merely transferred to these
 rough and primitive places.
Your present rank of petty official
 is not worth a mention —
You may not escape a good whipping
 in the dust and dirt!
Many of our fellow-exiles are
 on the way back,
But the road to Heaven is dark and dangerous —
 hard for us to climb."

Come, stop your song now and listen to my song —
This song of mine is quite different from yours.
"Of all the year's bright moons, tonight's glows the brightest.
Man's life is fixed by fate, not his to order:
If we have wine and do not drink —
 of what use is the moonlight?"

昨者州前捶大鼓，嗣皇繼聖登夔皋。
赦書一日行千里，罪從大辟皆除死，
遷者追迴流者還，滌瑕蕩垢清朝班。
州家申名使家抑，坎軻祇得移荊蠻。
判司卑官不堪說，未免捶楚塵埃間。
同時輩流多上道，天路幽險難追攀。」
君歌且休聽我歌。我歌今與君殊科。
一年明月今宵多，人生由命非由他，
有酒不飲奈明何？

VISITING A TEMPLE ON HENG MOUNTAIN AFTER STAYING THE NIGHT AT A MONASTERY ON THE PEAK: A POEM INSCRIBED ON THE ENTRANCE GATE

Han Yu

The Five Sacred Mountains have their rank like the Three
    Dukes:
Four stand guard in a ring, Mount Song in the centre.
In the wild lands of the fiery south, the haunt of weird spirits,
Heaven bestowed on Heng Mountain the power to assume
    supremacy.
Scudding clouds and seeping mists are stored in its girdle,
The ultimate peak is so far, who can discern it?
I came here in autumn, just at the season of rains —
The air dull and foggy, the clean wind gone.
I steadied my thoughts and muttered a prayer, as if the spirits
    would answer —
Surely my upright mind would be able to move them?
Instantly the mist blew clear, a crowd of peaks emerged;
I saw a pinnacle above that held the blue vault of the sky.
'Purple Canopy' stretched out to touch 'Heaven's Pillar',
'Stone Granary' sprang up and piled beside 'Fire God':
The majesty of this shook my soul, I dismounted to prostrate
    myself.
By the pathway of pine and cypress I hastened to the holy
    temple.

謁衡嶽廟遂宿嶽寺題門樓

韓　愈

五嶽祭秩皆三公，四方環鎮嵩當中，
火維地荒足妖怪，天假神柄專其雄。
噴雲泄霧藏半腹，雖有絕頂誰能窮？
我來正逢秋雨節，陰氣晦昧無清風。
潛心默禱若有應，豈非正直能感通。
須臾靜掃眾峰出，仰見突兀撐青空。
紫蓋連延接天柱，石廩騰擲堆祝融。
森然動魄下馬拜，松柏一徑趨靈宮。

Its whitewashed walls and rosy cassia wood shimmered and
　　glinted with light;
There were frescoes of spiritual beings filled out in blue and
　　scarlet.
I climbed the steps with shoulders bowed to offer dried meat
　　and wine;
Through my humble offering I tried to show my heart's
　　sincerity.
Within the temple was an old man who could interpret the
　　spirit's will,
His eyes lit up, he kept bowing and peering;
He handed me the divination box and showed me how to cast;
He said, "That's the luckiest throw — the rest are not so good."

Though exiled to the barbarous wilds, luckily I haven't died
　　there.
Sufficient clothing and food are all I desire now:
To be Duke, Prince, General, Premier, I long gave up hope;
Even if the spirit granted me blessing, what would be the
　　use?
I shall lodge at night in a monastery — climb to an upper
　　room,
And when moon and stars have hid their brilliance in the
　　veils of sunrise,
Though monkeys chatter and bells toll, I shall not heed the
　　dawn,
Nor how the wintry sun effulgent climbs out of the east.

粉牆丹桂動光彩，鬼物圖畫填青紅。
升階傴僂薦脯酒，欲以菲薄明其衷。
廟內老人識神意，睢盱探伺能鞠躬。
手持盃珓導我擲，云此最吉餘難同。
竄逐蠻荒幸不死，衣食纔足甘長終。
侯王將相望久絕，神縱欲福難為功。
夜投佛寺上高閣，星月掩映雲曚曨，
猿鳴鐘動不知曙，杲杲寒日生於東。

SONG OF THE STONE DRUMS

Han Yu

Mr. Chang handed me this rubbing from the Stone Drums
And urged me to compose a 'Stone Drum Song'.
Shaoling has lost its Du Fu, Li Bai 'the immortal' is dead —
What can my poor talent do for the Stone Drums?

When the Zhou laws decayed and the Four Seas heaved in
    turmoil,
King Xuan rose in anger and brandished his sacred sword,
And wide swung the doors of Bright Hall to receive the
    congratulations
Of feudal princes with their swords and jangling pendants.
To the hunt at Qiyang galloped the brave and handsome,
Birds and game lay strewn over countless miles:
All was wonderfully chiselled in stone, to inform ten thousand
    generations.
Rock was broken from rough hillsides, shaped into drums;
Attendant ministers skilled in the arts, each of the first rank,
Were chosen to carve and inscribe them, and set them on
    the mountain.
Rain drenched, sun baked, wild fire burned them,
Spirits guarded, and drove away what would harm them.
Where could you have found this sheet of tracing?
Absolutely complete down to the finest stroke, with no error.

石　鼓　歌

韓　愈

張生手持石鼓文，勸我試作石鼓歌，
少陵無人謫仙死，才薄將奈石鼓何？
周綱陵遲四海沸，宣王憤起揮天戈。
大開明堂受朝賀，諸侯劍佩鳴相磨。
蒐於岐陽騁雄俊，萬里禽獸皆遮羅。
鐫功勒成告萬世，鑿石作鼓墮嵯峨。
從臣才藝咸第一，揀選撰刻留山阿。
雨淋日炙野火燎，鬼物守護煩撝呵。
公從何處得紙本？毫髮盡備無差訛。

But severe in expression, obscure in meaning, hard to understand,
The style of calligraphy neither 'official' nor 'tadpole' —
Of such antiquity, how could it escape disfigurement?
The strokes like living dragons, hewn with a keen sword,
Like phoenix flying and argus wheeling, a crowd of immortals
    descending,
Sea corals and jade trees with branches firmly entwined,
Or golden cords and iron wires strongly twisted and locked,
Like ancient tripods skipping into water or shuttles soaring
    like dragons.
Ignorant scholars collecting poems forgot to include these;
The two books of Solemn Songs were too narrow, lacked
    scope.
Confucius travelling westward did not reach Qin State —
He gathered a constellation of stars but missed the sun and
    moon!
How sad that I who love the old culture was born too late!
I look at the drums, and tears stream from my eyes.

I remember, long ago, being summoned to receive my
    doctorate,
The year when the reign title changed to Yuanhe.
An old friend with the army at You Fufeng
Advised me where these old drums were buried.
I brushed my cap, washed myself, and spoke with the overseer
    of sacrifices —
Objects so precious, how many could there be in existence?

辭嚴義密讀難曉，字體不類隸與蝌。
年深豈免有缺畫，快劍砍斷生蛟鼉，
鸞翔鳳翥眾仙下，珊瑚碧樹交枝柯，
金繩鐵索鎖紐壯，古鼎躍水龍騰梭。
陋儒編詩不收入，二雅褊迫無委蛇。
孔子西行不到秦，掎摭星宿遺羲娥。
嗟余好古生苦晚，對此涕淚雙滂沱！
憶昔初蒙博士徵，其年始改稱元和。
故人從軍在右輔，為我度量掘臼科，
濯冠沐浴告祭酒，如此至寶存豈多？

They should be wrapped in rugs and mats and transported
  forthwith:
All ten drums could be loaded on just a few camels.
And presented to the Imperial Temple, like the tripod of Gao;
Their splendour and value would increase a hundredfold.
Or if the royal bounty would present them to the University,
Many students could study and diligently decipher them.
In Han days, people came to the Capital over the great Passes,
  to look at the classical texts;
If these drums were set up in public, the whole country
  would scramble to see them.
We would scratch out the moss, scrape away lichen, expose
  the joints and corners,
Set them in a definite place, level and not aslant.
A great building with wide eaves should house them,
Where nothing could happen to them, as it did in the past
  years.
But the Court officials have grown old in service,
Will not comply with this obligation but keep procrastinating.
So herdboys use them for striking sparks, cows to rub their
  horns on;
Who would handle them now or stroke them with affection?
Days fade and months melt away, the drums returning to dust:
Six years I looked to the west, chanting my songs in vain.
Wang Xizhi's ordinary script with its bewitching style of
  brushwork
Can be had, several pages of it, for a few white geese!
Eight dynasties have passed since the Zhou, and wars have
  ceased:
Why does nobody look after these drums?

We are at peace now, days with no disturbance,
The authorities employ scholars and respect Confucius and
　　Mencius,
How can I bring this subject up for discussion?
I want to borrow an orator's mouth — words tumbling like a
　　cataract!

Here I end my song of the Stone Drums —
Alas, alas! my thoughts have gone wandering!

氈包席裹可立致，十鼓祇載數駱駝。
薦諸太廟比郜鼎，光價豈止百倍過。
聖恩若許留太學，諸生講解得切磋。
觀經鴻都尚填咽，坐見舉國來奔波。
剜苔剔蘚露節角，安置妥帖平不頗，
大廈深簷與蓋覆，經歷久遠期無佗。
中朝大官老於事，詎肯感激徒媕婀！
牧童敲火牛礪角，誰復著手為摩挲？
日銷月鑠就埋沒，六年西顧空吟哦！
羲之俗書趁姿媚，數紙尚可博白鵝。
繼周八代爭戰罷，無人收拾理則那？
方今太平日無事，柄任儒術崇丘軻。
安能以此上論列，願借辯口如懸河。
石鼓之歌止於此，嗚呼我意其蹉跎！

THE OLD FISHERMAN

Liu Zongyuan

An old fisherman sleeps at night
    under the western cliff;
At dawn he draws the clear water of Xiang
    and kindles the bamboos of Chu.
When the sun rises and the mists thin
    there is no one in sight,
One sound — the creak of his oars
    by the green hills and the green stream.
As I turn to look, the sky merges
    in the rippling current;
Cloud follows aimless cloud
    high over the cliff.

When the sun rises and the mists thin
    there is no one in sight,
One sound — the creak of his oars
    by the green hills and the green stream.
煙消日出不見人，欸乃一聲山水綠。

漁　翁

柳　宗　元

漁翁夜傍西巖宿，曉汲清湘然楚竹，
煙消日出不見人，欸乃一聲山水綠。
迴看天際下中流，巖上無心雲相逐。

EVERLASTING REGRET
Bai Juyi

Ming Huang, the great lover, longed for a peerless beauty;
Many years he ruled, and sought without finding.
There was in the Yang family a girl just grown to womanhood,
Reared in the women's chambers and still a stranger to men:
Heaven had graced her with a loveliness hard to forget —
One day she was chosen, to lie beside the Emperor.

One smiling, wayward glance
    spoke of a hundred allurements —
The painted beauties of the Six Palaces
    looked pale beside her.
With Spring yet cold, she was bathed in Hua Qing pool,
In the soft water of that warm spring
    they laved her smooth body,
Supported by her handmaids, bewitching in her frailty;
This was when she first received
    the Emperor's love.

With her cloudy hair, her flower-like face,
    and twinkling golden headdress,
Warm within the hibiscus bed-curtain
    she spends the Spring nights.
Oh Spring nights are too short! She sleeps till the sun is high:
From then on, her lord the Emperor
    held no more dawn audiences.
She shared his pleasures, attended at his feasts, no moment
    idle;
Companion of his Spring roaming, despot of his nights.

長 恨 歌

白 居 易

漢皇重色思傾國，御宇多年求不得。
楊家有女初長成，養在深閨人未識。
天生麗質難自棄，一朝選在君王側。
迴眸一笑百媚生，六宮粉黛無顏色。
春寒賜浴華清池，溫泉水滑洗凝脂，
侍兒扶起嬌無力，始是新承恩澤時。
雲鬢花顏金步搖，芙蓉帳暖度春宵；
春宵苦短日高起，從此君王不早朝。
承歡侍宴無閒暇，春從春遊夜專夜。

Three thousand beauties dwelt in the inner courts,
But his love of all three thousand
    was lavished on one body.
Adorning herself in a Gold Chamber, she waited for night to
    come;
Feasting in the Jade Tower, they grew drunk with wine and
    Spring.
All her sisters and brothers received rank and feoff,
Every glory and splendour shone on her household:
It made the fathers and mothers of the whole Empire
Prefer to rear girls instead of boys.
High up where Li palace reaches into the blue,
Immortal music drifted with the wind, now here, now there;
Lazy songs, interminable dances, to the music of lyres and
    flutes
Till the day's end — and the Emperor tired not of gazing...
Came the war drums of Yu Yang, making the earth quake;
Terror silenced 'The song of the rainbow skirt and the coat
    of feathers'.
Dust and smoke surged from the nine-fold city walls.
A thousand chariots, ten thousand horsemen, headed for the
    South-west,
With kingfisher banners nodding, nodding,
    they travelled then halted;
A hundred miles or more, west of the Imperial city
The six armies would march no farther — what was to be done?
The Lady Yang knit her brows and was killed in front of
    the horses.

後宮佳麗三千人，三千寵愛在一身。
金屋妝成嬌侍夜，玉樓宴罷醉和春。
姊妹弟兄皆裂土，可憐光彩生門戶。
遂令天下父母心，不重生男重生女。
驪宮高處入青雲，仙樂風飄處處聞。
緩歌慢舞凝絲竹，盡日君王看不足。
漁陽鼙鼓動地來，驚破霓裳羽衣曲。
九重城闕煙塵生，千乘萬騎西南行。
翠華搖搖行復止，西出都門百餘里，
六軍不發無奈何？宛轉蛾眉馬前死。

Her bright head-gear tumbled in the dirt
    and no one picked it up:
Kingfisher feathers, golden birds and combs of jade.
The Emperor hid his face, unable to save her
He turned to look, and blood mingled with his flowing tears!

Yellow dust blew wildly, dreary winds whistled,
The armies wound slowly up a cloud path
    and climbed into Sword Pass
On Emei mountain travellers were few;
How dully the banners flapped in that weak sunlight!
Deep green was the Sichuan river, and the mountains grey.
Day after day and night after night
    His Majesty sorrowed.
He sees the moon over the Travelling Palace,
    painful in its loveliness;
He hears the bells in the night rain
    tinkle with a heartbreaking sound.
The heavens turn and earth revolves; the Dragon Chariot
    came back.
Reaching the fatal spot, the Emperor could not go on —
There in the mud and dust at the foot of Ma Wei
He sees no more her jade-like face, only the empty death
    place:
Ruler and ministers look at each other and tears wet their
    robes,
As they turn east to the city gates, giving their horses rein...

花鈿委地無人收，翠翹金雀玉搔頭。
君王掩面救不得，迴看血淚相和流。
黃埃散漫風蕭索，雲棧縈紆登劍閣。
峨嵋山下少人行，旌旗無光日色薄。
蜀江水碧蜀山青，聖主朝朝暮暮情。
行宮見月傷心色，夜雨聞鈴腸斷聲。
天旋地轉迴龍馭，到此躊躇不能去。
馬嵬坡下泥土中，不見玉顏空死處。
君臣相顧盡沾衣，東望都門信馬歸。

There were the ponds, there the gardens, all just as before,
Hibiscus of Taiyi lake, willows of Weiyang palace —
Hibiscus like her face, willow-leaves like her eyebrows —
Seeing these things, how could he hold back the tears?
Or when the spring breeze opened peach and plum flower,
Or the autumn rains beat down the Wutong leaves?
In the South court of the Western palace, autumn grass grew
    thick,
Red leaves fell and covered the steps — no one swept them
    away.
The Players of the Pear Garden were all white-haired,
The eunuchs and waiting-maids of the Pepper Chamber
    growing old.
In the Palace at evening when fireflies flit, he ponders in
    silence;
The wick of his single lamp burns low, before sleep comes.
Slowly, slowly, bells and drums usher in the long night,
Faintly, faintly, glimmers the Milky Way before dawn breaks.
Cold are the mandarin duck roof-tiles, coated with frost
    flowers,
And cold the kingfisher quilt, for who will share it now?
Idly, idly a year had passed since the dead and living parted,
But her spirit had never returned to him in dreams.
Then a Taoist magician from Linqiong came to the palace
    gate,
Claiming that his mystic powers could summon departed
    spirits.
In pity for the Emperor's restless desire,
They ordered him to seek her diligently.

歸來池苑皆依舊，太液芙蓉未央柳。
芙蓉如面柳如眉，對此如何不淚垂？
春風桃李花開日，秋雨梧桐葉落時。
西宮南內多秋草，落葉滿階紅不掃。
梨園子弟白髮新，椒房阿監青娥老。
夕殿螢飛思悄然，孤燈挑盡未成眠。
遲遲鐘鼓初長夜，耿耿星河欲曙天。
鴛鴦瓦冷霜華重，翡翠衾寒誰與共？
悠悠生死別經年，魂魄不曾來入夢。
臨邛道士鴻都客，能以精誠致魂魄。
為感君王展轉思，遂教方士殷勤覓。

Borne on the air and cleaving the clouds,
    he flew like a flash of lightning:
Rose into the sky, penetrated the earth, searching everywhere;
He explored the blue realm above and the Yellow Springs below,
But in both immensities he could not find her.
Then he heard of a mystic mountain, rising from the sea —
A mountain set in vacancy, unsubstantial,
Where towers and chambers, marvellously wrought,
    soar into five-coloured clouds.
There lived a host of immortal spirits, graceful and gentle,
And among them one who was called Tai Zhen,
With skin like snow and flower-like face —
    perhaps it was she...

At the western wing of a gold mansion,
    he knocked at a jade gate,
And instructed 'Little Jade' to inform the Queen's hand-maid.
When she heard of the envoy from the Son of Heaven,
She started from her dream within the nine-flower bed-curtain,
Pushed aside the pillow, dressed in haste, rose and hesitated.
One by one the pearl curtains and the silver screens parted:
Freshly woken from sleep, with her cloudy hair awry,
And her flowery cap set crooked, she stepped down into the
    Hall.
As the wind caught her mystic sleeves and raised them
    fluttering,
Once more she seemed to be dancing "The rainbow skirt and
    the coat of feathers".
Her jade-like face so pitiful, criss-crossed with tears —
A spray of pear blossom in the spring rain.

排空馭氣奔如電，昇天入地求之徧，
上窮碧落下黃泉，兩處茫茫皆不見。
忽聞海上有仙山，山在虛無飄渺間。
樓閣玲瓏五雲起，其中綽約多仙子。
中有一人字太真，雪膚花貌參差是。
金闕西廂叩玉扃，轉教小玉報雙成。
聞道漢家天子使，九華帳裡夢魂驚，
攬衣推枕起徘徊，珠箔銀屏迤邐開。
雲鬢半偏新睡覺，花冠不整下堂來。
風吹仙袂飄飄舉，猶似霓裳羽衣舞。
玉容寂寞淚闌干，梨花一枝春帶雨。

Swallowing her grief and choking back her tears,
　　she bade him thank her Lord
Whose voice and face were so remote since their parting.
Love and tenderness long ended in the Court of Zhaoyang,
Days and months endless in the Palace of Penglai.
Turning to look down into the world of men,
She could not see Chang'an, only dust and mist.
With deep emotion she brought the old pledges he had given —
The enamel casket and the golden hairpin, to send with the
　　envoy:
One wing of the hairpin she kept and one side of the casket,
Breaking the gold of the hairpin, splitting the work of the
　　casket.
"Bid his heart endure like gold and enamel,
Then in Heaven or on earth we shall meet again!"
As the Taoist was leaving, she sent another tender message:
It told of a vow known only to their two hearts,
Made on the seventh day of the seventh moon in Changsheng
　　palace,
When they whispered together at midnight, all alone.
"In Heaven we shall be two birds with the wings of one;
On earth two trees with branches intertwined."
Heaven and earth are long enduring, but they will pass away
This sorrow will go on and on — it will never end.

回頭不見廛寰嶺不見長多見塵霧葬

Turning to look down into the world of men,
She could not see Chang'an, only dust and mist.
回頭下望人寰處，不見長安見塵霧。

含情凝睇謝君王，一別音容兩渺茫。
昭陽殿裡恩愛絕，蓬萊宮中日月長。
回頭下望人寰處，不見長安見塵霧。
惟將舊物表深情，鈿合金釵寄將去。
釵留一股合一扇，釵擘黃金合分鈿。
但教心似金鈿堅，天上人間會相見。
臨別殷勤重寄詞，詞中有誓兩心知。
七月七日長生殿，夜半無人私語時。
在天願作比翼鳥，在地願為連理枝。
天長地久有時盡，此恨綿綿無盡期。

THE GUITAR SONG

Bai Juyi

By the Xunyang river one night I was bidding a friend
    farewell:
In the maple leaves and reed heads autumn soughed harshly.
I, the host, dismounted; my guest was already aboard;
We poured the wine and wished to drink, but music was
    missing,
And the drinking brought us no cheer — in gloom we prepared
    to part;
Saw only the vague river reaches drenched in moonlight.
Suddenly from across the water we heard a guitar's sound —
I forgot to return home and my guest stayed his leaving.
We searched for the source of the music and asked the
    player's name:
The guitar notes broke off and, faltering, she tried to answer.
We drew our boat alongside and invited her aboard.
"More wine! Bring back the lamps! We'll start the feast
    again!"
We hailed and urged her a thousand times before she would
    rise and come,
Still half-concealing her face behind the guitar she carried.
She moved the pegs and tried the strings with two or three
    notes;
Even before the tune came there was passion in the sound.

琵琶行

白居易

潯陽江頭夜送客，楓葉荻花秋瑟瑟。
主人下馬客在船，舉酒欲飲無管絃。
醉不成歡慘將別，別時茫茫江浸月。
忽聞水上琵琶聲，主人忘歸客不發。
尋聲暗問彈者誰？琵琶聲停欲語遲。
移船相近邀相見，添酒回燈重開宴。
千呼萬喚始出來，猶抱琵琶半遮面。
轉軸撥絃三兩聲，未成曲調先有情。

String after string she swept and plucked, note upon note
    told her thoughts;
She seemed to say she had missed her dreams all her life long.
With furrowed brow she plied her fingers, thrumming on and
    on:
She told of all the painful stuff overflowing her heart.
She lightly plucked, slowly stroked, brushed and twanged the
    strings;
First it was the song of "Rainbow skirts", then "The six
    drums".
The thick strings fiercely thrummed, like a squall of rain;
The fine strings softly tinkled, like a secret whispered.
Fiercely thrummed, softly tinkled, note mingled with note,
Like big pearls and little pearls dropped on a jade plate.
Clear like the fluting of orioles hidden among flowers,
Or the low gurgle of a running brook bubbling over falls...
The bubbling waters froze still, the strings froze too:
As the strings froze and ceased to hum the tune died away.
Next she played a hidden grief — vague regret was born,
And this time the silences were more pregnant than the notes.
A silver vase suddenly smashed and water gushed out,
Then men in armour, pell-mell, rattled sword and spear.
At the song's end, from the guitar she drew out the central
    stop:
The four strings made one sound, as of rending silk...
There was silence in the east boat and silence in the west:
We saw only the autumn moon, white in the heart of the
    river.

眉
信
子
彈
三
絃
之
畫
心
事

甲
寅
眼

紙
德
沁
說
畫
半

With furrowed brow she plied her fingers,
   thrumming on and on:
She told of all the painful stuff overflowing her heart.
   低眉信手續續彈，說盡心中無限事。

絃絃掩抑聲聲思，似訴平生不得志。
低眉信手續續彈，說盡心中無限事，
輕攏慢撚抹復挑，初為霓裳後六么。
大絃嘈嘈如急雨，小絃切切如私語；
嘈嘈切切錯雜彈，大珠小珠落玉盤。
間關鶯語花底滑，幽咽流泉水下灘。
水泉冷澀絃凝絕，凝絕不通聲漸歇。
別有幽愁暗恨生，此時無聲勝有聲。
銀瓶乍破水漿迸，鐵騎突出刀槍鳴，
曲終收撥當心畫，四絃一聲如裂帛。
東船西舫悄無言，惟見江心秋月白。

Mutely she put the finger-caps back among the strings,
Smoothed out her dress, then rose with dignity in her face.
She told us her tale: as a girl she had come from Chang'an;
Her home had been at the foot of the Hama hill.
At thirteen she achieved mastery in the study of the guitar,
Being awarded the first rank in the School of Music.
Each time she played, even the experts applauded;
When she dressed in her finery, the lovely Qiuniang was
    envious.
Young sparks of Wuling wrangled to engage her:
For one song, scarlet silk more than one could measure.
Combs of silver and enamel smashed as they beat out the
    music;
Wine splashed on fluttering skirts of blood-red silk.
That was a year of joy and laughter, the next year too;
Autumn moon and spring breeze came and passed unheeded.
A young brother joined the army, then her aunt died.
Nights passed, dawns broke, her lovely face grew old.
Before her delapidated gate few carriages or horses stopped...
No longer young, she married and became a merchant's wife —
A merchant who thinks much of money, little of leaving her.
Last month, for buying tea, he went off to Fuliang,
And she had come to the river mouth, steering an empty boat,
With the clear moon encircling her boat on the cold river
    water.
Deep in the night she would suddenly dream about her
    youthful life,
And cry in her dream so that the tears criss-crossed her
    rouge.

沈吟放撥插絃中，整頓衣裳起斂容。
自言「本是京城女，家在蝦蟆嶺下住，
十三學得琵琶成，名屬教坊第一部；
曲罷常教善才服，妝成每被秋娘妒。
五陵年少爭纏頭，一曲紅綃不知數。
鈿頭銀篦擊節碎，血色羅裙翻酒污。
今年歡笑復明年，秋月春風等閒度。
弟走從軍阿姨死，暮去朝來顏色故。
門前冷落車馬稀，老大嫁作商人婦！
商人重利輕別離，前月浮梁買茶去，
去來江口守空船，繞船明月江水寒。
夜深忽夢少年事，夢啼妝淚紅闌干！」

Listening to her guitar had made me sigh already,
But to hear this story moved me more deeply still.
Both of us at the world's end, aimless, disappointed,
Meeting now: why need we have known each other before?
I for the past year had been away from the Capital,
Banished from home, often ailing, in this Xunyang.
And Xunyang is so wild a place, there's no music here,
No sound of strings or pipe the whole year through.
I live near Pencheng, a low damp spot,
With old bamboo and yellowing rushes grown up round my hut.
In such a place, from morn to dusk what is there to hear
But the cuckoos calling their hearts out and the monkeys'
    dreary chatter?
By the spring river at flowering time, and on moonlit autumn
    nights,
Often have I caught up wine and swallowed it alone.
Of course there are boatmen's songs and tunes on village pipes,
Like the babble of children or twitter of birds, tedious to hear.
But tonight, when I heard you, playing on the guitar,
It was like the sound of Immortals' music clear in my ears.
Do not go! Sit down and play another tune:
I will write a poem for you, a "Song of the guitar".
Moved by these words of mine she stood awhile,
Then sat and tore at the strings, drawing a rush of sound,
Sadder, more sorrowful than the tunes she had played before:
The whole company hearing it tried to hide their tears.
And who of us all, do you suppose, wept the most?
This prefect of Jiangzhou — my blue coat was wet!

我聞琵琶已歎息，又聞此語重唧唧！
同是天涯淪落人，相逢何必曾相識！
我從去年辭帝京，謫居臥病潯陽城。
潯陽地僻無音樂，終歲不聞絲竹聲。
住近湓城地低濕，黃蘆苦竹繞宅生。
其間旦暮聞何物？杜鵑啼血猿哀鳴，
春江花朝秋月夜，往往取酒還獨傾。
豈無山歌與村笛，嘔啞嘲哳難為聽。
今夜聞君琵琶語，如聽仙樂耳暫明。
莫辭更坐彈一曲，為君翻作琵琶行。
感我此語良久立，卻坐促絃絃轉急，
淒淒不是向前聲，滿座重聞皆掩泣。
座中泣下誰最多？江州司馬青衫濕！

THE HAN YU MEMORIAL STONE
Li Shangyin

In Yuanhe times the Son of Heaven, a god-like warrior,
Comparable only with the ancients Xuan and Xi,
Vowed to wipe out the wrongs of his forbears.
Tribute was brought to his palace from all the four quarters.

Huaixi for fifty years had been a bandit country:
Wolves gave birth to lynxes and lynxes to bears!
They seized the level lands, not the mountain and river
    regions,
Challenging the sun with their long swords and sharp spears.
But the Emperor had a wise minister — the minister called Du,
So protected by spirits that the bandits could not harm him.
With the premier's seal hung at his girdle, he took over
    command,
And led out the Imperial banners against the winds of ill
    omen.
Su, Wu, Gu and Tong became his teeth and talons;
Secretaries from of the Board of Rites followed with writing
    brushes.
His aide-de-camp was a wise and forceful person;
His hundred and forty thousand fought like leopards and tigers:
They advanced on Cai, captured the Khan, and displayed
    him in the Imperial temple.

The achievement was incomparable, the imperial favour
    unbounded.

韓　碑

李　商　隱

元和天子神武姿，彼何人哉軒與羲。
誓將上雪列聖恥，坐法宮中朝四夷。
淮西有賊五十載，封狼生貙貙生羆；
不據山河據平地，長戈利矛日可麾。
帝得聖相相曰度，賊斫不死神扶持。
腰懸相印作都統，陰風慘澹天王旗。
愬武古通作牙爪，儀曹外郎載筆隨。
行軍司馬智且勇，十四萬眾猶虎貔。
入蔡縛賊獻太廟。功無與讓恩不訾。

His Majesty declared: "Du, you deserve the highest honour —
Your subordinate, Han Yu, should write a record of this."
Yu made a deep kow-tow, then began to stamp and dance:
"Engraved writing on metal and stone is my especial art:
Writers of the old days called it the bold style of brushwork.
Though the task is not among my official duties,
Men of good will have always accepted an obligation."
To these words the Emperor assented, nodding repeatedly.
Yu then retired and fasted, seated in a small room;
He soaked his great brush in ink — Oh how fast it flowed!
He improved on the characters of the Yao and Shun canons of
    history,
Surpassed the style of the Qing-miao and Sheng-min poems.
The essay was composed with striking originality and written
    on a sheet of paper:
At daybreak, Yu made obeisance and laid it on the vermilion
    steps.
Presenting it he said: "I, your servant, have ventured
To sing these miraculous exploits and inscribe them as a
    monument."
The tablet was thirty feet high, the characters huge as
    saucers;
A stone turtle supported it, stone dragons coiled round it.

帝曰：「汝度功第一，　　汝從事愈宜為辭。」

愈拜稽首蹈且舞，　　「金石刻劃臣能為，

古者世稱大手筆。　　此事不係於職司，

當仁自古有不讓。」　　言訖屢頷天子頤。

公退齋戒坐小閣，　　濡染大筆何淋漓！

點竄堯典舜典字，　　塗改清廟生民詩。

文成破體書在紙，　　清晨再拜舖丹墀。

表曰「臣愈昧死上。」　　咏神聖功書之碑；

碑高三丈字如斗，　　負以靈鼇蟠以螭。

It had strange phrases and deep words that few could
    understand.
But a slander reached the Emperor that Yu had been showing
    favour:
With a hundred feet of rope the tablet was dragged down;
With coarse sand and great stones they ground the words
    away.
But the strength of Yu's intellect is like a natural force —
From the beginning it penetrated the hearts of men.
The Tang dish, the Confucian tripod, both had precious
    engravings:
Today those vessels are no more, but the words are
    remembered.
Alas, alas! the wise kings and the wise statesmen of old —
Compared with their brilliance we have lost the true light!
If this writing of Yu's had not remained for later years,
How could we aspire to the merits of the Three Emperors
    and Five Rulers?
I want to make ten thousand copies, recite it ten thousand
    times,
Till spittle flowed from my mouth and callouses grew on my
    hand!
They should be transmitted through seventy-two generations
As precious precepts in the holy places, foundations stones of
    royal mansions.

句奇語重喻者少，讒之天子言其私。
長繩百尺拽碑倒，麤砂大石相磨治。
公之斯文若元氣，先時已入人肝脾。
湯盤孔鼎有述作，今無其器存其辭。
嗚呼聖皇及聖相，相與烜赫流淳熙！
公之斯文不示後，曷與三五相攀追。
願書萬本誦萬遍，口角流沫右手胝。
傳之七十有二代，以為封禪玉檢明堂基。

POEMS WRITTEN FOR MUSIC

A SONG OF YAN COUNTRY
Gao Shi

In Han days, with the smoke of battle on the north-east
    border,
Han generals left their homes to smash the evil invader.
Their followers, in the natural daring of their young manhood,
Had received the special favour of the Son of Heaven.
To bang of gong and beat of drum they marched down
    Elm Pass;
Flags and banners wound through the defiles of Tablet Rock
    mountain.
Officers sent winged despatches speeding to the Northern
    desert;
The Tartar Khan's hunting fires glimmered on Wolf mountain.
Hill and stream were desolate, dreary at the frontier lands
When barbarian horsemen plunged down in a flurry of wind
    and rain:
Half our men in the front ranks fell, only half survived,
While pretty girls in the soldiers' tents still danced and sang.
In the great steppe with autumn ending, grasses shrivelled
    and died;
On a lonely wall in the sunset, only a few sentries.
But men who received the Emperor's blessing hold the enemy
    light;
They have spent their strength in the mountain passes without
    breaking through.

燕 歌 行

高 適

漢家烟塵在東北，漢將辭家破殘賊。
男兒本自重橫行，天子非常賜顏色。
摐金伐鼓下榆關，旌旗逶迤碣石間。
校尉羽書飛瀚海，單于獵火照狼山。
山川蕭條極邊土，胡騎憑陵雜風雨。
戰士軍前半死生，美人帳下猶歌舞。
大漠窮秋塞草衰，孤城落日鬥兵稀。
身當恩遇常輕敵，力盡關山未解圍。

In their coats of mail, they have served long on frontier
    guard.
How the jade tears must have fallen since the parting:
Little wives south of the Wall feel their hearts breaking!
Fighting men in northern Ji look back in vain.
Border winds whirling and swirling — how can they get
    across?
Far stretches of endless waste — is there anything beyond?
The breath of slaughter mounts in clouds all day long,
And all night the cold boom of gong sounds the watches.
Each sees the other's naked blade spattered with blood:
Those who face death in battle never looked for reward.
Do you not see the wastes of sand, the bitterness of the fight?
To this day we still remember with gratitude General Li.[1]

1. This General Li may have been Li Guang, the famous Han general
who led several campaigns against the Xiongnu, or Li Mu of Zhao
State under the Zhou, who had been particularly successful in
throwing back the Tartar invaders.

鐵衣遠戍辛勤久，　玉筯應啼別離後。
少婦城南欲斷腸，　征人薊北空回首。
邊風飄飄那可度，　絕域蒼茫更何有？
殺氣三時作陣雲，　寒聲一夜傳刁斗。
相看白刃血紛紛，　死節從來豈顧勳！
君不見沙場爭戰苦？至今猶憶李將軍。

AN OLD MARCHING SONG
Li Qi

In the white dawn, climbing the hills
    to watch for beacon fires,
In the yellow dusk, watering the horses
    by Jiao river brink,
We men hear only the boom of watches
    and sand darkens the wind
Where a princess once sang to a guitar
    all her secret pain.

Our camp on the wild moors, no city for countless miles,
Rain and snow, flake on flake, up to the immense desert.
Tartar geese fly over, night after night,
    mournfully honking,
And the Tartar soldiers' tears keep falling, falling.
We heard tell they are still holding
    Yumon Pass:
We must risk our lives and follow the light chariots.
Year on year the bones of the fallen
    lie beyond the wild border —
And all this that barbarian grapes should be brought
    to the Han Court!

古 從 軍 行

李 頎

白日登山望烽火，黃昏飲馬傍交河。
行人刁斗風沙暗，公主琵琶幽怨多。
野營萬里無城郭，雨雪紛紛連大漠。
胡雁哀鳴夜夜飛，胡兒眼淚雙雙落。
聞道玉門猶被遮，應將性命逐輕車。
年年戰骨埋荒外，空見葡萄入漢家。

THE LUOYANG GIRL
Wang Wei

A young girl from Luoyang lives across the way —
To judge from her face, hardly more than fifteen.
Her husband rides a piebald horse with jade bit;
Her maid brings her minced carp on a gold dish.
One can easily see her painted boudoir and red pavilion,
The rosy peach flowers and green willows that sway against
    the eaves.
Escorted to her carriage of the Seven Perfumes through
    silken hangings,
By a jewelled screen she is welcomed to the Nine Flowers
    bed-curtain.
But her husband is a gay dog — noble, rich and young,
Haughty and extravagant, surpassing Ji Lun[1]
Doting on his 'Blue Jade[2]', he taught her to dance himself,
And he gives away red corals with a lavish hand.
The spring dawn shows at her window before the brazier fire
    dies;
The brazier smoke spirals puff by puff, like tiny petals.
Their dallying over, there is no time for songs;
She puts on her finery just to sit before the incense sticks,
For her husband knows all the wealthy families in the city —
Day and night he frequents the Zhao's and the Li's[3]...

Who took pity on the girl of Yue[4] with the jade-like face
When she washed silk by the riverside in the time of her
    poverty?

1. Ji Lun: a notoriously rich man of Jin dynasty.
2. 'Blue Jade': a concubine of Runan Wang.
3. Zhao's and Li's: well-known wealthy families of the Han dynasty.
4. The girl of Yue: Xi Shi. See Wang Wei's poem of that name p.38.

洛　陽　女　兒　行

王　維

洛陽女兒對門居，纔可容顏十五餘。
良人玉勒乘驄馬，侍女金盤膾鯉魚。
畫閣朱樓盡相望，紅桃綠柳垂簷向。
羅幃送上七香車，寶扇迎歸九華帳。
狂夫富貴在青春，意氣驕奢劇季倫。
自憐碧玉親教舞，不惜珊瑚持與人。
春窗曙滅九微火，九微片片飛花璅。
戲罷曾無理曲時，妝成祇是薰香坐。
城中相識盡繁華，日夜經過趙李家，
誰憐越女顏如玉，貧賤江頭自浣紗。

AN OLD GENERAL

Wang Wei

In the days of his youth — between fifteen and twenty —
He chased a Tartar horse, seized it and rode it off,
He slew with his arrows a white-faced mountain tiger,
He could defy the blond-whiskered swaggerer of Ye.[1]
Single-handed he has carried a battle forward a thousand
    miles,
His one sword a match for a million.
When his Han soldiers stormed on like a crash of thunder,
The Tartar horsemen plunged and reared, fearing their
    spiked pitfalls.
Wei Qing was never beaten, but that was a stroke of luck;
That Li Guang had no success was the malice of fate.
When our general retired he began to look old and frail,
Lost his grip on business and his hair grew white.
In past days his whizzing arrow could hit a bird's eye;
Now his left arm is knotted like a willow trunk.
At times he will sell melons by the roadside,
Or he learns to plant willows before his gate.
A tangle of aged trees borders his narrow lane;
Cold spiritless hills front his bare windows.
But if he prayed at Shule, a spring would spurt up;
He was never a drunkard like that Yingchuan person.

老 將 行

王 維

少年十五二十時，步行奪得胡馬騎。
射殺山中白額虎，肯數鄴下黃鬚兒。
一身轉戰三千里，一劍曾當百萬師。
漢兵奮迅如霹靂，虜騎崩騰畏蒺藜。
衛青不敗由天幸，李廣無功緣數奇。
自從棄置便衰朽，世事蹉跎成白首，
昔時飛箭無全目，今日垂楊生左肘。
路旁時賣故侯瓜，門前學種先生柳。
蒼茫古木連窮巷，寥落寒山對虛牖。
誓令疏勒出飛泉，不似潁川空使酒。

Below Helan mountain armies are massing like clouds,
Feathered despatches carried at the gallop day and night.
An official of the Three River Provinces calls up the young
    men;
Imperial edicts have despatched five Generals on different
    routes.
The old man polishes his armour to the brightness of snow,
Grasps his jewelled sword and twirls it with star flashes:
He would like to find a Yan bow and shoot the barbarian chief,
Ashamed that the din of Yue armies should reach our
    Emperor.
In time past they did not despise the Prefect of Yunzhong[2] —
Still fit for one more fight, to keep his record honourable.

1. The swaggerer of Ye was Cao Chang, son of Cao Cao, founder of
   Wei dynasty; Wei Qing and Li Guang were both Han Generals.
   The reference to Shule concerns another Han General, Geng Gong,
   who was beseiged by Tartars in Shule. His prayer for water was
   miraculously answered by the appearance of a spring. The Ying-
   chuan person was General Guan Fu, also of Han dynasty, who came
   from Yingchuan and was a heavy drinker and a bad character.
2. The Prefect of Yunzhong was Wei Shang of Han. He was retired
   in old age from the Prefectship of Yunzhong, but restored when the
   Tartars began to advance. (see also the Notes)

賀蘭山下陣如雲，羽檄交馳日夕聞。
節使三河募年少，詔書五道出將軍。
試拂鐵衣如雪色，聊持寶劍動星文。
願得燕弓射大將，恥將越甲鳴吾君，
莫嫌舊日雲中守，猶堪一戰立功勳。

THE SOURCE OF THE PEACH FLOWER STREAM
Wang Wei

A fisherman drifts with the current, entranced by the spring hills,
On either bank, peach flowers line an ancient ford.
He sits watching the pink trees, does not heed the distance,
Floats to the clear stream's end — suddenly finds other men;
Cautiously enters a mountain cleft, a dark and twisting way;
The mountain gapes and he looks out on a huge level plain.
Afar he sees a place of clouds and trees massed together,
Nearby he meets a thousand homes overshadowed with
    bamboo and flowers.
Woodcutters tell him their names in the speech of Han dynasty,
People had not changed from the Qin style of dress:
All of them used to live at the source of Wuling river,
Coming to another world, they worked fields and orchards.
When the moon glows under the pines, there is peace at their
    lattices;
When the sun rises from the cloud-wrack, dogs and roosters
    clamour.
Amazed to hear of a stranger from the world, they throng
    to see him,
Compete in hospitality and ask about his home town.
At first light they sweep the lanes of fallen blossom;
At night-fall fishermen and woodcutters return along the
    stream.

桃源行

王維

漁舟逐水愛山春，兩岸桃花夾古津。
坐看紅樹不知遠，行盡清溪忽值人。
山口潛行始隈隩，山開曠望旋平陸。
遙看一處攢雲樹，近入千家散花竹。
樵客初傳漢姓名，居人未改秦衣服。
居人共住武陵源，還從物外起田園。
月明松下房櫳靜，日出雲中雞犬喧。
驚聞俗客爭來集，競引還家問都邑。
平明閭巷掃花開，薄暮漁樵乘水入。

Long ago they fled the world, left human company,
Sought the life of immortal spirits and never went back.
Within that cleft, which of them remembered the affairs of
    men?
Others saw but a distant mountain, bare and half in cloud.

Not guessing it was a visionary place and hard to find,
The fisherman felt unbearable longing for his own village.
He scrambled out through the chasm, heedless of hill and
    stream:
Should he leave home once more, to make the long journey,
He had been there before, he thought, and could not lose the
    way —
How could he know the peaks and valleys would have changed
    places?
Of that time he just remembers entering deep in a mountain —
By what branch of the clear stream can he reach those misty
    woods?
Spring arrives, the whole river is awash with peach petals,
But he cannot distinguish the magic source — where shall he
    seek it?

初因避地去人間，更問神仙遂不還。
峽裡誰知有人事？世中遙望空雲山；
不疑靈境難聞見，塵心未盡思鄉縣。
出洞無論隔山水，辭家終擬長游衍。
自謂經過舊不迷，安知峰壑今來變。
當時只記入山深，清溪幾曲到雲林。
春來遍是桃花水，不辨仙源何處尋？

THE DANGERS OF THE SICHUAN ROAD
Li Bai

Aah!
Alas!
What terrors!
How perilous, how steep!
It is harder to walk the Sichuan road
    than to climb the blue sky!
Since Can Cong and Yu Fu
Shaped a kingdom in those formless wastes
Forty-eight thousand years have gone by,
Yet from thence to the frontiers of Qin
    there is no human dwelling.
Only westward, from the Great White Mountain,
    was a bird-way,
Cutting through the Emei ranges,
But the earth crumbled, rocks crashed down,
    and strong men perished.[1]
Afterwards, they set sky-ladders and hanging bridges, linked
    together.
Above are the peaks where six dragons turn back the sun;
Below, the churning streams that clash and burst into foam.
The yellow cranes' flight cannot reach across,
And the monkeys, trying to clamber over, gibber piteously.
How the road coils in the Pass of Green Mud!
With nine turns in a hundred steps,
    it twists past crag and chasm.

The dangers of the Sichuan road
蜀　道　難

蜀 道 難

李 白

噫，吁，嚱，　　　　　危乎高哉！
蜀道之難，　　　　　難於上青天。
蠶叢及魚鳧，　　　　　開國何茫然！
爾來四萬八千歲，　　　不與秦塞通人烟。
西當太白有鳥道，　　　可以橫絕峨眉巔。
地崩山摧壯士死，　　　然後天梯石棧方鈎連。
上有六龍迴日之高標，　下有衝波逆折之迴川。
黃鶴之飛尚不得過，　　猿猱欲度愁攀援。
青泥何盤盤，　　　　　百步九折縈巖巒。

Reaching for Orion, passing the Well star,
    I look up and gasp for breath,
Then beating my breast, I sit and heave a long sigh...

Oh if you travel westward, friend, when would you return?
Dangerous is the way and the rocks cannot be scaled!
You shall see only sad birds, chirping on ancient trees,
The male fluttering after the female,
    back and forth through the woods.
You shall hear no voice but the cuckoo's
    calling to the moon at evening
Weary of the empty mountains.
It is harder to walk the Sichuan road
    than to climb the blue sky:
The mere tale of it will drain the colour from youth's cheeks.
Between sky and mountain tops, there is not a foot's space;
Withered pines hang headlong over precipitous cliffs;
Flying cataracts and rushing torrents mingle their din —
They smash on the cliffs and boil among the rocks,
    like thunder in ten thousand valleys.
How fearful is this place!
Alas, traveller from afar,
What brings you here?
Sword Ledge is a lofty rugged spot:
If one man kept the Pass,
Ten thousand could not break through.
The guardians of the Pass are strangers to you —
They may act like wolves and jackals.

飛湍瀑流爭喧豗
砯崖轉石萬壑雷

Flying cataracts and rushing torrents mingle their din —
They smash on the cliffs and boil among the rocks,
  like thunder in ten thousand valleys.
飛湍瀑流爭喧豗，砯崖轉石萬壑雷。

扪參歷井仰脅息，　以手撫膺坐長歎，
問君西遊何時還？　畏途巉岩不可攀。
但見悲鳥號古木，　雄飛從雌繞林間。
又聞子規啼夜月，　愁空山。
蜀道之難難於上青天，使人聽此凋朱顏。
連峯去天不盈尺，　枯松倒掛倚絕壁。
飛湍瀑流爭喧豗，　砯崖轉石萬壑雷。
其險也若此！　嗟爾遠道之人，胡為乎來哉？
劍閣崢嶸而崔嵬，　一夫當關，萬夫莫開；
所守或匪親，　化為狼與豺。

By daylight, one flees from savage tigers,
At night, from long serpents
Who grind their fangs and suck blood
And raven on men like hemp.
Men say the Brocade City[2] is a place for pleasure,
But it would be better to hurry home,
For it is harder to walk the Sichuan road than to climb
the blue sky.
I turn and look to the west
and heave a long sigh...

1. Five strong men were sent by an ancient king of Shu (modern
Sichuan) to fetch five daughters of the king of Qin.
2. Chengdu, capital of Sichuan.

朝避猛虎，　　　　　夕避長蛇，

磨牙吮血，　　　　　殺人如麻。

錦城雖云樂，　　　　不如早還家。

蜀道之難難於上青天，側身西望長咨嗟。

ENDLESS LONGING

Li Bai

(I)

Remembering you always
At Chang'an.
Autumn crickets chirp
    beneath the golden railing of the well,
The light frost strikes chill
    and how bleak is the bamboo sleeping-mat!
My lonely lamp burns dull, thoughts grow confused;
Rolling up the blind to watch the moon
    I sigh for you in vain.

She who is lovely as a flower is held
    where the clouds begin.
Above is the blue mystery
    of the distant sky
And beneath, the surge and ripple
    of clear water.
Heaven is far and the way long —
    bitter for the soul's flight;
Even in dream it is hard for my spirit
    to cross the mountain passes.
Remembering you always
Shatters my heart!

長 相 思

李 白

長相思，　　　在長安。
絡緯秋啼金井闌，微霜淒淒簟色寒。
孤燈不明思欲絕，卷帷望月空長歎。
美人如花隔雲端，上有青冥之長天，
下有淥水之波瀾。
天長路遠魂飛苦，夢魂不到關山難。
長相思，　　　摧心肝。

(II)

The colours of day pale,
    flowers fill with mist,
Moonlight flows like silk, my grief
    is unsleeping.
The Zhao zither is put to rest
    on its phoenix-carved stand;
I want to play the Shu lute[1]
    with the mandarin-duck strings.[2]
There is meaning in this song
    but none to understand;
I wish it could follow the spring wind
    to Yanran Mountain!
I dream of you far, far away,
    remote as the blue sky.
My calm untroubled eyes of the old days
Now fill with tears, flowing like a spring.
O if you doubt my heart is breaking,
Come back, and look into my bright mirror!

---

1. Sima Xiangru was a Shu man, specially skilled at lute-playing.
2. The strings were attuned in pairs: mandarin duck and drake are symbolic of conjugal fidelity.

（二）

日色已盡花含烟，　　月明如素愁不眠。

趙瑟初停鳳凰柱，　　蜀琴欲奏鴛鴦絃。

此曲有意無人傳。　　願隨春風寄燕然。

憶君迢迢隔青天，昔時橫波目，今作流淚泉。

不信妾腸斷，　　　歸來看取明鏡前。

THE DIFFICULTIES OF THE JOURNEY

Li Bai

(I)

In my golden cup, clear wine
    costing ten thousand a flagon;
In my jade dish, choice foods
    worth ten thousand cash,
Yet I throw down the chopsticks and push aside the cup,
    unable to eat.
I draw my sword and glance around,
    troubled and confused at heart.

I want to cross the Yellow river
    but ice chokes its waters;
I tried to climb Taihang mountain
    but snow darkened the sky.
Sometimes I come to dangle my hook
    beside a mountain stream,
Then in a dream I'd board a boat
    and set course for the sun...
Oh hard is the way!
Hard is the way!
There were so many branches —
Where are they now?
A time will come to ride along the wind
    and cleave the waves;
I shall hoist my cloud-sail and cross the waste of seas.

行　路　難

李　白

金樽清酒斗十千，玉盤珍羞直萬錢。
停杯投筯不能食，拔劍四顧心茫然。
欲渡黃河冰塞川，將登太行雪暗天。
閒來垂釣坐溪上，忽復乘舟夢日邊。
行路難，行路難，多岐路，今安在？
長風破浪會有時，直挂雲帆濟滄海。

(II)

The broad highway is like the azure sky:
I alone cannot find my way there.
I am ashamed to have consorted with
    the young sparks of Chang'an,
And gambled on 'red chickens' and 'white dogs'[1]
    for pears and chestnuts.
Yet think of Feng Huan[2] who thrummed his sword
    and sang a bitter song;
Of Zou Yang[3] who trailed his skirts in a prince's hall
    without satisfying his heart!
In Huaiyin market-place they mocked the great Han Xin[4];
Nobles of the Han court were jealous of Mr. Jia[5].
Have you not heard of Zhao Wang in days gone by,
    how he venerated Guo Wei[6] —
He stooped low and swept the floor to welcome him,
    without suspicion.
Ju Xin and Yue Yi were brought into royal favour,
And they strained nerve and sinew to perform the utmost
    service.
But Zhao Wang's white bones are twined around with creeping
    weeds:
Who will sweep his yellow gold pavilion now?
Oh the way is too hard!
Let us go home!

1. 'Red chickens' and 'white dogs': cock fights and dog fights.
2. Feng Huan: a scholar of the Warring States period who tried to earn a living by his singing in the house of a rich nobleman, Meng Chang.
3. Zou Yang: a Han dynasty scholar who tried in vain to get worthy employment in a Prince's household.

4. Han Xin: a great general of Han dynasty who as a youth was put to shame in a fight by the local butcher.
5. Mr. Jia: Jia Yi, a statesman of Han dynasty who rose to high office but was sent into exile in Changsha through the machinations of enemies at Court.
6. Guo Wei was a minister under Zhao Wang, ruler of Yan state, at whose order Guo designed the Gold Pavilion (in which a thousand pieces of gold were incorporated). The pavilion was built for the reception of scholars from all over the kingdom, and the Yan Court become a centre of learning and culture. Among the scholars who were attracted to Yan by its reputation were Ju Xin and Yue Yi; they were well received and given high rank by Zhao Wang.

（二）

大道如青天，　　　　　我獨不得出。

羞逐長安社中兒，　　　赤雞白狗賭梨栗。

彈劍作歌奏苦聲，　　　曳裾王門不稱情，

淮陰市井笑韓信，　　　漢朝公卿忌賈生。

君不見昔時燕家重郭隗，擁篲折節無嫌猜；

劇辛樂毅感恩分，　　　輸肝剖膽效英才。

昭王白骨縈蔓草，　　　誰人更掃黃金臺？

行路難，　　　　　　　歸去來！

(III)

If you have ears, do not wash them in Ying river[1] waters!
If you have a mouth, do not eat the bracken on Shouyang[2]!
To keep one's honour in this dirty world,
    better dispense with fame:
What use is a lonely eminence, like the moon's or the clouds?
When I think of the ablest men since ancient times
Who won their glory but failed to retire — all came to grief.
Zixu's[3] corpse was flung into the river Wu,
Qu Yuan[4] threw himself into the Miluo river.
The highly talented Lu Ji[5], could he preserve his life?
Li Si[6] met a bitter fate by not retiring in time.
Can we hear the cry of cranes any more at Hua Ting?
No use to speak of the blue falcon of Shang Cai.
Have you not heard of Zhang Han[7] of Wu, a broad-minded
    scholar?
In the autumn wind he suddenly remembered the road east
    of the river.
It is better to enjoy a cup of wine during one's life:
What use is a thousand years of glory
    when you are dead?

1. Ying river: a hermit called Xu You was invited by Emperor Yao
   to take over the government. The suggestion was so distasteful
   that Xu washed his ears in the river.
2. The bracken on Shouyang: Bo Yi and Shu Qi, two princes of Shang
   dynasty, did not wish to become subjects of the Zhou, and fled to
   the Shouyang hills.
3. Zixu: Wu Zixu of the Spring and Autumn period. His prince, the
   ruler of Wu state would not accept his advice not to make war on
   Yue state. He committed suicide and his body was put in a sack
   and thrown into the river.

4. Qu Yuan: The famous poet and statesman of Chu state in the Spring and Autumn period, whose advice was rejected and who drowned himself in the Miluo.
5. Lu Ji of Jin was put to death by Chengdu Wang, a Prince of Sichuan. When he was dying, he wished he could hear the cry of the cranes as he had heard them at Hua Ting in his youth.
6. Li Si: First Minister under Qin Shi Huangdi. He was impeached by the eunuch Zhao Gao and executed in the market-place in 208 B.C. Before meeting his death he regretted that he would never go out of the gate at Shangcai again with a yellow dog at his heels and a blue falcon on his wrist.
7. Zhang Han: A leading minister to the ruler of Qi state, who gave up his position to return to his country retreat.

（三）

有耳莫洗潁川水，　　　有口莫食首陽蕨。
含光混世貴無名，　　　何用孤高比雲月？
吾觀自古賢達人，　　　功成不退皆殞身。
子胥既棄吳江上，　　　屈原終投湘水濱。
陸機雄才豈自保？　　　李斯稅駕苦不早，
華亭鶴唳詎可聞？　　　上蔡蒼鷹何足道。
君不見吳中張翰稱達生，秋風忽憶江東行。
且樂生前一杯酒，　　　何須身後千載名？

INVITATION TO WINE
Li Bai

Do you not see the waters of the Yellow river
    streaming from the sky —
How they rush tumbling to the sea
    and never return?
Do you not see, within the high tower,
    someone who sorrows for his white hair
        before the bright mirror? —
In the morning like black silk, at evening turned to snow?
In human life, when hopes are won,
    we should drink our joys to the end,
Not leave the golden wine-jar
    empty in the moonlight.
The things that Heaven made must have a use;
Though I squander a thousand gold pieces,
    time may restore them.

Boil the sheep! Kill the ox! Let us be merry!
Three hundred cupfuls of wine we must drink this time!
Master Cen[1]!
Doctor Danqiu[2]!
I am bringing the wine —
Don't put down your cups!
I shall sing you a snatch of song:
Listen to me please.

Gongs and drums, costly dishes, little I prize them;
I only want the long dream of wine and never to wake.

將　進　酒

李　白

君不見黃河之水天上來，　奔流到海不復回！
君不見高堂明鏡悲白髮，　朝如青絲暮成雪。
人生得意須盡歡，　　　　莫使金樽空對月！
天生我材必有用，　　　　千金散盡還復來。
烹羊宰牛且為樂，　　　　會須一飲三百杯。
岑夫子，丹邱生，　　　　將進酒，杯莫停！
與君歌一曲，　　　　　　請君為我傾耳聽！
鐘鼓饌玉不足貴，　　　　但願長醉不願醒！

Through all the ages, the good and wise were passed
    over in silence;
Only the mighty drinkers left a name behind.
Think of the Prince of Chen[3] in former days,
    feasting at Ping-le palace —
The wine at ten thousand a flagon,
    the endless jesting and laughter...

How can a host complain he is short of money?
I must hasten to buy the wine to put before my friends.
My horse dappled with the five colours
And my thousand-guinea furs —
I will call the boy to barter them for a splendid wine
That you and I may forget for sorrows of all the ages.

1. Master Cen: the poet Cen Shen
2. Doctor Danqiu: the Taoist hermit Yuan Danqiu. Both were friends
    of Li Bai.
3. The Prince of Chen: Cao Zhi, a prince of Wei in the Three Kingdoms
    period (220-265), notorious in his youth for his dissipation and love
    of luxury.

古來聖賢皆寂寞，唯有飲者留其名。
陳王昔時宴平樂，斗酒十千恣歡謔。
主人何為言少錢？徑須沽取對君酌！
五花馬，　　　　千金裘，
呼兒將出換美酒，與爾同銷萬古愁！

BALLAD OF THE ARMY WAGONS
Du Fu

Wagons rumble,
Horses neigh,
Marching men, each with bow and arrows at the waist.
Fathers and mothers, wives and children
    rush to bid them farewell
Till Xianyang bridge disappears in the dust.
Stumbling and clutching at their clothes,
    they bar the way in tears:
The sound of wailing rises into the clouds.

A bystander on the roadside questions a soldier:
The soldier merely replies, "Another conscription".
"Some of us at fifteen went north to guard the River;
Reaching forty, sent west to work the farms.
When we left, the village Elder bound our heads;
White-haired we return, still on Border duty —
That Border where blood has flowed to fill a sea,
And the Emperor's craving for territory is still unsatisfied.
Have you not heard, Sir, about the two hundred districts east
    of our mountains,
How thistle and medlar are creeping over thousands of villages?
Even where the women are sturdy, able to hoe and plough,
The grain grows anywhere — boundaries are all broken down.
It is even worse for the Qin soldiers, enduring the bitterness
    of battle,
Driven this way and that, no better than dogs or fowls.

兵 車 行

杜 甫

車轔轔，馬蕭蕭，　　　　行人弓箭各在腰。
耶孃妻子走相送，　　　　塵埃不見咸陽橋。
牽衣頓足攔道哭，　　　　哭聲直上干雲霄。
道旁過者問行人，　　　　行人但云點行頻。
或從十五北防河，　　　　便至四十西營田。
去時里正與裹頭，　　　　歸來頭白還戍邊。
邊庭流血成海水，　　　　武皇開邊意未已。
君不聞漢家山東二百州，千村萬落生荊杞？
縱有健婦把鋤犂，　　　　禾生隴畝無東西。
況復秦兵耐苦戰，　　　　被驅不異犬與雞。

Even though a local Elder may question us,
Humble soldiers, dare we express resentment?
Only look at the present winter —
Still no relief for the Guanxi forces,
Local officials urgently pressing for taxes:
Where are the taxes to come from?
It seems that bearing sons is a bad business;
Better to have borne girls instead.
Girls can marry in the neighbourhood;
Boys will lie buried among common grasses.

Have you not seen, Sir, near the Kokonor,
The white bones of those long dead
    that no man gathers?
New ghosts murmur, the old ones sob:
You can hear them on dull days
    in the sound of the rain."

長者雖有問，　　役夫敢申恨？
且如今年冬，　　未休關西卒。
縣官急索租，　　租稅從何出？
信知生男惡，　　反是生女好；
生女猶得嫁比鄰，生男埋沒隨百草。
君不見青海頭，　古來白骨無人收？
新鬼煩冤舊鬼哭，天陰雨濕聲啾啾。

A BALLAD OF LOVELY WOMEN

Du Fu

The third day of the third moon, the spring air fresh,
Chang'an lake-side is thronged with lovely women,
Voluptuous in beauty, thoughts aloof, gentle and elegant,
Gleaming skin smooth and fine, bones and flesh in symmetry,
Dresses of silk gauze shining in the late Spring sun,
Woven with peacocks in gold thread and unicorns in silver.
On their heads, what do they wear?
Leaves made of kingfisher feathers garlanding their temples.
At their backs what do we see?
Pearl-embroidered trains, perfectly shaped to fit.
Among the many-coloured marquees are kinswomen of the
    Empress,
Favoured with the titles, Duchesses of Guo and Qin.
Purple steaks of camel-hump are lifted from a turquoise
    cauldron,
Fresh silvery fish served on crystal dishes.
But the chopsticks of rhinoceros horn are plied languidly
    now,
And delicate morsels are sliced by tinkling knives to no
    purpose.
Mounted eunuchs gallop up, without stirring the dust,
Sent from the Imperial kitchens with the eight dainties in
    succession.
While the flutes and pipes speak mournfully, invoking spirits,
The throng and press of guests overflows the green-sward.
Last of all a horseman approaches, measured and slow,
Dismounts at the pavilion and steps up the embroidered carpet.
Willow-fluff falls like snow, covering the white duckweed;
Bluebirds fly off, carrying red veils.
His power is immeasurable: keep your fingers out of the fire!
Beware of approaching the Premier, to incur his anger!

麗 人 行

杜 甫

三月三日天氣新，長安水邊多麗人。
態濃意遠淑且真，肌理細膩骨肉勻。
繡羅衣裳照暮春，蹙金孔雀銀麒麟。
頭上何所有？　　翠微匎葉垂鬢脣。
背後何所見？　　珠壓腰衱穩稱身。
就中雲幕椒房親，賜名大國虢與秦。
紫駝之峰出翠釜，水精之盤行素鱗。
犀筯厭飫久未下，鸞刀縷切空紛綸。
黃門飛鞚不動塵，御廚絡繹送八珍。
簫管哀吟感鬼神，賓從雜遝實要津。
後來鞍馬何逡巡，當軒下馬入錦茵。
楊花雪落覆白蘋，青鳥飛去銜紅巾。
炙手可熱勢絕倫，慎莫近前丞相嗔。

LAMENT BY THE RIVERSIDE
Du Fu

An old fellow of Shaoling, crying silently,
Shuffles along a bend of Winding River
   in the spring sun.
Locked are the thousand gates of the palaces
   by the riverside:
For whom now do the slender willows, the tender reeds
   renew their green?
I remember the old days when the rainbow banners
   streamed into South Park,
And the whole park grew brilliant with a thousand colours,
And the First Lady of Zhaoyang palace
Shared the Emperor's carriage,
   attending at his side.

Before the carriage rode the Court beauties,
   bearing bows and arrows,
Clattering by on white horses that
   champed their golden bits.
Leaning back to face the sky,
   they would loose their arrows at the clouds —
With a single arrow drop a pair of birds in flight!

Those shining eyes and sparkling teeth —
   where are they now?
Blood has defiled her restless ghost,
   she can never return!
The clear Wei flows east, the Sword Cliffs lead deep into the
   west;
One is gone, the other stays: the link is broken.

As I ponder human life,
    the tears wet my breast:
Oh river grasses, river flowers,
    when will there be an end?
At twilight the Tartar horsemen
    fill the city with dust:
I want to go to the south of the city
    but keep looking towards the north.

哀 江 頭

杜 甫

少陵野老吞聲哭，春日潛行曲江曲。
江頭宮殿鎖千門，細柳新蒲為誰綠？
憶昔霓旌下南苑，苑中萬物生顏色。
昭陽殿裡第一人，同輦隨君侍君側。
輦前才人帶弓箭，白馬嚼齧黃金勒；
翻身向天仰射雲，一箭正墜雙飛翼。
明眸皓齒今何在，血污遊魂歸不得。
清渭東流劍閣深，去住彼此無消息！
人生有情淚霑臆，江草江花豈終極？
黃昏胡騎塵滿城，欲往城南望城北。

LAMENT FOR A PRINCE OF THE IMPERIAL FAMILY
Du Fu

To the city walls of Chang'an came white-headed crows;
By night they flew to Yan-qiu gate and perched there cawing,
Then made for the homes of men and pecked at the great eaves,
Where high officials galloped off to escape the Tartars.
Golden whips snapped in two and nine horses died,
Yet his own flesh and blood could not flee with the Emperor.

With a precious jade and green coral hanging at his girdle,
How pitiful to see the young prince
      weeping by the roadside!
Ask him, but he dare not tell his name:
He will just plead distress and beg to be your servant.
A hundred days now he has skulked in thorns and brambles:
On every part of his body the flesh is torn.
The descendants of Emperor Gao all have prominent noses —
The Dragon's seed are not like common men.
Wolves and jackals roam the city while the dragon lives in
     the wilds:
The young prince must guard his person, precious as a
     thousand taels!
I dare not speak with him long, so near the cross-roads,
But for his sake I will stay with him here a moment.

Last night the east wind carried the stench of blood,
And from the east, camel bands crowded the old Capital.
The northerners were the strong ones, staunch of body and
     hand,
The fearless fighters of old — why have they grown so feeble?
I heard tell that the Son of Heaven had already abdicated,
Whose kingly virtue won over our Uigur allies;

At Huamen they gashed their faces and swore to wipe out
   his shame,
But be careful not to speak of this — there are enemies about!
Woe, alas, poor prince, be on your guard,
And may the kindly influence of the Five Tombs never
   forsake you!

哀 王 孫

杜 甫

長安城頭頭白烏，夜飛延秋門上呼。

又向人家啄大屋，屋底達官走避胡。

金鞭斷折九馬死，骨肉不得同馳驅。

腰下寶玦青珊瑚，可憐王孫泣路隅；

問之不肯道姓名，但道困苦乞為奴。

已經百日竄荊棘，身上無有完肌膚，

高帝子孫盡隆準，龍種自與常人殊。

豺狼在邑龍在野，王孫善保千金軀。

不敢長語臨交衢，且為王孫立斯須。

昨夜東風吹血腥，東來橐駝滿舊都；

朔方健兒好身手，昔何勇銳今何愚？

竊聞天子已傳位，聖德北服南單于。

花門劙面請雪恥，慎勿出口他人狙！

哀哉王孫慎勿疏，五陵佳氣無時無！

SECTION 3

Five-character 'regulated' verse

SACRIFICING TO CONFUCIUS AND MOURNING HIM, WHEN PASSING THROUGH LU

Emperor Xuanzong

How is it with you, Master Kong,
Who strove for your beliefs a whole age long?
This place is still the Zou family's ground,
Your home became a palace for the Dukes of Lu.
You sighed for a phoenix and lamented your ill luck,
You grieved for the unicorn and mourned the failure of
  your teaching.
As I watched the libation poured between two columns
I thought of your dream — all was just the same!

The Chinese phoenix (*feng*) was said to appear when a sage ascended
the throne or when the right principles were going to triumph.   On
one occasion Confucius said to his disciples: "The phoenix does not
appear — it is all over with me!" (Analects Book IX, 8).
On another occasion some hunters brought him a dead unicorn (*qilin*).
This creature was also said to portend a successful reign.
Confucius wrote a poem about it:
"What made you come at the wrong time, only to die?
Unicorn, unicorn, my heart is full of pity!"
Shortly before he died, Confucius told his disciples he had dreamt of
a large temple where a sacrifice was being offered between two pillars,
and he foresaw in this his approaching death.

經魯祭孔子而歎之

唐 玄 宗

夫子何為者？栖栖一代中。
地猶鄹氏邑，宅即魯王宮。
歎鳳嗟身否，傷麟怨道窮！
今看兩楹奠，當與夢時同。

LOOKING AT THE MOON AND LONGING FOR
A DISTANT LOVER

Zhang Jiuling

A clear moon climbs over the sea;
To its farthest rim
    the whole sky is glowing.
Lovers complain — how endless is the night!
Their longing thoughts rise till the dawn.

I blow out the candle
    to enjoy the clear radiance,
Slip on my clothes
    for I feel the dew grow thick.
Since I cannot gather a handful of moonlight
    to give you,
I shall go back to sleep
    and hope to meet you in a dream!

望 月 懷 遠

張 九 齡

海上生明月，天涯共此時。
情人怨遙夜，竟夕起相思。
滅燭憐光滿，披衣覺露滋。
不堪盈手贈，還寢夢佳期。

FOR VICE-PREFECT DU, ON HIS BEING
APPOINTED TO SICHUAN
Wang Bo

From these watch-towers that protect
    the Three Qins,
Through blown mists we see
    the five streams of Shu.
My thoughts are on the coming parting from you,
Both travelling to distant posts.
But if the world holds a friend who knows your heart,
The sky's end is as near as the next village,
So do not linger here
    where the road forks,
Crying bitterly, as children do.

送杜少府之任蜀州

王 勃

城闕輔三秦，風烟望五津。
與君離別意，同是宦游人。
海內存知己，天涯若比鄰。
無為在岐路，兒女共沾巾。

ON HEARING A CICADA IN PRISON
Luo Binwang

Earth spins westward;
    a cicada starts to twitter,
Stirring deep memories
    in this exile from the south.
I cannot bear to hear that
    dark-winged shape
Chirping to me,
    a white-haired prisoner.
It is hard for it to rise
    out of the heavy dew;
Its voice is easily drowned
    in the strong wind...
None will admit the
    purity of its nature,
And who will explain
    what is in my heart?

在 獄 詠 蟬

駱 賓 王

西陸蟬聲唱，南冠客思深。
不堪玄鬢影，來對白頭吟。
露重飛難進，風多響易沉。
無人信高潔，誰為表予心？

A WALK IN EARLY SPRING WITH SECRETARY-OF-STATE LU OF JINLING

Du Shenyan

We two are just wandering officials
Taken unaware by the freshness of season and scene:
Pink clouds rising from the sea at daybreak;
Spring edging the river with plum and willow.

Mild air excites the golden oriole;
Clear light twinkles in green duckweed.
Suddenly I hear you singing an old tune
And home thoughts fill my eyes with tears.

和晉陵陸丞相早春游望

杜審言

獨有宦遊人，偏驚物候新。
雲霞出海曙，梅柳渡江春。
淑氣催黃鳥，晴光轉綠蘋。
忽聞歌古調，歸思欲沾襟。

THE GARRISON AT HUANGLONG

Shen Quanqi

We heard tales of the guards at Huanglong —
Year after year, not a soldier relieved.
How pitiful that the moon on women's chambers
Keeps shining too on the Han soldiers' camp!

A young wife today
    felt spring longing;
Her man last night
    remembered her with love.
Ah! who will lead out the flags and drums
To fall upon Dragon city[1]?

1. Dragon City: a stronghold of the Xiongnu tribes in the north-west.

雜　詩

沈　佺　期

聞道黃龍戍，頻年不解兵，
可憐閨裡月，長在漢家營。
少婦今春意，良人昨夜情，
誰能將旗鼓，一為取龍城。

WRITTEN ON THE WALL OF THE POST-HOUSE, NORTH OF DAYU PASS

Song Zhiwen

About the tenth moon
  the wild geese fly south:
Here is their farthest mark,
  I heard men say.
But my road
  is still far from its end —
When shall I turn back again?

How voiceless is the river
  with the tide on the ebb!
The fever-mists do not lift
  over these murky woods.
In the morning, from the top of the pass,
  I shall look towards my home:
I should see the plum trees flowering
  all along the field dykes.

題大庾嶺北驛

宋 之 問

陽月南飛鴈，傳聞至此迴。
我行殊未已，何日復歸來？
江靜潮初落，林昏瘴不開。
明朝望鄉處，應見隴頭梅。

AT AN INN BELOW BEIGU MOUNTAIN
Wang Wan

A traveller's track leads down
    the leafy mountain;
A passing boat pushes up
    the green river.
The tide is running high — wide the expanse
    from shore to shore;
In the face of the wind
    a single sail bellies.

Sunlight on the sea
    rises from night's traces;
Spring touches the river
    as in all the past years...
Letters from home,
    where will they reach me now?
Perhaps the wild geese making for Luoyang
    will carry a message.

次 北 固 山 下

王 灣

客路青山下，行舟綠水前。
潮平兩岸闊，風正一帆懸。
海日生殘夜，江春入舊年，
鄉書何處達？歸雁洛陽邊。

AT A BUDDHIST RETREAT BEHIND POSHAN TEMPLE

Chang Jian

At first light I entered the ancient temple
As the high woods shone in the sunrise.
Winding ways had led me to this quiet place:
An Abbot's cell deep in trees and flowers.

Mountain sunshine makes the birds merry;
Shadows in the deep pool clear our minds.
The myriad noises are all hushed now
And I hear only the toll of the bells.

題破山寺後禪院

常 建

清晨入古寺，初日照高林；
曲徑通幽處，禪房花木深。
山光悅鳥性，潭影空人心。
萬籟此俱寂，惟聞鐘磬音。

FOR THE CENSOR DU FU

Cen Shen

Together we advance up the vermilion steps,
Each to his office, separated by the purple myrtle[1].
At dawn, we enter behind the imperial attendants;
At dusk depart, redolent of Palace incense.

I grieve for my white hairs,
    like petals falling.
I envy you the blue skies,
    you soaring bird!
Under our wise ruler, little is neglected:
Thus there are few memorials to consider.

---

1. The purple myrtle: in the Grand Secretariat of the Palace, myrtle
   bushes separated left and right departments. Du Fu belonged to the
   left, Cen Shen to the right.

寄左省杜拾遺

岑 參

聯步趨丹陛，分曹限紫薇。
曉隨天仗入，暮惹御香歸。
白髮悲花落，青雲羨鳥飛。
聖朝無闕事，自覺諫書稀。

FOR MENG HAORAN

Li Bai

I love this Master Meng!
All under heaven have heard of his ways,
How a bright-cheeked youth,
    he scorned a carriage and cap,
And white-haired he lies
    beneath the pines and clouds.
Often tipsy by moonlight
    like the ancients,
Beguiled by flowers
    he cares not a jot for princes.
Who can reach the heights of so great a mountain?
We can but admire its fragrance and purity.

贈 孟 浩 然

李 白

吾愛孟夫子，風流天下聞，
紅顏棄軒冕，白首臥松雲。
醉月頻中聖，迷花不事君。
高山安可仰？徒此挹清芬。

A PARTING BEYOND THORN-GATE MOUNTAIN
Li Bai

From way beyond Thorn-gate mountain
I travelled with you into the land of Chu:
This is where the moorland mountains end
And the streams flow on into the immense plain.

Now under the moon,
    mirror that sails the skies,
And the swelling clouds that weave sea-palaces,
I bid you goodbye: a thousand miles you sail away
On the river that carries you
    to your old home.

渡　荊　門　送　別

李　白

渡遠荊門外，來從楚國遊。
山隨平野盡，江入大荒流。
月下飛天鏡，雲生結海樓。
仍憐故鄉水，萬里送行舟。

TAKING LEAVE OF A FRIEND
Li Bai

Blue hills rearing over the north wall;
White water swirling to the east of the city:
This is where you must leave me —
A lone puff of thistledown
    on a thousand-mile journey.
Ah the drifting clouds
    and the thoughts of a wanderer!
The setting sun
    and emotions of old friends.
A wave of the hand now
    and you are gone.
Our horses whinnied to each other at parting.

送 友 人

李 白

青山橫北郭，白水繞東城，
此地一為別，孤蓬萬里征。
浮雲遊子意，落日故人情，
揮手自茲去，蕭蕭班馬鳴。

ON HEARING JUN, A MONK FROM SHU, PLAY THE LUTE

Li Bai

A monk from Shu, clasping a Luqi lute,
Descends the west face of Emei peak.
He sweeps his hand over the strings for me
And I seem to hear pines sigh in a thousand ravines,
And a running stream
    that washes the ache from my heart.
The faint notes blend with the icy bells.
I had not noticed the dusk on the green mountains:
How many folds are hidden
    in the autumn clouds?

聽蜀僧濬彈琴

李 白

蜀僧抱綠綺，西下峨眉峯；
為我一揮手，如聽萬壑松。
客心洗流水，餘響入霜鐘。
不覺碧山暮，秋雲暗幾重。

ANCHORING AT NIGHT BY NIUZHU AND
REMEMBERING THE PAST

Li Bai

Night at Niuzhu, on the West River,
A sapphire sky without a fleck of cloud.
I climb on deck
    and gaze at the autumn moon,
Vaguely meditate on General Xie.[1]

I too know how to chant poetry,
Only there are none like him to listen.
Tomorrow at dawn
    I'll hoist sail and depart:
Oh, how the maple leaves keep falling, falling!

1. General Xie Shang of Jin dynasty, a poet and scholar as well as
a soldier, was stationed in the Niuzhu region. One moonlight night
when boating on the river, he heard someone chanting poems in
another boat. It turned out to be the young poet Yuan Hong, who
later became famous. The general invited him into his boat and
praised his talent.

夜泊牛渚懷古

李 白

牛渚西江夜，青天無片雲，
登舟望秋月，空憶謝將軍。
余亦能高詠，斯人不可聞。
明朝掛帆去，楓葉落紛紛。

MOONLIT NIGHT
Du Fu

There will be moon tonight
    over Fuzhou.
In the women's rooms
    she is gazing at it alone.
From afar,
    I pity my little children:
·They do not know yet
    about Chang'an.
In the sweet mists
    her cloud-like hair is damp;
In the clear shining
    her jade-white arms are cold.
When shall we two lean beside
    the filmy curtain
With moonlight on us both
    and the tear-stains dry?

Du Fu's family was then at Fuzhou; he himself was held in
Chang'an by An Lushan's rebel army.

今庭廓卅月闰中
祇獨看鄜

There will be moon tonight
  over Fuzhou.
In the women's rooms
  She is gazing at it alone.
今夜鄜州月，閨中祇獨看。

月　夜

杜　甫

今夜鄜州月，閨中祇獨看。
遙憐小兒女，未解憶長安。
香霧雲鬟濕，清輝玉臂寒。
何時倚虛幌，雙照淚痕乾。

SPRING PROSPECT
Du Fu

The kingdom is ruined —
    only hills and streams are there as before.
In the city it is spring;
    grass and foliage grow dense.
Grieving for the times,
    flowers splash their tears;
Shocked by the partings,
    birds seem terrified!
For three months on end beacon fires flared.
Letters from home rated ten thousand gold pieces.

When I scratch my white head,
    I find the hair so scanty,
There will soon be hardly enough
    to hold the hairpin.[1]

---

1. The Chinese gentleman of Tang times wore his hair in a knot on top of the head.

春　望

杜　甫

國破山河在，城春草木深；
感時花濺淚，恨別鳥驚心。
烽火連三月，家書抵萬金，
白頭搔更短，渾欲不勝簪。

SPENDING A SPRING NIGHT AT MY OFFICE
Du Fu

It is dusk:
flowers darken the Palace walls.
"Jiu, jiu" chitter the birds
flying over to roost.
Above a thousand doorways
the stars hang spinning;
The moon's light grows stronger
as it nears the Ninth Heaven.

Sleepless,
I listen for the key in the golden lock;
I fancy those are jade horse-bells
carried on the wind.
Early tomorrow
I have a memorial for the Emperor —
I keep asking:
    "How is the night going?"

Du Fu wrote this while holding the office of Remembrancer to Emperor
Suzong. The imperial audiences were held at dawn, so that the court
officials had to be ready before daybreak. The jade horse-bells were
attached to the bridles of the officials coming to the audience.

春 宿 左 省

杜 甫

花隱掖垣暮，啾啾棲鳥過。
星臨萬戶動，月傍九霄多，
不寢聽金鑰，因風想玉珂。
明朝有封事，數問夜如何？

A SAD RECOLLECTION
Du Fu

I left the capital by the Gate of Golden Light, in the second year of Zhide, and by an unfrequented road reached Fengxiang. In the first year of Qianyuan, having been relieved of my post as censor, I was sent to Huazhou as a minor official. In order to take leave of relations and friends, I left by this same gate, and felt sad about those past events.

This was the road of the tribute-bearers in the past.
Lately the western outskirts swarmed with Tartar
    soldiers:
Even now the remembrance strikes terror.
There must be some who lost their wits with fright!

I returned to the capital
    in the Emperor's entourage:
Surely it is not His Majesty's wish
    to send me away?
Without talent, and with life ebbing daily,
I rein in my horse
    to gaze at the thousand palace gates.

The Tartars were the followers of An Lushan who raised a rebellion against Emperor Xuanzong and invested the capital of Chang'an in 755. Du Fu had been held there for some time but managed to make his escape in 757 (the second year of Zhide), and to join the court of the new Emperor, Suzong, at Fengxiang. For his loyalty he was given the post of Censor, but in 758 (the first year of Qianyuan) was demoted, possibly because his patron, the loyal minister Fang Huan, had himself fallen into disgrace. The rebels had in the meantime been driven out of Chang'an, and the court had returned.

至德二載甫自京金光門出，間道歸鳳翔。乾元初，從左拾遺移華州掾，與親故別。因出此門，有悲往事。

杜　甫

此道昔歸順，西郊胡正繁。

至今猶破膽，應有未招魂。

近侍歸京邑，移官豈至尊！

無才日衰老，駐馬望千門。

THINKING OF MY BROTHERS ON A NIGHT OF MOONLIGHT

Du Fu

The bang of war-drums halts a traveller's step.
Autumn at the frontier,
    and the honk of a solitary wild-goose.
From tonight there will be white dews,
And how the moon will glow
    over my old village!

Brothers I have, but they are all scattered;
No home to ask —
    "Are they alive or dead?"
Letters I sent will never reach them now;
Besides, the armies are still embattled.

月 夜 憶 舍 弟

杜 甫

戍鼓斷人行，邊秋一雁聲。
露從今夜白，月是故鄉明。
有弟皆分散，無家問死生。
寄書長不達，況乃未休兵！

AT THE WORLD'S END, THINKING OF LI BAI
Du Fu

Cold is the wind that rises
    over this remote region;
Old friend, tell me your thoughts!
When will a wild goose reach me here
From the rivers-and-lakes
    where the autumn waters are brimming?

Writing is at odds with worldly success,
Forest demons exult to have men come by.
You should join your plaints
    with the spirit of Qu Yuan —
Drop a poem for him into the Miluo!

Du Fu commiserates with his friend on his lack of recognition, and
reminds him of another great poet whose merits were ignored, and
who drowned himself in the Miluo river.

天末懷李白

杜 甫

涼風起天末，君子意如何？
鴻雁幾時到，江湖秋水多。
文章憎命達，魑魅喜人過。
應共冤魂語，投詩贈汨羅。

TAKING LEAVE OF GENERAL YAN, WRITTEN AT FENGJI POST-HOUSE
Du Fu

I came a long way with you:
  here we must part
Where the blue hills blankly
  answer my sadness.
When shall we raise our wine-cups
  again together,
Or stroll in the moonlight
  as we did last night?

The people of all these parts
  regret your going;
You have served with honour
  under three reigns.
Now I return alone to my river-village
To spend in solitude my remaining years.

奉濟驛重送嚴公四韻

杜 甫

遠送從此別，青山空復情。
幾時盃重把，昨夜月同行。
列郡謳歌惜，三朝出入榮。
江村獨歸處，寂寞養殘生。

ON LEAVING MARSHAL FANG'S TOMB

Du Fu

In a strange town, and on the move again,
I stayed my horse
    to take leave of your lonely grave.
Approaching in tears,
    I moistened the ground with my weeping,
Low in the sky were
    broken fragments of cloud.

Could I sit at chess with Grand Tutor Xie,
Or bring a precious sword to the Lord of Xu!
But I see only
    forest flowers falling,
And hear the orioles
    call this traveller good-bye.

Xie An, (320-385), a premier of East Jin dynasty, was playing chess
with his nephew when the title of Grand Tutor was bestowed on him.
Prince Jizha of Wu state, a contemporary of Confucius, knew that his
friend, the Lord of Xu, admired a fine sword which he possessed.
When the Prince visited Xu state, intending to present the sword to
his friend, he found the Lord of Xu had already died. He went to his
grave and hung the sword there.

別 房 太 尉 墓

杜 甫

他鄉復行役，駐馬別孤墳。
近淚無乾土，低空有斷雲。
對棋陪謝傅，把劍覓徐君；
惟見林花落，鶯啼送客聞。

THOUGHTS WHILE TRAVELLING AT NIGHT
Du Fu

A faint wind
    through the fine grasses
    on the shore;
High mast
    and lonely boat
    in the night.
The stars reach down to the wide level fields,
The moon rushes on
    in the swing of the Great River.

Shall I ever make a name in poetry?
Old and sick,
    it is time for me to retire.
Driven this way and that like —
    what shall I say?
Like a solitary gull
    blown between earth and sky!

旅 夜 書 懷

杜 甫

細草微風岸，危檣獨夜舟。
星垂平野闊，月湧大江流。
名豈文章著？官應老病休。
飄飄何所似，天地一沙鷗。

ON CLIMBING YUEYANG TOWER

Du Fu

I long heard of Dongting lake:
Only now have I climbed the Yueyang tower.[1]
Wu and Chu, east and south,
    break in the ripples;
Heaven and earth are day and night afloat.

From friends and family no word comes.
Old and sick, I have but my solitary boat.
Barbarian cavalry are
    north of the Border mountains:
I lean on the parapet and my tears flow.

1. The Yueyang tower was a gate-tower on the city wall of Yuezhou,
   overlooking the Dongting lake. The barbarian cavalry are an allusion
   to the Tibetan invasion of 768.

登 岳 陽 樓

杜 甫

昔聞洞庭水，今上岳陽樓。
吳楚東南坼，乾坤日夜浮。
親朋無一字，老病有孤舟！
戎馬關山北，憑軒涕泗流。

FROM MY RETREAT ON THE RIVER WANG, FOR PEI DI

Wang Wei

The colours of the cold mountain
    have turned to emerald;
The autumn river gurgles on
    day after day.
Leaning on my staff
    before the wicket gate,
I hear the cicadas' chirp
    carried on the evening wind.
Beyond the ferry-head
    the sun is just setting;
A solitary plume of smoke
    rises above the village.
I met you just now, tipsy as Jie Yu:[1]
How wildly you sang to me — a "Mr. Five-Willows[2]"!

---

1. Jie Yu was an eccentric recluse of Confucius' time, famous for drinking.
2. 'Mr. Five-Willows' was the nickname of Tao Yuanming, a scholar-poet of Jin dynasty who retired from office to enjoy the simplicity of country life and write poetry, and with whom Wang Wei now compares himself.

輞川閒居贈裴秀才迪

王　維

寒山轉蒼翠，秋水日潺湲，
倚杖柴門外，臨風聽暮蟬。
渡頭餘落日，墟里上孤烟。
復值接輿醉，狂歌五柳前。

AUTUMN EVENING IN A MOUNTAIN HUT

Wang Wei

Rain freshly fallen on the bare mountain;
The air full of autumn in the dusk,
A bright moon peers between the pines;
A clear stream bubbles over the stones.

Clamour in the bamboos —
    the washer-girls are returning;
The lotus stirs
    and down come the fisher-boats.
Though the sweet grass of spring has withered,
Why not linger here, my prince of friends?

山 居 秋 暝

王 維

空山新雨後，天氣晚來秋；
明月松間照，清泉石上流。
竹喧歸浣女，蓮動下漁舟。
隨意春芳歇，王孫自可留。

WRITTEN ON RETURNING FROM MOUNT SONG
Wang Wei

A clear stream ribbons through the long moors.
My horse and carriage amble on, clop clop.
The water flows
    as if it had a will;
Birds homing at dusk
    keep me company.
There are crumbling walls
    down by the ancient ford;
The autumn hills
    are awash in the sunset.
It was a long descent from the peak of Mount Song:
On reaching home I shall close my door on the world.

歸 嵩 山 作

王 維

清川帶長薄，車馬去閑閑，
流水如有意，暮禽相與還。
荒城臨古渡，落日滿秋山；
迢遞嵩山下，歸來且閉關。

THE ZHONGNAN RANGE

Wang Wei

Tai Yi peak,
    near to the Imperial city,
Joins the great range
    stretching to the sea's verge,
As I turn to look,
    the white clouds gather;
Blue mists close on
    views I admired.
The middle ridge divides
    two kinds of landscape;
Dull and fine days change
    the prospect of the valleys.
Desiring to find a human dwelling
    for the night,
I question a woodcutter
    on the far bank of the stream.

終 南 山

王 維

太乙近天都，連山到海隅。
白雲迴望合，青靄入看無。
分野中峰變，陰晴眾壑殊。
欲投人處宿，隔水問樵夫。

A REPLY TO ASSISTANT-PREFECT ZHANG
Wang Wei

In my later years
    I care only for quiet;
The ten thousand affairs
    no longer concern me.
Communing with myself
    I find no plan:
I only know
    I must return to the old woods.

A pine wind
    will loosen the girdle of my gown,
A mountain moon
    glitter on my lute.
You question me about
    success and failure?
Listen —
    a fisherman's song drifting up the estuary!

酬　張　少　府

王　維

晚年惟好靜，萬事不關心。
自顧無長策，空知返舊林。
松風吹解帶，山月照彈琴；
君問窮通理，漁歌入浦深。

ON MISSING MY WAY TO THE MONASTERY OF HEAPED FRAGRANCE

Wang Wei

I cannot find the monastery of Heaped Fragrance,
Miles up now
    into the clouds of the summit.
There is no footpath through the ancient woods.
Where did the bell sound, deep in the mountain?
The voice of the torrent gulps over jagged stones;
Sunlight hardly warms the bluish pines.
As dusk deepens in these unfathomable mazes,
I practise meditation
    to subdue the dragon of desire.

過 香 積 寺

王 維

不知香積寺，數里入雲峯。
古木無人徑，深山何處鐘？
泉聲咽危石，日色冷青松。
薄暮空潭曲，安禪制毒龍。

ON SEEING MR. LI OFF TO ZIZHOU[1]
Wang Wei

On countless precipices
   trees brush the sky
And cuckoos clamour
   among a thousand hills.
A whole night's rain on the mountains
Brings hundreds of cascades
   leaping off the tree-tops.

Chinese girls
   would offer you gifts of *tong* cloth,
But those men of Ba
   bring only their grievance about the *taro* fields.
Wen Weng[2] instructed them in our culture,
But surely you will not depend
   on a scholar of the past?

1. Part of Sichuan; Ba is also an old name for this extreme west of China. To be sent there on government service was, at that time, regarded as tantamount to exile.
2. A Han dynasty offical who became Governor of what is now Sichuan, and was the first to develop and civilize it.

送梓州李使君

王　維

萬壑樹參天，千山響杜鵑。
山中一夜雨，樹杪百重泉。
漢女輸橦布，巴人訟芋田，
文翁翻教授，不敢倚先賢。

A VIEW OF THE RIVER HAN
Wang Wei

Passing the three Xiangs,
    on the Chu border,
Its nine tributaries meeting at Jing Gate,
This river streams over the edge of the world!
The colours of the mountain
    come and are gone in it.
Cities seem to waver up the foreshore;
The distant sky trembles
    in the river ripples.
Here in Xiangyang
    the scenery is so lovely,
It intoxicates this old mountain hermit!

漢　江　臨　眺

王　維

楚塞三湘接，荊門九派通。
江流天地外，山色有無中。
郡邑浮前浦，波瀾動遠空。
襄陽好風日，留醉與山翁。

MY COUNTRY RETREAT ON SOUTH MOUNTAIN
Wang Wei

In middle age
I came to love the Way[1],
Growing old,
I live by the South mountain.
When fancy stirs
I wander there alone
Among delights
known only to myself.

I walk to where the stream
dwindles
And sit watching the clouds
rise up and up...
Maybe I shall meet
an old man of the woods
And we shall talk and laugh
and forget to go home.

1. The essence of Taoist teaching, as expounded in the *Dao De Jing* (The Way and its Power).

行到水山窮處 坐看雲起時

辛未夏 葊峯

I walk to where the stream
  dwindles
And sit watching the clouds
  rise up and up...
行到水窮處，坐看雲起時。

終 南 別 業

王 維

中歲頗好道，晚家南山陲。
興來每獨往，勝事空自知。
行到水窮處，坐看雲起時。
偶然值林叟，談笑無還期。

BY DONGTING LAKE FOR FIRST MINISTER ZHANG

Meng Haoran

In the eighth month, the lake is calm and full,
Brimming the valley, indistinguishable from the sky.
Its mists obscure the Yunmeng marshes;
Its swell shudders on the walls of Yueyang.

I want to cross, but there's no boat to row.
In this idle life I'm ashamed at not serving.
As I sit and watch an angler with his line,
Foolishly I envy him his fishes!

臨洞庭上張丞相

孟浩然

八月湖水平，涵虛混太清；
氣蒸雲夢澤，波撼岳陽城。
欲濟無舟楫，端居恥聖明；
坐觀垂釣者，徒有羨魚情。

ON CLIMBING MOUNT XIAN WITH SOME FRIENDS

Meng Haoran

Human affairs have their ebb and flow:
One comes, another goes — that is man's history.
But this great landmark of Nature's remains.
We too have come to climb it.
We can pick out the fish-dam in the shallows
  at low tide,
And the flooded marshes of Yunmeng
  under cold skies.
Yang Hu's[1] memorial stone stands here yet:
When I have read it I wipe away some tears.

1. Yang Hu (d. 278) was a governor of Xiangyang in Hubei, much beloved by the people. A memorial stone was raised to him on Mount Xian, a hill to the south of Xiangyang, at his death, and many wept when they visited it.

與諸子登峴山

孟浩然

人事有代謝，往來成古今；
江山留勝迹，我輩復登臨。
水落魚梁淺，天寒夢澤深。
羊公碑尚在，讀罷淚沾襟。

DRINKING AT THE TAOIST PRIEST MEI'S
HERMITAGE

Meng Haoran

In my forest hut I grieved at spring's passing,
Drew the bed-curtain to scan the glory of things.
Suddenly appeared a bluebird messenger[1]
Who led me to the home of Chi Song.
The alchemist's furnace was just starting to blaze,
And the magic peach-tree breaking into blossom.
Could it preserve for us the glow of youth,
How we should drench ourselves in the Immortals' wine!

1. Bluebirds were messengers of Xi Wang Mu, the queen of the Taoist
   heaven. Here it evidently stands for a servant sent by the Taoist
   Mei, who is himself represented by Chi Song, an Immortal.

宴梅道士山房

孟　浩　然

林臥愁春盡，搴帷覽物華。
忽逢青鳥使，邀入赤松家，
丹竈初開火，仙桃正發花。
童顏若可駐，何惜醉流霞！

ON RETIRING TO SOUTH MOUNTAIN AT THE
YEAR'S END

Meng Haoran

I have ceased to present petitions at the Capital
And return to my shabby hut on South Mountain.
With my small talent, a wise Ruler discards me;
Being often ill, old friends forget to come.

Age hurries on
　　with its white hairs;
Green spring presses hard on
　　the year's end.
I cannot sleep
　　for the long memories that sadden:
The pine moon wastes its light on my window.

歲 暮 歸 南 山

孟 浩 然

北闕休上書，南山歸敝廬。
不才明主棄，多病故人疎。
白髮催年老，青陽逼歲除！
永懷愁不寐，松月夜窗虛。

ON STOPPING AT AN OLD FRIEND'S HOMESTEAD
Meng Haoran

My old friend prepared a chicken with millet,
Inviting me to visit his country home,
Where the green of the trees
    girdles the village
And beyond the walls the blue hills begin.

We opened your windows to inspect the kitchen-garden,
Took some wine, and spoke of mulberries and flax.
Wait until the Autumn Festival:
I shall come again,
    to enjoy your chrysanthemums.

過 故 人 莊

孟 浩 然

故人具雞黍，邀我至田家。
綠樹村邊合，青山郭外斜。
開軒面場圃，把酒話桑麻。
待到重陽日，還來就菊花。

WRITTEN IN THE QIN COUNTRY, FOR A BUDDHIST
PRIEST, MASTER YUAN

Meng Haoran

To live on a mountain was often my desire,
With three paths to my hut,
   but I lack the money.
I never chose to dwell on the northern plains;
I think with longing of my Master at East Wood.
Spent is my yellow gold on costly fuel,
Waning my power of will as the years go.
At evening, when a cool wind passes,
I hear the cicadas,
   and they make my sorrow more.

秦中寄遠上人

孟　浩　然

一邱常欲臥，三徑苦無資。
北土非吾願，東林懷我師，
黃金燃桂盡，壯志逐年衰。
日夕涼風至，聞蟬但益悲！

MOORING AT NIGHT ON THE TONGLU RIVER, AND REMEMBERING AN OLD FRIEND AT GUANGLING

Meng Haoran

I hear the monkeys howl
    on the dark mountain
And the grey river
    rushing by in the night.
Wind talks among the leaves
    on either bank;
The moon lights my solitary boat.

This Jiande is not my region:
I think of an old companion at Guangling.
Two streams of tears begin to flow
As I look far
    to the west of the water.

The Tonglu is a river in Zhejiang, and Jiande a district in that province.
Guangling is in Jiangsu and thus "far to the west" of the poet's mooring.

宿桐廬江寄廣陵舊游

孟 浩 然

山暝聽猿愁，滄江急夜流。
風鳴兩岸葉，月照一孤舟。
建德非吾土，維揚憶舊遊。
還將兩行淚，遙寄海西頭。

PARTING FROM WANG WEI

Meng Haoran

Lonely, lonely, what is there to hope for —
Day after day
    returning here alone?
If I want to go
    searching for fragrant herbs
I grieve to lack my old friend's company.

Who will stand aside for me
    on the public road?
Those who know my heart
    are rare in this world.
It is best to keep this solitary life —
I am shutting again
    my old garden gate.

留 別 王 維

孟 浩 然

寂寂竟何待！朝朝空自歸，
欲尋芳草去，惜與故人違。
當路誰相假？知音世所稀。
祇應守寂寞，還掩故園扉。

FEELINGS AT THE BEGINNING OF WINTER

Meng Haoran

Leaves are falling,
   the wild-geese pass southward,
A north wind blows cold
   on the river.
My home is by the
   winding Xiang stream,
Far distant from
   the piled clouds of Chu.

My homesick tears are spent
   in a land of strangers!
I watch a solitary sail
   by the sky's rim.
I am lost
   and want to ask the way:
There is only the level sea
   and the formless dusk.

早 寒 有 懷

孟 浩 然

木落雁南度，北風江上寒。
我家襄水曲，遙隔楚雲端。
鄉淚客中盡，孤帆天際看。
迷津欲有問，平海夕漫漫。

CLIMBING TO THE MONASTERY ON GENERAL WU'S TERRACE AND SURVEYING THE PROSPECT ON AN AUTUMN DAY

Liu Changqing

To this ancient terrace
   crumbled by the years
I come in autumn
   with a homesick heart.
Few travellers pass
   this temple in the wilds
Perched between misty peaks
   and deep-cut streams.

Evening light rests
   on age-old ramparts;
A gong's cold boom
   fills the leafless trees.
I am saddened by those Southern dynasty affairs —
Only the Long River is with us still.

In the period of the Northern and Southern dynasties (420-589), North China was ruled by invading northern tribes, and the South by a series of short-lived dynasties: Song, Qi, Liang and Chen. General Wu served the Chen.

秋日登吳公台上寺遠眺

劉 長 卿

古臺搖落後，秋入望鄉心，
野寺來人少，雲峰隔水深。
夕陽依舊壘，寒磬滿空林。
惆悵南朝事，長江獨至今。

SEEING OFF GOVERNOR LI ON HIS RETIREMENT
TO HANYANG

Liu Changqing

Ruined and broken, leader of the Southern expeditions,
You used to command a hundred thousand.
Dismissed from office and without employment,
In old age you ponder the years of your glory.
Alone you pacified the three borders:
How lightly you held life, only your sword could tell.
Over the shoreless waters of Han and Yangtze
The sun is setting now and where will you go?

送李中丞歸漢陽別業

劉 長 卿

流落征南將，曾驅十萬師。
罷官無舊業，老去戀明時！
獨立三邊靜，輕生一劍知。
茫茫江漢上，日暮欲何之？

ON SEEING WANG THE ELEVENTH
LEAVE FOR THE SOUTH

Liu Changqing

I look for you in the spreading mist and waters;
I wave you away and weep.
Where is the swift bird winging?
Blue hills stare blankly down on me.
Down the Long River
    your single sail draws away;
Sun sets on the spring glory
    of the five lakes.
Do any notice me on this river strand
As I watch the white duckweed[1],
    remembering you sadly?

1. Floating duckweed is an accepted symbol for the rootless wanderer.

餞別王十一南游

劉 長 卿

望君煙水闊，揮手淚沾巾。
飛鳥沒何處？青山空向人。
長江一帆遠，落日五湖春，
誰見汀州上，相思愁白蘋。

LOOKING FOR CHANG, THE TAOIST RECLUSE OF
SOUTH STREAM

Liu Changqing

Everywhere along the path I followed,
On the moss
    I saw the print of your wooden shoes.
White clouds clung around your quiet islet,
Scented grasses blocked your idle door.
When the rain passed,
    I noticed the beauty of the pine trees;
Following the hill-path
    I reached the stream's source.
The flowers, the torrent, and thoughts of meditation
Composed one harmony —
    there was no need of speech.

尋南溪常道士

劉 長 卿

一路經行處，莓苔見屐痕。
白雲依靜渚，芳草閉閒門。
過雨看松色，隨山到水源。
溪花與禪意，相對亦忘言。

WRITTEN AT NEW YEAR

Liu Changqing

Homesick thoughts
    embitter the New Year;
Alone at the sky's end
    my tears are springing.
Old age will find me
    still in the service of strangers;
Spring will be back again
    before this exile.

Mountain apes
    my company day and night,
Sharing wind and mist
    with the riverside willows,
I am like the imperial tutor
    banished to Changsha[1] —
Ah! how many more years yet?

1. Jia Yi, a statesman under Emperor Wen of Han dynasty. His warnings
   and proposals for reform angered the Emperor who sent him as a
   petty official to Changsha, then an uncivilized place. While there
   he served as tutor to Prince Liang.

新 年 作

劉 長 卿

鄉心新歲切，天畔獨潸然。
老至居人下，春歸在客先。
嶺猿同旦暮，江柳共風煙；
已似長沙傅，從今又幾年。

FAREWELL TO A BUDDHIST MONK RETURNING
TO JAPAN

Qian Qi

You came to China, a follower of Pratvaya;
The way you travelled was like a path in a dream.
Afloat on grey seas to the sky's rim,
You are leaving now in a light boat of *dharma*.

Moon and wave partake of the Buddhist peace,
Fish and dragon hear you chanting sutras.
I watch with compassion the spark of your single lamp
Clear shining to my eyes a thousand leagues away.

送僧歸日本

錢　起

上國隨緣住，來途若夢行；
浮天滄海遠，去世法舟輕。
水月通禪寂，魚龍聽梵聲。
惟憐一燈影，萬里眼中明。

WRITTEN IN MY STUDY AT GUKOU, FOR THE CENSOR MR. YANG

Qian Qi

Torrents and ravines girdle my thatched hut;
Morning clouds glide past my creeper-curtain.
The bamboos are very touching
    after fresh rain;
The mountains lovely in the evening light.

A lazy egret comes in early to roost;
The autumn blossom here is slow to fall.
My house-boy has swept the wistaria from the path
For yesterday I invited an old friend.

谷口書齋寄楊補闕

錢　起

泉壑帶茅茨，雲霞生薜帷。
竹憐新雨後，山愛夕陽時。
閒鷺棲常早，秋花落更遲。
家僮掃蘿徑，昨與故人期。

A LUCKY MEETING ON THE RIVER HUAI WITH AN OLD FRIEND FROM LIANGZHOU

Wei Yingwu

Both travellers once
  on the Han and Yangtze,
From every meeting we were sure
  to return tipsy!
Since last we parted
  like clouds drifting,
Ten years have passed
  like the flowing stream.

Our joy and affection are
  just as before,
Only our hair is thinner
  and sprinkled with grey.
Why should we not return home together,
Up this Huai river, facing the autumn hills?

淮上喜會梁州故人

韋　應　物

江漢曾為客，相逢每醉還。
浮雲一別後，流水十年間。
歡笑情如舊，蕭疎鬢已斑。
何因不歸去，淮上對秋山。

A FAREWELL TO LI CAO IN THE EVENING RAIN

Wei Yingwu

On Chu river in the fine rain
As evening bells sound from Nanjing,
Limply, limply hang the sodden sails;
In a murky sky
    birds flap slowly over.
The opening to the sea is lost in the thick air,
Far along the ferry, trees drip with moisture:
At the moment of parting
    feeling has no bounds,
Tears fall on our jackets
    like threads of rain.

賦得暮雨送李曹

韋　應　物

楚江微雨裡，建業暮鐘時。
漠漠帆來重，冥冥鳥去遲。
海門深不見，浦樹遠含滋。
相送情無限，沾襟比散絲。

A REPLY TO CHENG YAN'S POEM, WRITTEN IN THE SAME MEASURE

Han Hong

The dawn wind creeps under my sleeping mat.
In the empty city, pools of pale moonlight.
One autumn goose crosses the Milky Way;
In a thousand homes, mallet thuds on washing-stone.

One can tell it is deep in autumn.
Trying over my rhymes, I long put off sleep.
All the while I was humming your graceful lines
And did not notice the crows already cawing.

In the autumn, the padded winter clothes were taken out and washed.
Thus the sound of clothes being slapped on the washing-stone indicated
the approach of winter.

酬程延秋夜即事見贈

韓 翃

長簟迎風早，空城澹月華。
星河秋一雁，砧杵夜千家。
節候看應晚，心期臥亦賒。
向來吟秀句，不覺已鳴鴉。

POEM

Liu Shenxu

The way leads into white clouds
    and disappears;
The spring day is long
    as this glassy stream
Bearing away its freight
    of fallen petals —
Their scent follows the flow of the water
    into the distance.

A hermit's door
    fronts the mountain path,
A study set secretly
    in willow trees;
Full sunlight ever flickers
    on this quiet place —
Its clear shining
    blazes on my garments.

闕　題

劉　眘　虛

道由白雲盡，春與清溪長。
時有落花至，遠隨流水香。
閒門向山路，深柳讀書堂。
幽映每白日，清輝照衣裳。

ON MEETING AT AN INN AN OLD FRIEND FROM MY VILLAGE IN JIANGNAN

Dai Shulun

Autumn here
    and a moon again at the full.
Night thickens the city walls
    a thousand-fold.
Once more
    we meet in Jiangnan,
Half in doubt —
    does it happen in a dream?

A wind in the branches
    startles the sleeping magpies;
In the wet grass
    freezing insects cower.
We wayfarers ought to drink deep
For the dreaded morning bell
    will part us again.

江鄉故人偶集客舍

戴 叔 倫

天秋月又滿，城闕夜千重。
還作江南會，翻疑夢裡逢。
風枝驚暗鵲，露草覆寒蟲，
羈旅長堪醉，相留畏曉鐘。

FAREWELL TO LI DUAN

Lu Lun

Dying grass
 in our familiar fields
Adds a melancholy
 to the parting.
Your road leads
 beyond the storm clouds;
I shall return
 into the evening snow.

Early orphaned,
 I was soon a wanderer;
Through many disasters
 I came to know you late.
Hiding our tears,
 speechless we face each other:
What can we hope for
 in the wind and dust[1]?

1. 'Wind and dust' is a synonym for disturbed conditions in the world.

送 李 端

盧 綸

故關衰草遍，離別正堪悲。
路出寒雲外，人歸暮雪時。
少孤為客早，多難識君遲，
掩泣空相向，風塵何所期？

JOY AT MEETING A COUSIN AND SPEAKING OF THE SEPARATION

Li Yi

After ten years of
    chaos and separation,
I have met you again,
    a full-grown man.
I asked your family,
    startled at first to see you:
As you spoke your name
    I remembered your face from the past.
All the changes in life
    since we parted
Kept us talking
    till the evening bells.
Tomorrow
    when you take the Baling road,
What deeps of autumn mountain
    will divide us!

喜見外弟又言別

李 益

十年離亂後，長大一相逢；
問姓驚初見，稱名憶舊容。
別來滄海事，語罷暮天鐘。
明日巴陵道，秋山又幾重。

PARTING FROM HAN SHEN AFTER STAYING AT THE YUNYANG TAVERN

Sikong Shu

Old friends, but parted by river and sea,
Divided many a time by stream and hill,
We suddenly meet, amazed, suspect we are dreaming,
Lament with each other, ask how the years have passed.
Cold shines the rain in the beam of our single lamp;
Drifting mists muffle the dense bamboos.
Feeling tomorrow's grief again before us,
We pass from hand to hand the 'parting cup'.

雲陽館與韓紳宿別

司 空 曙

故人江海別，幾度隔山川。
乍見翻疑夢，相悲各問年。
孤燈寒照雨，深竹暗浮煙；
更有明朝恨，離杯惜共傳。

JOY AT SEEING MY COUSIN LU LUN COMING TO STAY

Sikong Shu

The night is still, no neighbours near
In this wild place — my poor old croft.
Yellow-leaved trees stand in the rain
And white-haired men under a lamp.

Sunk in loneliness these many years
I was ashamed to beg your company,
But all our lives we cherished each other;
We were closer even than brothers.

喜外弟盧綸見宿

司 空 曙

靜夜四無鄰，荒居舊業貧；
雨中黃葉樹，燈下白頭人。
以我獨沈久，愧君相見頻；
平生自有分，況是霍家親。

TAKING LEAVE OF A FRIEND WHO IS RETURNING
NORTH AFTER THE REBELLION

Sikong Shu

In the Rebellion, we came south together;
In quieter times, you turn north alone.
Your hair has whitened here in strange country,
But soon you will see the green hills of home.

By a waning moon you will pass the ruined ramparts,
Sleep at the frontier pass under a crowd of stars,
With shivering birds and fast-fading grasses
Your sad companions everywhere.

賊平後送人北歸

司 空 曙

世亂同南去，時清獨北還。
他鄉生白髮，舊國見青山。
曉月過殘壘，繁星宿故關。
寒禽與衰草，處處伴愁顏。

AT THE TEMPLE TO THE FIRST RULER OF SHU

Liu Yuxi

To your heroic spirit, generations
Paid reverence here for a thousand years.
When the land was divided —
    a pot with three feet,
It was your merit to restore
    the ancient coinage of Han.
With your minister Zhuge Liang
    you founded a kingdom,
But the son you bore
    could not compare in brilliance,
And when Shu fell, your former singing-girls
Came to dance before the Palaces of Wei.

This commemorates Liu Bei, the first ruler of Shu, one of the Three
Kingdoms, the others being Wu and Wei. Shu was eventually conquered
by Wei.

蜀先主廟

劉禹錫

天地英雄氣，千秋尚懍然，
勢分三足鼎，業復五銖錢。
得相能開國，生兒不象賢。
淒涼蜀故妓，來舞魏宮前。

ON AN OLD FRIEND LOST IN TIBET

Zhang Ji

Last year, while beating off the Yuezhi[1],
Your whole army was lost
    below a city wall:
News snapped between Tibet and China;
The dead parted for ever from the living.

No one retrieved your useless tent;
Your horse strayed back —
    he knew your tattered flag.
Were I sure you were gone,
    I would sacrifice to your spirit
Instead of howling my grief to the far skies.

1. A tribe inhabiting part of Tibet.

沒蕃故人

張 籍

前年戍月支，城下沒全師；
蕃漢斷消息，死生長別離。
無人收廢帳，歸馬識殘旗。
欲祭疑君在，天涯哭此時。

GRASS

Bai Juyi

How the wild grasses spread over the plain!
Year after year they wither to sprout afresh:
Even heath fires cannot burn them up —
When the spring winds blow they rise again.
Their scent creeps on to the ancient road;
Their immaculate green clasps the ruined wall.
Now as I bid my noble friend farewell
I find the endless grasses
  heavy with regret.

草

白 居 易

離離原上草，一歲一枯榮，
野火燒不盡，春風吹又生。
遠芳侵古道，晴翠接荒城。
又送王孫去，萋萋滿別情。

STAYING AT AN INN

Du Mu

Staying at an inn with no companions,
I grew melancholy in my reveries.
The cold light of a lamp and
    thoughts of bygone things...
The honk of a strayed wildgoose
    jerked me from joyless sleep;
Dawn put an end to a dream
    of my distant home.
No news of my kin for a whole year now.
But the grey river was fair
    in the hazy moonlight,
With a fisher-boat at anchor
    near the outer gate.

旅　宿

杜　牧

旅館無良伴，凝情自悄然。
寒燈思舊事，斷鴈警愁眠。
遠夢歸侵曉，家書到隔年。
滄江好煙月，門繫釣魚船。

INSCRIBED ON THE POST-HOUSE AT TONG PASS,
ON MY AUTUMN TRIP TO THE CAPITAL

Xu Hun

At dusk the red leaves drift down with a sigh
Past the long arbour and my gourdful of wine;
Spent clouds are sailing back to Tai Hua,
Light rain passes over Zhong Tiao.
The trees' brilliance follows the Pass into the distance,
The river's racket making for the sea sounds far away.
Tomorrow I shall reach the Imperial city;
Till then, I can dream of being a fisherman or woodcutter.

秋日赴闕題潼關驛樓

許　渾

紅葉晚蕭蕭，長亭酒一瓢。
殘雲歸太華，疏雨過中條。
樹色隨關迥，河聲入海遙。
帝鄉明日到，猶自夢漁樵。

EARLY AUTUMN

Xu Hun

All night
    the voice of autumn hovers;
A west wind breaks from
    the blue convolvulus.
The last glow-worms creep
    into the jade-white dew;
The first wild-geese brush
    the Milky Way.

Tall trees are still mist-bound
    in the dawn;
More of the far hills appear
    in the clarity of morning.
By the fall of a single leaf[1]
    here in Huainan,
I can feel waves rising
    on lake Dongting.

1. There is a well-known Chinese saying: 'When a single leaf falls from the wutong tree, one knows it is autumn'.

早　秋

許　渾

遙夜汎清瑟，西風生翠蘿。
殘螢棲玉露，早鴈拂銀河。
高樹曉還密，遠山晴更多。
淮南一葉下，自覺洞庭波。

THE CICADA

Li Shangyin

Pure of nature, eating only sparely,
Vainly it spins out a plaintive tune.
By the fifth watch,
    the chirps grow faint and cease
On a green indifferent tree.

Unlucky in office,
    I drifted with the stream;
Others have cleared
    my weed-choked fields.
I thank you singer for your true example:
My home too
    shall wear its poverty with honour.

The cicada was held to be the purest of insects, living only on dew.
It is advising the poet to live in poverty at home rather than risk the
uncertainties of official life.

蟬

李 商 隱

本以高難飽，徒勞恨費聲。
五更疏欲斷，一樹碧無情。
薄宦梗猶汎，故園蕪已平；
煩君最相警，我亦舉家清。

WIND AND RAIN

Li Shangyin

Dispiriting, this "Precious Sword" essay[1]
For a wanderer
    almost at the year's end!
Once more leaves yellow
    in the wind and rain.
The old fluting and twanging sound
    from the Blue Pavilions[2].
My new friends lead a heartless social life;
With old friends I am deprived of intimacy.
My heart yearns
    for the wine of Xinfeng:
How many jugs should I need
    to settle my sorrows?

1. The "Precious Sword" essay was presented by the scholar Guo Zhen to the Tang Empress Wu Zhao (r. 690-704). It compares a good scholar with a valuable sword, and was in effect a plea for a position at court.
2. The Blue Pavilions were the houses of singing girls.

風　雨

李　商　隱

淒涼寶劍篇，羈泊欲窮年。
黃葉仍風雨，青樓自管絃。
新知遭薄俗，舊好隔良緣。
心斷新豐酒，銷愁又幾千。

FALLEN FLOWERS

Li Shangyin

The guests are all gone
    from the high pavilion,
In the small garden
    a tumult of petals is whirling;
They fall in heaps
    upon the winding footpaths
And drift away
    to escort the setting sun.
They break my heart —
    I cannot sweep them up;
From my eager eyes
    Spring still slips away:
My sensitive mind is crushed
    by its passing —
All I am left with is a jacket
    wet with tears!

落　花

李　商　隱

高閣客竟去，小園花亂飛，
參差連曲陌，迢遞接斜暉。
腸斷未忍掃，眼穿仍欲歸。
芳心向春盡，所得是沾衣。

THOUGHTS IN THE COLD

Li Shangyin

Since you have gone
    the flood rose level with my sills,
Cicadas are mute,
    dew clings thick on the branches.
This is the season when
    I spin long thoughts,
Leaning at the window
    while time passes.

The northern Wain[1] is distant
    as the spring,
Messengers from Nanling
    slow in coming.
At the edge of the world
    I read my fate in dreams
And I fancy —
    you have found a new friend!

1. Meaning his friend in Nanling.

涼　思

李　商　隱

客去波平檻，蟬休露滿枝。
永懷當此節，倚立自移時。
北斗兼春遠，南陵寓使遲，
天涯占夢數，疑誤有新知。

AT BEI JING LUO MONASTERY

Li Shangyin

The sun drops west
    into Yan hills.
At a thatched hut
    I seek the hermit monk.
In all these falling leaves
    where is my friend?
The path is lost in billows
    of cold mist.

Alone in the dusk
    he is striking the stone gong:
I lean upon my staff
    and listen idly.
Frail dust
    set in this human world,
I cease to concern myself
    with love and hate.

北　菁　蘿

李　商　隱

殘陽西入崦，茅屋訪孤僧。
落葉人何在？寒雲路幾層。
獨敲初夜磬，閒倚一枝藤。
世界微塵裡，吾甯愛與憎？

425

TAKING LEAVE OF A FRIEND GOING EAST
Wen Tingyun

At this deserted fort yellow leaves keep dropping.
You are determined to leave the old country.
With a lively wind blowing you to Hanyang ferry,
By sunrise you will reach Yingmen mountain.

But how many friends are left here by the Yangtze?
Your lone boat disappears into the horizon.
When shall we greet each other again?
A jar of wine will lighten my parting gloom.

送 人 東 遊

温 庭 筠

荒戍落黃葉，浩然離故關，
高風漢陽渡，初日郢門山。
江上幾人在？天涯孤櫂還。
何當重相見？樽酒慰離顏。

AUTUMN HUT BY THE RIVER BA

Ma Dai

In the Ba valley wind and rain have ceased;
I see the evening wild-geese, line on line.
Leaves falling
    from the trees of a strange village,
A cold lamp
    for a man alone in the night.

White dew drips in the empty garden;
A monk is my neighbour beyond these lonely walls.
I have stayed a long while in this peasant hut:
When will they summon me home?

灞 上 秋 居

馬 戴

灞原風雨定，晚見雁行頻。
落葉他鄉樹，寒燈獨夜人。
空園白露滴，孤壁野僧鄰。
寄臥郊扉久，何年致此身？

BY THE RIVER CHU, REMEMBERING THE PAST
Ma Dai

Pale sunlight threads the dew-filled air;
The last rays slip below Chu mountain.
Monkeys screech
    in the trees by Dongting lake
Where someone steers his boat of magnolia wood.

A clear moon is rising over the wide marsh;
Grey mountains press upon the churning current.
I cannot find the spirit of the clouds[1]:
All night long, alone, I mourn the autumn.

1. This rather mysterious poem contains a political allegory. The spirit
of the clouds (who figures in one of the 'Nine Songs' by the ancient
poet Qu Yuan) represents the Emperor Xuanzong who fled before
the rebel armies of An Lushan. The latter can be recognised in the
'grey mountains' (*shan* = mountain).

楚 江 懷 古

馬 戴

露氣寒光集，微陽下楚邱。
猿啼洞庭樹，人在木蘭舟。
廣澤生明月，蒼山夾亂流。
雲中君不見，竟夕自悲秋。

NEWS FROM THE FRONTIER

Zhang Qiao

Bugles have ceased to brag
    in the clear autumn,
The troops are at rest
    under the Drum Towers.
Spring-like winds meet
    at a green grave[1];
White fire of the sun
    sinks over Liangzhou.

No soldiers bar the way
    to the Great Desert —
Travellers can journey
    to the farthest borders:
But Tibetans have a temper
    like this stream —
Ever striving to pour southward.

1. The grave of Wang Zhaojun, a Chinese princess who was married
   for political reasons, and against her will, to a barbarian chieftain.
   It was said that after her death, her grave alone remained green
   among the dry grasses of the steppe.

書 邊 事

張 喬

調角斷清秋，征人倚戍樓。
春風對青塚，白日落梁州。
大漠無兵阻，窮邊有客游。
蕃情似此水，長願向南流。

REFLECTIONS ON NEW YEAR'S EVE
Cui Tu

Farther and farther on the Three Ba[1] road;
Uneasy rest for this much-traveled body.
Flecks of snow tonight
    in the tangle of mountains;
A single lamp
    and the company of strangers.
Day by day
    farther from my own kind;
Gradually
    more intimate with servants:
How to endure this drifting rootless life?
And tomorrow will be the New Year.

1. The Three Ba's were Bajun, Badong and Baxi, all in the far west of Sichuan.

除 夜 有 懷

崔 塗

超遞三巴路，羈危萬里身。
亂山殘雪夜，孤燭異鄉人。
漸與骨肉遠，轉於僮僕親。
那堪正飄泊，明日歲華新。

THE SOLITARY WILD-GOOSE

Cui Tu

Line after line vanish over the Border:
I wonder where you are bound for, lonely one?
In the evening rain you scream for your lost companions;
On the freezing pond, you hesitate to drop down.

You skim by misty islets, low in the darkness;
The frontier moon creeps coldly after you.
I pray you will not meet a fowler's arrow:
The lone flier must be on his guard!

孤　　雁

崔　塗

幾行歸塞盡，念爾獨何之？
暮雨相呼失，寒塘欲下遲。
渚雲低暗渡，關月冷相隨。
未必逢矰繳，孤飛自可疑。

GRIEVANCE IN THE SPRING PALACE
Du Xunhe

Early I learned the snare of beauty and grace.
Listless before the mirror I add powder and rouge:
My charms delight an emperor no longer.
How can I adorn myself to please him?

Birds chirp and twitter when the wind is warm;
Flower shadows deepen when the sun is high.
And year after year, the girls by Yue stream
Still dream of plucking hibiscus.

The beautiful Xi Shi was discovered washing silk by Yue stream and became the favourite of the King of Wu. The imperial bed-curtains were embroidered with hibiscus flowers, as we learn from Bai Ju-yi's 'Everlasting regret': "Warm within the hibiscus bed-curtain she spends the spring nights." The warm wind and strong sun are emblems of the imperial favour.

春　宮　怨

杜　荀　鶴

早被嬋娟誤，欲妝臨鏡慵。
承恩不在貌，教妾若為容？
風暖鳥聲碎，日高花影重，
年年越溪女，相憶采芙蓉。

NIGHT THOUGHTS AT ZHANG TAI

Wei Zhuang

Clear lute-notes accuse the long night;
Grief from the wind and rain coils in the strings.
Alone in the lamplight, I hear the Chu horns,
And watch the last of the moon sink on Zhang Tai.

The sweet-smelling grass is almost at its close.
But my old friend has not yet come.
Letters from home cannot reach me now,
For the autumn wild-geese have turned south.

章臺夜思

韋　莊

清瑟怨遙夜，繞弦風雨哀。
孤燈聞楚角，殘月下章臺。
芳草已云暮，故人殊未來。
鄉書不可寄，秋雁又南迴。

A VISIT TO LU HONGJIAN, WITHOUT FINDING HIM

The monk Jiaoran

Though your new home is on the city border,
A wild path leads to it
    through mulberries and hemp.
Chrysanthemums you planted by the fence
    a while ago
Are not flowering yet, though autumn has come.

I tap on your door — no answering yelp from your dog,
I turn to go, hailing your neighbour to the west:
He tells me, you have made for the hills,
That you return each day
    only when the shadows lengthen.

尋陸鴻漸不遇

皎 然

移家雖帶郭，野徑入桑麻。
近種籬邊菊，秋來未著花。
扣門無犬吠，欲去問西家。
報道山中去，歸來每日斜。

SECTION 4

Seven-character 'regulated' verse

YELLOW CRANE PAVILION

Cui Hao

Long ago a sage vanished
    riding a yellow crane:
Here is only an empty trace —
    Yellow Crane Pavilion.
Once the yellow crane had left
    it never returned again:
For a thousand years, only white clouds
    in the endlessness of space.

Glass-clear streams thread
    the Hanyang woodlands,
Fragrant grasses spring and spread
    on Parrot Island,
But where shall I find my old village
    in the sunset?
Waves and mist on the river
    make one mournful.

This pavilion on the Yangtze at Wuchang is said to commemorate the
spot where Wang Zuqiao, an immortal, flew up to heaven on a yellow
crane.

Long ago a sage vanished
   riding a yellow crane:
Here is only an empty trace —
   Yellow Crane Pavilion.
   昔人已乘黃鶴去，此地空餘黃鶴樓。

黃　鶴　樓

崔　顥

昔人已乘黃鶴去，此地空餘黃鶴樓。
黃鶴一去不復返，白雲千載空悠悠。
晴川歷歷漢陽樹，芳草萋萋鸚鵡洲；
日暮鄉關何處是？煙波江上使人愁。

PASSING HUAYIN
Cui Hao

The sharp heights of Great Hua[1]
    overlook Xianyang;
The three peaks, heaven-pointing,
    no man could have fashioned.
Before the temple of Emperor Wu
    clouds are about to part;
Over 'Immortals' Palm'
    rain begins to clear.
Northward, river and mountain pillow
    the perilous Qin Pass;
From the west, the courier road leads
    to the Han temple on the plain.
Let me beg you wayfarers, seekers of fame and profit —
Stay rather here and learn to lengthen your days.

1. Great Hua, one of the Five Sacred Mountains, had three peaks: 'Hibiscus,' 'Bright Star' and 'Jade Maiden'. 'Immortals' Palm' was another peak of the same range. The Han temple was where the State sacrifices to Heaven and Earth were performed.

行　經　華　陰

崔　顥

岧嶢太華俯咸京，天外三峯削不成。
武帝祠前雲欲散，仙人掌上雨初晴。
河山北枕秦關險，驛路西連漢畤平。
借問路旁名利客，何如此處學長生。

LOOKING TOWARD JIMEN PASS

Zu Yong

Once past the Yan tower
    my heart was afraid;
Pipes and drums banged and wailed;
    in the Han general's camp.
Heaped snow, mile on mile,
    shone with a cold glare,
War flags on the three borders
    fluttered in the grey of dawn.

Across the battlefield, beacon fires
    disturb the Tartar moonlight;
From the fringe of the sea cloudy hills
    cluster round Jizhou.
In youth I was no clerk to throw down my pen,
But if need arise I too will beg a long rope.

Ban Chao of Han was a copyist in his boyhood, but he threw away
his writing-brush to join the army and fight invading tribes. Later he
became a famous general.
Zhong Jun, also of Han, before going to the wars took off his student
cap and asked for a lasso, with which he strangled the King of the Nanyue.

452

望 薊 門

祖 詠

燕臺一去客心驚，笳鼓喧喧漢將營。
萬里寒光生積雪，三邊曙色動危旌。
沙場烽火侵胡月，海畔雲山擁薊城。
少小雖非投筆吏，論功還欲請長纓。

ON SEEING WEI WAN OFF TO THE CAPITAL
Li Qi

I heard travellers at daybreak
    singing the songs of farewell;
Last night the first snow
    reached Yellow River...
I can't bear to hear the wild-geese
    in this mood of sadness
Just when my friend must pass
    into the clouded hills.

When dawn glows in the frontier city
    you will feel winter pressing;
Towards evening in the Royal park
    you will hear the washerwomen's pounding.
No longer is Chang'an a city for pleasure;
Months and years are passing — hopelessly squandered.

The honk of wild geese passing south, and the washing of the heavy
winter clothing were both signs of autumn and were associated with
melancholy emotion.

454

送 魏 萬 之 京

李 頎

朝聞遊子唱驪歌，昨夜微霜初度河。
鴻雁不堪愁裡聽，雲山況是客中過。
關城曙色催寒近，御苑砧聲向晚多。
莫是長安行樂處，空令歲月易蹉跎。

CLIMBING WANG XIAN TERRACE ON THE DOUBLE NINTH: PRESENTED TO VICE-PREFECT LIU
Cui Shu

Emperor Wen of the Han
had a high terrace[1];
Today I climbed it
as the colours of morning broke.
Clouds and hills of the Three Jins
all lay to the north,
Wind and rain from the Two Tombs
blew in from the east.

The guardian of the frontier gate —
who would know him now?
The old man of the river
departed and never returned.
But I want to go in search of Peng Ze[2] —
Get happily fuddled with him
on chrysanthemum-flower wine!

1. Legend says that Lao Zi, the founder of Taoism, rode away to the west and disappeared, but the guardian at the frontier gate made him first write down his principles. This was the 'Dao De Jing' (The Way and its Power). Emperor Wen of Han, wishing to understand this mystical book, sent for a certain old magician living by a river to interpret it. The place where they met was afterwards called Wang Xian Tai — Consulting Magician Terrace.
2. Peng Ze is the official title of the hermit poet Tao Qian, a lover of chrysanthemums.

九日登望仙臺呈劉明府

崔　曙

漢文皇帝有高臺，此日登臨曙色開。
三晉雲山皆北向，二陵風雨自東來。
關門令尹誰能識，河上仙翁去不回。
且欲近尋彭澤宰，陶然共醉菊花杯。

ON CLIMBING PHOENIX TOWER AT JINLING

Li Bai

Phoenixes once played on Phoenix Tower.
The birds have left it bare now —
    only the river flows on.
At the Palace of Wu,
    silent paths
    buried under grass and blossom;
Men of Jin in their fine attire
    become ancient grave-mounds.

The Three Peaks reach halfway
    into the blue;
Between two arms of the river
    White Egret Island.
Everywhere drifting clouds that
    dull the sunlight:
Chang'an is invisible
    and that saddens me.

登金陵鳳凰台

李 白

鳳凰台上鳳凰遊，鳳去台空江自流。
吳宮花草埋幽徑，晉代衣冠成古丘。
三山半落青天外，二水中分白鷺洲。
總為浮雲能蔽日，長安不見使人愁。

SEEING OFF ASSISTANT-MAGISTRATE LI, DEGRADED TO XIAZHONG, AND ASSISTANT-MAGISTRATE WANG, DEGRADED TO CHANGSHA

Gao Shi

Alas my friends, what are your
    thoughts now at parting?
Stay your horses and drink
    while I speak of your places of exile.
At Wu Gorge the monkeys' howling
    will often draw your tears;
How much news can the migrant geese
    carry from Hengyang?

Autumn sails will carry you far
    up Green Maple river;
Old trees grow sparely
    near White Emperor city,
Yet in this blessed time the royal favour
    falls like dew and rain:
Do not falter — we part,
    but only for a while.

送李少府貶峽中王少府貶長沙

高 適

嗟君此別意何如？駐馬銜杯問謫居。
巫峽啼猿數行淚，衡陽歸雁幾封書。
青楓江上秋帆遠，白帝城邊古木疏。
聖代即今多雨露，暫時分手莫躊躇。

FOLLOWING THE METRE OF THE COURT OFFICIAL
JIA ZHI'S 'DAWN AUDIENCE AT DA MING PALACE'

Cen Shen

Cock-crow on the imperial road,
    dawn strikes cold.
Orioles flute in the royal city
    but the colours of spring are passing.
At the morning bell from Golden Gate
    myriad doors spring wide;
Fabulous weapons on the jade stairs
    guard a thousand officials.
Flowers reach our sword pendants,
    stars begin to set;
Dew is not dry on the willows
    as they brush our banners.

All alone by Phoenix lake
    stands the poet —
Composing to the air 'Spring sunlight',
    hard for others to cap!

和賈至舍人早朝大明宮之作

岑 參

雞鳴紫陌曙光寒，鶯囀皇州春色闌；
金闕曉鐘開萬戶，玉階仙仗擁千官。
花迎劍佩星初落，柳拂旌旗露未乾。
獨有鳳凰池上客，陽春一曲和皆難。

ANOTHER, ON THE SAME THEME
Wang Wei

The red-capped watchman, like the cock,
  announces the dawn,
The Master of the Robes advances
  with the Imperial garments and precious furs;
The Palace doors swing wide, nine-fold
  like the gates of Heaven,
Officials of countless States bow
  before the headdress with the pearl tassels.
Sunbeams spread and shimmer
  over the 'fairy palms'[1],
Fragrant incense swirls
  around the Dragon robes.

After the audience you must inscribe
  the five-coloured edict[2] —
I can hear your pendants jingle
  as you return past Phoenix lake.

1. Fairy palms: mysterious figures erected by Emperor Wu of Han with cupped hands to collect the dew.
2. Five-coloured edict: i.e. written on paper of five colours.

和賈至舍人早朝大明宮之作

王 維

絳幘雞人報曉籌，尚衣方進翠雲裘。
九天閶闔開宮殿，萬國衣冠拜冕旒。
日色纔臨仙掌動，香煙欲傍袞龍浮。
朝罷須裁五色詔，佩聲歸到鳳池頭。

AFTER THE EMPEROR'S POEM ON SPRING SCENERY
Wang Wei

River Wei twists in coils
    along the old Qin boundary;
Yellow mountain rears as of old
    above the palace of Han.
The Emperor's carriage bowls past
    a thousand courtyard willows,
And over a carved bridge with vistas
    of the Imperial flower gardens.

High in the clouds, twin turrets
    of the royal domain;
In falling rain spring foliage
    shelters the homes of the people.
His majesty takes advantage of the warm air
    to make an official journey —
It is not just a pleasure-outing
    to enjoy the scenery.

奉和聖製從蓬萊向興慶閣道中留春雨中春望之作應制

王　維

渭水自縈秦塞曲，黃山舊繞漢宮斜。
鸞輿迥出千門柳，閣道迴看上苑花。
雲裡帝城雙鳳闕，雨中春樹萬人家。
為乘陽氣行時令，不是宸遊翫物華。

WRITTEN AT MY COUNTRY RETREAT BY THE RIVER WANG, AFTER HEAVY RAIN

Wang Wei

Days of rain in the empty woods,
    wavering chimney smoke —
They are stewing vegetable and steaming millet
    to send to the eastern acres.
Over the still flooded fields
    a white heron flies,
In the leafy woods of summer
    pipes a golden oriole.

I have practised quietude in the mountains
    contemplating the 'morning glory';
For my simple meal under the pines
    I gather dewy ferns.
An old countryman now, I've abandoned
    the struggle for gain —
Why are those seagulls
    still suspicious of me?

積雨輞川莊作

王 維

積雨空林煙火遲，蒸藜炊黍餉東菑。
漠漠水田飛白鷺，陰陰夏木囀黃鸝。
山中習靜觀朝槿，松下清齋折露葵，
野老與人爭席罷，海鷗何事更相疑？

PRESENTED TO THE PALACE OFFICIAL GUO

Wang Wei

Sunset glows on your high pavilion
　　and deep doorway,
Peach and plum trees cluster thick,
　　willow catkins fly;
In the Palace, a slow-tolling bell
　　signals the evening,
In the Censor's department, birds twitter —
　　there are few clerks left.
At daybreak, jade pendants swinging,
　　you will hurry to the Gold Court;
At dusk you receive the Imperial Order
　　and bow low at the Palace gate.
I should force myself to serve with you
　　were it not for old age —
Being ill, I need to rest
　　and shall take off my Court robes.

酬 郭 給 事

王 維

洞門高閣靄餘暉，桃李陰陰柳絮飛。
禁裡疏鐘官舍晚，省中啼鳥吏人稀。
晨搖玉佩趨金殿，夕奉天書拜瑣闈。
強欲從君無那老，將因臥病解朝衣。

A PREMIER OF SHU

Du Fu

Where shall I seek the shrine of the famous Premier?
Beyond the walls of Brocade city,
    where the cypress grow darkly.
Green grass paints the steps
    with spring's own colour,
Golden orioles fill the leaves
    with their sweet idle notes.

In three visits the Ruler pressed him
    to make a plan for government;
Through two reigns the old statesman's heart
    supported and steadied the kingdom,
But before his last campaign could succeed
    he passed away,
Making brave men ever since
    shed tears.

The Premier was Zhuge Liang, the famous general and statesman of
Shu in the 'Three Kingdoms' period. Liu Bei, the first ruler of Shu
Kingdom went twice to his hut to ask for advice; only at the third
occasion did he agree to take up office. He remained Premier under
Liu Bei's successor, Liu Chan. He died while commanding an expedition
against Wei Kingdom.

蜀　相

杜　甫

丞相祠堂何處尋？錦官城外柏森森。
映階碧草自春色，隔葉黃鸝空好音。
三顧頻煩天下計，兩朝開濟老臣心。
出師未捷身先死，長使英雄淚滿襟。

A GUEST ARRIVES

Du Fu

North of my hut, south of my hut,
    the spring floods are out,
Flocks of gulls my only callers
    day after day.
My path is deep in petals,
    not swept for guests;
You were the first today
    to open my thorn-wood gate.

With the market so far
    there's little choice for supper;
In our poor home
    we have only a pot of home-brew:
If you'd like to drink with
    an old neighbour of mine,
I'll call over the fence —
    he will help us finish the wine.

客　至

杜　甫

舍南舍北皆春水，但見群鷗日日來。
花徑不曾緣客掃，蓬門今始為君開。
盤飧市遠無兼味，樽酒家貧只舊醅。
肯與鄰翁相對飲，隔籬呼取盡餘杯。

LOOKING AT THE COUNTRYSIDE

Du Fu

West mountain white with snow,
    the Three Towns filled with armour.
I stand on the south bank of the sparkling river
    by Myriad Mile Bridge:
From sea to sea, only fury and dust;
    kept from my kindred
I am weeping at the sky's end
    for loneliness and exile.

I can only expect life's decline
    attended by much sickness,
With nothing of the least value
    to offer the Imperial Court.
At times I ride out of the city
    and gaze to the limit of sight —
I can't bear the spectacle of human affairs
    worsening from day to day.

野　　望

杜　甫

西山白雪三城戍，南浦清江萬里橋。
海內風塵諸弟隔，天涯涕淚一身遙。
惟將遲暮供多病，未有涓埃答聖朝。
跨馬出郊時極目，不堪人事日蕭條。

ON HEARING OF THE RECOVERY OF HENAN
AND HEBEI BY GOVERNMENT TROOPS

Du Fu

Near Jiange I suddenly hear
    Hebei is retaken:
At the news my tears well up
    and wet my gown.
I turn to look at my wife and children —
    where's my grief gone?
I sweep aside the Poetry Classic —
    joy is driving me wild!
I sing lustily in the broad daylight
    and drink without measure.
The verdant spring shall be my fellow
    on the glad journey home:
I'll sail at once through the Ba Gorge then Wu Gorge,
    on past Xiangyang, and make for Luoyang.

聞官軍收河南河北

杜 甫

劍外忽傳收薊北，初聞涕淚滿衣裳。
卻看妻子愁何在？漫卷詩書喜欲狂。
白日放歌須縱酒，青春作伴好還鄉。
即從巴峽穿巫峽，便下襄陽向洛陽。

CLIMBING A HEIGHT

Du Fu

A sharp wind,
    the sky high,
    gibbons' mournful screeching;
Blue islets,
    white sands,
    sea-birds wheeling.
Without cease
    falling leaves
    drift down with a whisper;
Without end
    the Long River
    washes endlessly by.

Miles from home,
    mourning the autumn,
    always a wanderer,
An old man,
    often sick,
    I have climbed this height alone.
My hardships
    and bitter regrets
    have added frost to my temples:
In my unhappiness
    I push aside
    the cup of rough wine.

登　高

杜　甫

風急天高猿嘯哀，渚清沙白鳥飛迴。
無邊落木蕭蕭下，不盡長江滾滾來。
萬里悲秋常作客，百年多病獨登臺。
艱難苦恨繁霜鬢，潦倒新停濁酒杯。

CLIMBING A TOWER
Du Fu

Flowers beside the high tower
    sadden a wanderer's heart.
From a world beset with troubles
    I have climbed up here.
The spring colours of Brocade River
    bring all nature before me;
In shifting clouds over Jade Rampart
    the whole of history passes...

With the Imperial Court
    firmly set in the north,
Brigands from the western mountains
    should cease their sallies.
The pitiful Second Ruler[1]
    still has his temple here.
As the sun goes down
    I shall hum a Liangfu song[2].

1. The Second Ruler of Shu (one of the Three Kingdoms) was enshrined in the same temple as the great general Zhuge Liang.
2. The song was one which Zhuge was fond of reciting when still living in retirement.

登　樓

杜　甫

花近高樓傷客心，萬方多難此登臨。
錦江春色來天地，玉壘浮雲變古今。
北極朝廷終不改，西山寇盜莫相侵。
可憐後主還祠廟，日暮聊為梁父吟。

SPENDING THE NIGHT AT THE GENERAL'S HEADQUARTERS

Du Fu

Clear autumn at Headquarters;
　　the wu-tong trembles by the well.
I am lodged alone in this river city;
　　my candle gutters and fades.
All night long the bugle's tones
　　speak their own sadness;
The moon's orb hangs in the sky —
　　who has the heart to watch it?

Driven on by the winds and dust
　　I lost touch with home.
In this desolate frontier country
　　even the roads are hazardous.
I have endured my loneliness
　　for ten years now:
Chased from the nest I snatch a moment's peace
　　on this solitary bough.

宿　府

杜　甫

清秋幕府井梧寒，獨宿江城蠟炬殘。
永夜角聲悲自語，中天月色好誰看？
風塵荏苒音書絕，關塞蕭條行路難。
已忍伶俜十年事，強移棲息一枝安。

NIGHT AT THE PAVILION

Du Fu

Sun and moon vie to shorten the day
    at the year's end;
To the horizon, frost and snow have settled
    this bitter night.
Drums and bugles of the fifth watch
    sound desperately sad;
Shadows of the stars tremble
    in the waters of the Three Gorges.

In many homes over the countryside
    they are crying for the war dead;
In some parts, fishermen and woodcutters
    hum the barbarians' songs.
'Sleeping Dragon' and 'Restive Horse[1]'
    ended under the yellow earth —
Useless to lament our human lot,
    even that letters cease to come.

1. 'Sleeping Dragon' and 'Restive Horse' were the nicknames of two famous generals: Zhuge Liang of Shu Kingdom and Gongsun Shu a war-lord of the first century.

閣　夜

杜　甫

歲暮陰陽催短景，天涯霜雪霽寒宵。
五更鼓角聲悲壯，三峽星河影動搖。
野哭幾家聞戰伐，夷歌數處起漁樵。
臥龍躍馬終黃土，人事音書漫寂寥。

REMEMBERING THE PAST

Du Fu

(I)

Fleeing and parting, north and east
    a concourse of wind and dust.
I drift anchorless south and west,
    between earth and sky.
Pavilions and towers by the Three Gorges
    drenched in sun and moonlight;
Tartars of the Five Streams dressed
    in the colours of mountain and cloud.

The Xiongnu pay allegiance to our Emperor
    but are not to be trusted;
This wandering poet, grieving for the times.
    still cannot return.
Yu Xin's[1] whole life was a rough and stormy one —
In old age he wrote poems of homesickness
    for his own river region.

1. Yu Xin, a 6th century poet who wrote when China was divided
   into north and south. Among his best poems is a *fu*, 'Lament for
   Jiang-nan' (the region south of the Yangtze).

詠　懷　古　跡

杜　甫

支離東北風塵際，漂泊西南天地間。
三峽樓台淹日月，五溪衣服共雲山。
羯胡事主終無賴，詞客哀時且未還。
庾信平生最蕭瑟，暮年詩賦動江關。

(II)

Deeply I understand Song Yu's[1] lament for unrest and decay;
The force and elegance of his style are an example to me still.
Despairing I look back a thousand autumns and share his tears,
Lonely and poor both, in different generations, other ages.
His old country hut is no more, his writings
    are vaguely remembered:
Was it a dream that he wrote of morning clouds and
    evening rain over this ruined terrace?
Most grievous is it that the Chu palaces are utterly decayed —
A boatman points out the spot, but I doubt if one can still tell.

1. Song Yu was a poet at the court of Prince Qingxiang of Chu
   (298-265 B.C.), and a disciple of the great Chu poet, Qu Yuan. He
   is said to be the author of 'Jiu Bian' (The Nine Arguments) in the
   collection of 'Chu Ci' (Songs of the South).

其　二

搖落深知宋玉悲，風流儒雅亦吾師。
悵望千秋一灑淚，蕭條異代不同時。
江山故宅空文藻，雲雨荒臺豈夢思。
最是楚宮俱泯滅，舟人指點到今疑。

(Ⅲ)

Through a maze of hills, a crowd of valleys,
    I came to Thorn Gate;
The hamlet where Zhaojun grew to womanhood
    is there still.
She left the Palace of Han for
    the northern border desert:
All that remains — a green grave
    facing the dull dusk.

Her portrait concealed the truth
    of her spring-wind face;
Vainly her ghost with its jingling jewels
    returned under the moon.
Years ago she made a Tartar song to the guitar
That expressed all the passion of her bitterness.

Wang Zhaojun was a beauty at the court of Emperor Yuan of Han.
This Emperor chose his favourites from the portraits made by the court
painter, who increased the beauty of the sitters according to the size
of their bribe. Zhaojun was of too noble a character to use bribery
and when a Tartar chieftain was to be placated by the offer of a Han
princess in marriage, Zhaojun was chosen as being the ugliest. At the
farewell feast, when he saw her for the first time, the Emperor found
she was the most beautiful of all, but it was too late to save her. At
her death she was buried near the Chinese boundary, and the grass
on her grave was said to remain always green.

其　　三

群山萬壑赴荊門，生長明妃尚有村，
一去紫台連朔漠，獨留青塚向黃昏。
畫圖省識春風面，環佩空歸月下魂；
千載琵琶作胡語，分明怨恨曲中論。

(IV)

When the Lord of Shu invaded Wu Kingdom,
    he passed the Three Gorges,
And till his death year remained in the Palace
    of Endless Peace.
I can picture his kingfisher banners in these empty mountains;
His Jade Court a wraith in this deserted temple...
River herons have nested in pine and fir
    around the ancient shrine;
Only an old peasant shambles up to
    present the annual offering.
Zhuge Liang's ancestral temple still stands near,
So the Prince and Minister share the same sacrifice.

其 四

蜀主征吳幸三峽，崩年亦在永安宮。
翠華想像空山裡，玉殿虛無野寺中。
古廟杉松巢水鶴，歲時伏臘走村翁。
武侯祠屋長鄰近，一體君臣祭祀同。

(V)

Zhuge's great name passed down to all the world;
Men pay reverence to the portrait of this grave and
noble statesman.
At the carving of the Three Kingdoms
he depended on cunning stratagems,
Like a single feather against the clouds of all the ages.
Among his peers he counted Yi and Lü;
In directing affairs he surpassed Xiao and Cao.
Fate turned; it was no longer possible
to restore the House of Han:
With singleness of purpose he offered his
life — accepted death.

The references are to Yi Yin a statesman of Shang dynasty, Lü Shang
of Zhou dynasty, Xiao He and Cao Shen of early Han.
Zhuge is, of course, the famous general of Shu kingdom in the 'Three
Kingdoms' period.

其　五

諸葛大名垂宇宙，宗臣遺像肅清高。
三分割據紆籌策，萬古雲霄一羽毛。
伯仲之間見伊呂，指揮若定失蕭曹，
運移漢祚終難復，志決身殲軍務勞。

ON PARTING AGAIN FROM THE TWO OFFICIALS, XUE THE SIXTH AND LIU THE EIGHTH, IN JIANGZHOU

Liu Changqing

At this stage of life why dream
    of receiving the imperial mandate?
Human affairs are nothing to me —
    I had better learn tipsy songs!
There's a fine moon on the river,
    the northern geese passing,
Naked trees in Huainan
    show more of the Chu hills.

How thankful I am to rest my body
    near Cangzhou.
White hair faces me in the mirror —
    there's no help for it!
Our strength is failing by now —
    we are all old men:
I am touched that you still bid me
    beware of wind and wave.

江州重別薛六柳八二員外

劉 長 卿

生涯豈料承優詔？世事空知學醉歌。
江上月明胡鴈過，淮南木落楚山多。
寄身且喜滄州近，顧影無如白髮何！
今日龍鍾人共老，媿君猶遣慎風波。

ON PASSING JIA YI'S HOUSE AT CHANGSHA

Liu Changqing

Here for three years you sojourned,
    banished from office;
All you left to the ages, your grief,
    like the exile from Chu.
I search for a trace of you still
    in the autumn grass,
Look in vain through wintry trees
    in the sunset.

Emperor Wen was pious
    but he lacked benevolence;
The waters of Xiang are unfeeling —
    how can they know my lament?
In this deserted spot
    where hill and stream
    share the desolation,
I pity you and wonder
    what brought you
    to this edge of the world?

Jia Yi, statesman and scholar of Han dynasty, was banished to Changsha by Emperor Wen. While there he wrote a poem in memory of Qu Yuan ('the exile from Chu'), who had also been misunderstood by his ruler, and had drowned himself in the river (see also Liu Changqing's poem 'Written at New Year', p. 378).

長沙過賈誼宅

劉　長　卿

三年謫宦此棲遲，萬古惟留楚客悲。
秋草獨尋人去後，寒林空見日斜時。
漢文有道恩猶薄，湘水無情弔豈知？
寂寂江山搖落處，憐君何事到天涯？

COMPOSED ON A JOURNEY FROM XIA KOU TO PARROT ISLAND ONE EVENING, WHILE CONTEMPLATING YUEYANG: FOR MR. YUAN THE CENSOR

Liu Changqing

No mist round the island
    and no waves breaking;
Memories of the exile from Chu[1]
    add an impalpable sadness.
In the sunset over Han
    birds pass wheeling;
The autumn waters of Dongting
    join the remote sky.

Horns are blown in the cold
    in a solitary hill-town;
My boat is moored tonight
    by a lonely river-outpost.
Disquieted about the Han fortunes,
    Jia Yi sent up memorials,
But was banished to Changsha,
    an object of pity to all the ages.

1. See note to the previous poem.

自夏口至鸚鵡洲夕望岳陽寄元中丞

劉　長　卿

汀洲無浪復無烟，楚客相思益渺然。
漢口夕陽斜度鳥，洞庭秋水遠連天。
孤城背嶺寒吹角，獨戍臨江夜泊船。
賈誼上書憂漢室，長沙謫去古今憐。

PRESENTED TO THE PALACE OFFICIAL, MR. PEI

Qian Qi

The second month; golden orioles
    flutter in the Imperial gardens.
Spring in the Forbidden City
    and a sombre morning...
The clang of bells from Chang Le Palace
    dies away beyond the flowers,
The colour of the willows by Dragon Pool
    deepens in the rain.

Kindly sunshine cannot dispel
    the bitterness of my condition;
I was always eager to offer the Emperor
    my duty.
For ten years I kept sending up my writings —
    still unaccepted:
White-haired now, I am mortified to face you
    in your official regalia.

贈闕下裴舍人

錢　起

二月黃鸝飛上林，春城紫禁曉陰陰。
長樂鐘聲花外盡，龍池柳色雨中深。
陽和不散窮途恨，霄漢常懸捧日心。
獻賦十年猶未遇，羞將白髮對華簪。

FOR LI DAN AND YUAN XI

Wei Yingwu

Last year in the flowering time
    we met and parted;
Now flowers blossom again
    and another year gone!
Human affairs twisted and tangled,
    hard to judge the way,
And spring sadness clouds my spirit
    when I sleep alone.

With a body full of ailments,
    I dream of the home fields;
The fugitives in the district
    Make me ashamed of my pay.
Someone said, you wanted to come —
    and we could talk together:
How often must I watch from west pavilion
    the moon coming to the full?

寄李儋元錫

韋應物

去年花裏逢君別，今日花開又一年。
世事茫茫難自料，春愁黯黯獨成眠。
身多疾病思田里，邑有流亡愧俸錢。
聞道欲來相問訊，西樓望月幾回圓。

COMPOSED AT THE TAOIST MONASTERY OF XIAN YOU

Han Hong

From Xian Terrace where I glimpsed
    the Immortals' cities and towers,
Nature seems drear and cold
    after the night storms.
The colours of the mountain merge afar
    with the twilit woods of Qin;
The Han palace washing-stones
    speak of autumn approaching.

How still the empty altars
    where worn pines throw their shadows!
How secret this tiny glade
    which spring will sweeten with new grass!
Why seek elsewhere for other-worldly teaching?
Here among men there is also a Cinnabar Hill.

The first line refers to the five cities and twelve towers of the Taoist immortals; the Cinnabar Hill of the last line is another of their legendary dwellings.

同 題 仙 遊 觀

韓 翃

仙臺初見五城樓，風物凄清宿雨收。
山色遙連秦樹晚，砧聲近報漢宮秋。
疎松影落空壇靜，細草春香小洞幽。
何用別尋方外去？人間亦自有丹邱。

SPRING THOUGHTS
Huangfu Ran

The piping of orioles and twitter of swallows
    announce a new year.
To Ma Yi and Long Dui
    a thousand mile road.
My home is in a towered city close to the Han park;
My heart follows the bright moon into Tartar skies.
On my loom I have woven my endless sorrow
    into brocade;
In the upper chamber, sprays of blossom
    mock my solitary sleep.
I ask General Dou, Commander of the Cavalry,
When will he turn the banners
    and carve his exploits on Swallow Rock.

Lady Su Hui of Jin (265-419) wove a love poem on silk for her husband General Dou Tao who was guarding the Northern borders against the Tartars. It was composed of 800 characters, and many hundred poems have been discovered in it by reading the characters in different directions.

春　思

皇　甫　冉

鶯啼燕語報新年，馬邑龍堆路幾千。
家住層城鄰漢苑，心隨明月到胡天。
機中錦字論長恨，樓上花枝笑獨眠。
為問元戎竇車騎，何時返旆勒燕然。

EVENING AT EZHOU

Lu Lun

Through a break in the cloud I glimpse
    distant Hanyang —
Still a day's journey
    for our lonely sail.
All day the merchants dozed
    sure of the waves' calm;
Tonight the boatmen chatter
    feeling the pull of the tide.

Regret at San Xiang, my hair fades
    with the colours of autumn;
Under the moonlight, my heart travels back
    ten thousand miles
To my old homestead, left a shambles
    by the fighting,
And still I must endure the bang of war-drums
    across the river.

晚 次 鄂 州

盧綸

雲開遠見漢陽城，猶是孤帆一日程。
估客晝眠知浪靜，舟人夜語覺潮生。
三湘愁鬢逢秋色，萬里歸心對月明。
舊業已隨征戰盡，更堪江上鼓鼙聲。

ON CLIMBING A TOWER ON LIUZHOU CITY WALL, PRESENTED TO THE SUB-PREFECTS OF ZHANG, TING, FENG AND LIAN

Liu Zongyuan

High tower on a city wall
    facing the waste lands;
Sea and sky and melancholy thoughts —
    equally endless.
A rough wind troubles the hibiscus by the moat,
Fine rain invades the creepers on the wall.
Dense trees on the mountain-ridge,
    screen the thousand-mile vista,
The river's flow twists like the nine entrails.
Together we came to this land of the Yue
    who tattoo their bodies;
Alas that letters from home seldom reach us!

登柳州城樓寄漳汀封連四州刺史

柳　宗　元

城上高樓接大荒，海天愁思正茫茫。
驚風亂颭芙蓉水，密雨斜侵薜荔牆。
嶺樹重遮千里目，江流曲似九迴腸。
共來百越文身地，猶自音書滯一鄉。

AT XISAI MOUNTAIN, REMEMBERING THE PAST

Liu Yuxi

When Wang Jun's war junks
    slid down from Yizhou
The majesty of Jinling
    passed into the dark.
A thousand feet of chains were sunk
    in the river bed,
But flags of surrender appeared
    on the city of Nanjing.

How often in human life are we touched
    by events from the past!
The mountain's image as of old is pillowed
    on the cold current.
These days, within the four seas
    all are one family;
Only the old forts, empty, dreary,
    are left to the reeds and the autumn.

Wang Jun was a general of Jin dynasty at the time of the Three
Kingdoms, who brought his warships down the Yangtze from Sichuan
to attack Wu Kingdom. Jinling, Capital of Wu, had been defended by
heavy chains laid across the river.

西 塞 山 懷 古

劉 禹 錫

王濬樓船下益州，金陵王氣黯然收。
千尋鐵鎖沉江底，一片降幡出石頭。
人世幾回傷往事？山形依舊枕寒流。
從今四海為家日，故壘蕭蕭蘆荻秋。

ELEGY

Yuan Zhen

(I)

Youngest daughter of the Xies —
    She whom they loved the best,
When you wed this poor Qian Lou[1]
    a hundred things vexed you,
Yet seeing I need clothes
    you would ransack your wicker baskets;
When I coaxed you to buy me wine
    you pledged a gold hairpin.
Wild plants made our meals
    and long beans tasted sweet;
Fallen leaves helped for fuel —
    we relied on the old locust-tree.
Now my official pay is more than a hundred thousand
But for you I can only perform sacrifice
    and offer prayers.

Qian Lou, a noted scholar of the 'Spring and Autumn' period who
preferred a life of poverty to seeking high office.

遣　悲　懷

元　稹

謝公最小偏憐女，自嫁黔婁百事乖；
顧我無衣搜藎篋，泥他沽酒拔金釵。
野蔬充膳甘長藿，落葉添薪仰古槐，
今日俸錢過十萬，與君營奠復營齋。

(II)

In the old days you and I
    mocked the business of dying —
Now, before my eyes,
    it has all come to pass.
Nearly all your clothes have been given away,
Your embroidery is still here
    that I cannot bear to unfold...
I still remember your sweetness
    and am kind to the maids and servants;
Since you came into my dreams
    I had paper money burnt for you.[1]
I know this is a sorrow every man must have,
But those who knew poverty together
    a hundred memories hurt.

1. Special paper money is burnt for the dead, to supply their needs in the next world.

其　二

昔日戲言身後事，今朝都到眼前來。
衣裳已施行看盡，針線猶存未忍開。
尚想舊情憐婢僕，也曾因夢送錢財；
誠知此恨人人有，貧賤夫妻百事哀。

(Ⅲ)

Listless I sit, grieving for you
    and grieving for myself;
Of my hundred ailing years
    how many are left?
Deng You[1] had no sons, and accepted his fate,
Pan Yue[2] lost a wife, and lavished poetry on her.

What hope can I have
    in the dark of our common grave-mound?
It is hard to imagine
    reunion in that other life.
All night
    I shall lie with unclosed eyes
To repay you
    for a lifetime of furrowed brows.

1. Deng You of Jin dynasty, when fleeing from bandits with his wife, son and nephew, was obliged to abandon one of the children. Since he himself might have another son, and his brother was dead, he sacrificed his own child. He had no more sons, but his act was considered meritorious.
2. Pan Yue, a poet of Jin dynasty, famous for his elegies to his wife.

其 三

閒坐悲君亦自悲，百年多病幾多時？
鄧攸無子尋知命，潘岳悼亡猶費詞。
同穴窅冥何所望？他生緣會更難期。
唯將終夜長開眼，報答平生未展眉。

FEELINGS WHILE LOOKING AT THE MOON WHEN SEPARATED FROM MY BROTHERS

Bai Juyi

Hard times, a famine year,
    a worthless patrimony;
We brothers wayfarers
    to the west and the east.
Our fields and gardens run to waste
    after the fighting,
Kinsmen wandering homeless
    on the high roads.

In my own shadow I trace
    the far-flying wild geese;
Torn from my roots I drift
    like autumn's winged seeds
Surely we are all watching the bright moon
    with falling tears
On this night of homesickness spent
    in five different places.

自河南經亂，關內阻饑，兄弟離散，各在一處。因望月有感，聊書所懷，寄上浮梁大兄、於潛七兄、烏江十五兄，兼示符離及下邽弟妹。

白　居　易

時難年荒世業空，弟兄羈旅各西東。

田園寥落干戈後，骨肉流離道路中。

弔影分為千里鴈，辭根散作九秋蓬。

共看明月應垂淚，一夜鄉心五處同。

THE INLAID ZITHER[1]

Li Shangyin

By chance the inlaid zither
    has fifty strings;
Every string with its fret
    evokes the golden years;
Zhuangzi dreaming at dawn
    he was a butterfly[2],
King Wang's[3] heart
    haunting the cuckoos in Spring,
Grey seas and moonshine,
    tears of pearl[4],
Sultry sun on Lantian[5],
    smoke rising from the jade...
Moods that must wait for memory to strengthen,
Only at the time, these were mysteries.

1. The zither with fifty strings was an ancient musical instrument on which tunes sounded infinitely sad. It is thought that Jinse ('Gilded Zither') was the name of one of the poet's women friends, cut off in her prime without even reaching fifty (in accordance with her name). This would explain the obscurity of the allusions, which would thus be personal ones.
2. Zhuangzi, Taoist philosopher, tells how he once dreamt he was a butterfly and on waking could not be sure whether he was a man who had had a dream or a butterfly who was dreaming of being a man.
3. King Wang was an ancient ruler of Sichuan who lost his kingdom and whose spirit was changed into a cuckoo at his death. The cuckoo's call is said to sound like 'O to go back again!'
4. Mermaids were said to shed tears of pearl.
5. Lantian is a mountain in Shanxi where ancient jade was found.

錦　瑟

李　商　隱

錦瑟無端五十絃，一絃一柱思華年。
莊生曉夢迷蝴蝶，望帝春心托杜鵑。
滄海月明珠有淚，藍田日煖玉生烟。
此情可待成追憶，只是當時已惘然。

TO...

Li Shangyin

Last night under the starlight,
    last night in the wind!
To the west, your painted pavilion,
    To the east, my hall of cassia...
Our bodies have not the wings
    of the many-coloured phoenix,
But our hearts know the other truly
    in every part.

We sat 'guessing fingers',
    the wine of spring warm;
Changing place we played at riddles;
    candles glowed red.
Alas! I heard the morning drum —
    must speed to the Court,
Spurred horse to Orchid Tower,
    a piece of rootless tumbleweed.

無　題

李　商　隱

昨夜星辰昨夜風，畫樓西畔桂堂東，
身無彩鳳雙飛翼，心有靈犀一點通。
隔座送鉤春酒暖，分曹射覆蠟燈紅。
嗟余聽鼓應官去，走馬蘭台類轉蓬。

A PALACE OF THE SUI DYNASTY

Li Shangyin

The old Palace by the purple fountains
    locked in mist and cloud-wrack.
The Emperor had coveted Yangzhou
    to make his royal dwelling,
But the jade seal was not his destiny —
    it passed to the Horned Sun.[1]
His embroidered sails could have reached
    the edge of the world.

No fireflies sparkle
    on these rotten grasses now,
Only crows come at dusk
    to age-old weeping willows.
If he should meet Houzhu of Chen[2]
    beneath the earth
Will he remind him, I wonder,
    of 'the backyard flowers'?

1. The Horned Sun refers to the first Emperor of Tang who overthrew
   Emperor Yang Di of Sui (605-617), one of the most extravagant
   and luxury-loving of all Chinese rulers.
2. Houzhu was Emperor of Chen State (583-589) in the 'Northern and
   Southern dynasties' period. Like Tang Xuanzong, he lost his kingdom
   through his obsession for a Court beauty. In the ensuing rebellion,
   he hid with her in a dry well, but they were discovered and
   assassinated (see Zheng Tian's 'At Ma Wei Hill', p.752). The song
   of 'The backyard flowers' was composed for her (See also Du Mu's
   'Mooring on Qinhuai river', p.718).

隋　宮

李　商　隱

紫泉宮殿鎖煙霞，欲取蕪城作帝家。
玉璽不緣歸日角，錦帆應是到天涯。
於今腐草無螢火，終古垂楊有暮鴉。
地下若逢陳後主，豈宜重問後庭花。

TO...

Li Shangyin

Coming was an empty word — you are gone
    and left no trace.
Moonlight falls aslant the tower,
    the fifth watch clangs...
I dream of a far parting, cry out
    but cannot summon you;
I write to you in such haste,
    the ink won't thicken[1].

Candlelight half illumines
    golden kingfisher feathers,
Smell of musk drifts faintly
    through embroidered hibiscus.
Master Liu already regretted
    the distance to the Immortals' mountain[2] —
I am ten thousand times farther
    from that Paradise.

1. Chinese ink is prepared by the user, by grinding a solid ink-block with water on an ink-stone.
2. Liu Chen of Han with his friend Yuan Zhao visited 'Heavenly Terrace' mountain, where he saw two female spirits of extraordinary beauty. He stayed there half a year and then returned home to find seven generations had passed.

無　　題

李　商　隱

來是空言去絕蹤，月斜樓上五更鐘。
夢為遠別啼難喚，書被催成墨未濃。
蠟照半籠金翡翠，麝薰微度繡芙蓉，
劉郎已恨蓬山遠，更隔蓬山一萬重。

TO...

Li Shangyin

Sa, sa the East wind,
    a fine rain comes;
Beyond the hibiscus pool
    a faint growl of thunder.
A gold toad bites on the lock —
    incense drifts through;
A jade tiger hauls on the rope
    when you draw well-water.

Jia's daughter peeped through a screen
    at young secretary Han[1],
Lady Mi left her cushion
    for the gifted Prince of Wei[2].
Our spring desire can never vie with the opening blossom —
For a pinch of heart's longing, a pinch of ashes!

1. Lady Jia, the younger daughter of Jia Chong a Premier of Jin dynasty, who fell in love with her father's handsome young secretary, Han Shou.
2. Lady Mi, a spirit of Luo river. The Prince of Wei was Cao Zhi who wrote a famous poem, the *Luo Shen fu*, on the spirit of Luo river.

其　二

李　商　隱

颯颯東風細雨來，芙蓉塘外有輕雷。
金蟾齧鏁燒香入，玉虎牽絲汲井迴。
賈氏窺簾韓掾少，宓妃留枕魏王才。
春心莫共花爭發，一寸相思一寸灰。

AT CHOU BI POST-HOUSE

Li Shangyin

Birds and monkeys still revere your bamboo despatches.
Wind and cloud ever protect your palisades.
In vain created Commander of armies,
    wielder of inspired brush,
In the end you saw your King carried away in a cart.
Guan Zhong and Yue Yi[1], able statesmen,
    would not shame you;
Guan Yu and Zhang Fei[2] were killed in battle —
    who can escape?
Some year, when I pass your shrine near Brocade city,
I shall read your 'Song of the Sacred Mountain',
    regretting you.

The poem is addressed to General Zhuge Liang, general, statesman
and scholar of the Three Kingdoms period, in the service of Liu Bei,
first King of Shu. The second King of Shu, whom he also served,
was defeated and captured. His 'Song of the Sacred Mountain' was a
poem about Mount Tai which he composed in retirement before entering
the King's service.
1. Guan Zhong and Yue Yi: statesmen of Zhou dynasty.
2. Guan Yu and Zhang Fei: famous generals of Shu kingdom.

籌 筆 驛

李 商 隱

猿鳥猶疑畏簡書，風雲常為護儲胥。
徒令上將揮神筆，終見降王走傳車。
管樂有才元不忝，關張無命欲何如！
他年錦里經祠廟，梁父吟成恨有餘。

TO...

Li Shangyin

Hard it was to see each other —
    harder still to part!
The east wind has no force,
    the hundred flowers wither.
The silkworm dies in spring
    when her thread is spun;
The candle dries its tears
    only when burnt to the end.

Grief at the morning mirror —
    cloud-like hair must change;
Verses hummed at night,
    feeling the chill of moonlight...
Yet from here to Paradise
    the way is not so far:
Helpful bluebird,
    bring me news of her!

無　　題

李　商　隱

相見時難別亦難，東風無力百花殘。
春蠶到死絲方盡，蠟炬成灰淚始乾。
曉鏡但愁雲鬢改，夜吟應覺月光寒。
蓬萊此去無多路，青鳥殷勤為探看。

SPRING RAIN

Li Shangyin

Dispirited I lie, dressed in white for the new spring.
At Baimen, a dreary life filled with frustration.
Rain blots out your red pavilion,
    cold to the sight;
Lamplight wavers on a beaded blind —
    you are there alone!
Ah the long road between
    and grief that our spring is passing!
Night wanes and your faint form enters my dream.
Jade earrings sealed in a letter —
    how can they reach you?
Endless miles of cobweb cloud, a lone goose flying.

春　雨

李　商　隱

悵臥新春白袷衣，白門寥落意多違。
紅樓隔雨相望冷，珠箔飄燈獨自歸。
遠路應悲春晼晚，殘宵猶得夢依稀。
玉璫緘札何由達，萬里雲羅一雁飛。

TO...

Li Shangyin

Phoenix tails on scented silk,
    filmy fold on fold;
Blue pattern on round canopy
    she stitches deep in the night.
A moon-shaped fan
    could hardly hide her blush,
His coach rumbled by like thunder —
    words could not reach her.

It is still and lonely now,
    the glowing wick burnt black;
No message comes
    though pomegranate flowers are red.
A dappled horse is just tethered
    at the bank of trailing willows —
Where should she wait for a favourable wind
    to blow from the south-west?

無　題

李　商　隱

鳳尾香羅薄幾重，碧文圓頂夜深縫。
扇裁月魄羞難掩，車走雷聲語未通。
曾是寂寥金燼暗，斷無消息石榴紅。
斑騅只繫垂楊岸，何處西南任好風？

TO...

Li Shangyin

Heavy curtains hang deep
    in my hall of Never Grieve[1];
I stir from sleep, the grey night
    bit by bit lengthens.
Life with the wraith of Wu Shan
    was a dream from the start[2];
No husband ever
    with the little maid of Blue Brook[3].

Wind and wave do not realise
    the frailty of water-cresses;
Does moon or dew teach cassia petals
    their fragrance?
A true saying, that all love is profitless,
Yet I cannot help heartache
    turning to clear passion.

1. Never Grieve: a well-known singing-girl.
2. The goddess of Wu mountain gave herself to King Huai in a dream.
3. The story of the little maid of Blue Brook is told in a popular ballad.

其　二

李　商　隱

重帷深下莫愁堂，臥後青宵細細長。
神女生涯原是夢，小姑居處本無郎。
風波不信菱枝弱，月露誰教桂葉香。
直道相思了無益，未妨惆悵是清狂。

FERRYING SOUTH AT LIZHOU
Wen Tingyun

Placidly the bare waters
    face the sunset,
Jagged islets blend a sober green
    with the mountain mists.
A horse neighs over the ripples
    as I watch them pole away,
Men rest beside the willows, waiting
    for the ferry's return.

A forest of dune-grasses and
    a flock of gulls veering,
Acres of river-meadows and
    a single egret winging.
Who has the wisdom to embark
    and search for Fan Li[1]?
He alone learnt to forget
    on the misty waters
    of the Five Lakes.

1. A minister in the 'Spring and Autumn' period who helped the king
of Yue to defeat Wu kingdom. Afterwards he went sailing on the
Five Lakes with Xi Shi, the Wu King's beautiful concubine.

利 州 南 渡

溫 庭 筠

澹然空水對斜暉，曲島蒼茫接翠微。
波上馬嘶看棹去，柳邊人歇待船歸。
數叢沙草群鷗散，萬頃江田一鷺飛。
誰解乘舟尋范蠡？五湖煙水獨忘機。

SU WU'S TEMPLE

Wen Tingyun

His spirit has vanished — Su Wu,
    former envoy of the Han;
An old shrine, a high tree, both decrepit.
Wild geese lost in the clouds,
    moon in Tartar skies,
He with his sheep on the field paths
    in the grass and mist of the Border.

No military honours on the Imperial terrace
    at his homecoming;
In the freshness of youth he had left
    with envoy's cap and sword.
The spirit at Maoling could not see him
    receive the Marquisate:
By the autumn waves he wept hopelessly
    for the unreturning stream.

Emperor Wu Di of Han (140-87 B.C.) sent Su Wu to negotiate with
the Xiongnu tribes. He was held captive in Mongolia for 19 years,
and lived as a shepherd. In 86 B.C. he was able to return to China,
in the first year of Emperor Zhao Di, Wu Di being already dead and
buried at Maoling.

548

蘇　武　廟

溫　庭　筠

蘇武魂銷漢使前，古祠高樹兩茫然。
雲邊雁斷胡天月，隴上羊歸塞草煙。
迴日樓臺非甲帳，去時冠劍是丁年。
茂陵不見封侯印，空向秋波哭逝川。

A PALACE POEM

Xue Feng

Within the Twelve Pavilions
    someone has dressed for the morning;
On Looking-for-Fairies tower
    she looks for the Emperor.
Golden beasts gripping the door-chains
    are cold to the touch;
The bronze-dragon water-clock
    tells that day is far.

She has combed out her cloud-like hair
    turning before the mirror;
She has changed her filmy gown
    and added more perfume.
She catches a glimpse of the royal bed-chamber,
    where the screens part:
Court attendants in jacket and trousers
    are straightening the Emperor's bed.

宮　詞

薛　逢

十二樓中盡曉粧，望仙樓上望君王；
鎖銜金獸連環冷，水滴銅龍畫漏長。
雲髻罷梳還對鏡，羅衣欲換更添香。
遙窺正殿簾開處，袍袴宮人掃御床。

THE POOR GIRL

Qin Taoyu

In her thatched hut, she knows nothing of scented silks;
She longs to employ a go-between, wistful in her loneliness.
"Who am I to love the fashionable and gifted?
All of them pity me, too pinched for powder and paint."

She may dare to vaunt her wizardry with the needle,
But not vie with the girls who paint their eyebrows long.
In bitter resentment, year after year,
    she stitches her gold thread,
Making wedding-gowns for other girls.

貧　女

秦韜玉

蓬門未識綺羅香，擬托良媒亦自傷。
誰愛風流高格調，共憐時世儉梳妝。
敢將十指誇鍼巧，不把雙眉鬥畫長。
苦恨年年壓金線，為他人作嫁衣裳。

WRITTEN FOR MUSIC

ALONE

Shen Quanqi

In the Lu household is a little wife
    sweet as the wild cherry;
They were close as a pair of swallows
    perched on a tortoise-shell beam.
At the ninth moon when the pounding of washing
    hurries leaves from the trees,
She thinks of him with the Expedition
    ten years in Liaoyang.

From north of White Wolf river
    news cut off;
In the south of Red Phoenix city
    autumn nights endless.
How can she bear her heartache,
    alone, unable to see him?
Still less when the bright moon glares
    on her silk bed-curtains.

樂 府
獨 不 見

沈 佺 期

盧家少婦鬱金香，海燕雙棲玳瑁梁。
九月寒砧催木葉，十年征戍憶遼陽。
白狼河北音書斷，丹鳳城南秋夜長。
誰謂含愁獨不見，更教明月照流黃。

SECTION 5

Five-character 'cut-shorts'

THE DEER ENCLOSURE

Wang Wei

On the bare mountain
    I meet no one,
I only hear the echo
    of human voices.
Sunlight flickers
    through the dense wood
And shines full
    upon the green moss.

鹿　柴

王　維

空山不見人，但聞人語響，
返景入深林，復照青苔上。

HUT AMONG THE BAMBOOS

Wang Wei

Sitting alone
  in the hush of the bamboo grove
I thrum my lute
  and whistle lingering notes.
In the secrecy of the wood
  no one can hear —
Only the clear moon
  comes to shine on me.

Sitting alone
   in the hush of the bamboo grove
I thrum my lute
   and whistle lingering notes.
   獨坐幽篁裡，彈琴復長嘯。

竹　里　館

王　維

獨坐幽篁裡，彈琴復長嘯，
深林人不知，明月來相照。

FAREWELL

Wang Wei

Among the mountains
    we bade each other farewell;
The sun sank
    as I closed the wicket gate.
Grass will be green again
    another spring
But will my prince of friends
    return or no?

送　別

王　維

山中相送罷，日暮掩柴扉。
春草明年綠，王孫歸不歸？

REMEMBRANCE

Wang Wei

A red berry grows
    in the south country —
The boughs are full of them
    when spring arrives.
Gather some, I pray,
    and fill your pockets —
These are the best
    forget-me-nots!

相　　思

王　維

紅豆生南國，春來發幾枝；
願君多採擷，此物最相思。

POEM

Wang Wei

You came, Sir,
    from my old village —
You must know
    all the village affairs:
Tell me,
    was the winter-plum in flower
Before my gauze window
    on the day you left?

Tell me,
   was the winter-plum in flower
Before my gauze window
   on the day you left?
   來日綺窗前，寒梅著花未？

雜　詩

王　維

君自故鄉來，應知故鄉事，
來日綺窗前，寒梅著花未？

FAREWELL TO CUI THE NINTH
Pei Di

When you retire
    into the mountain mazes
You must learn the beauty
    of every hill and hollow.
Do not imitate the man from Wuling
Who lingered only a space
    at Peach Flower spring.

The fisherman in the story of Peach Flower stream (See Wang Wei's poem, p.240) was from Wuling, a district in Hunan.

送　崔　九

裴　迪

歸山深淺去，須盡邱壑美；
莫學武陵人，暫遊桃源裡。

LOOKING AT THE SNOW DRIFTS ON SOUTH MOUNTAIN

Zu Yong

How fair is the shadowed face
    of South mountain,
Its piles of snow afloat
    on the cloud-crests!
When the sky clears
    the fringes of the woods glitter,
But in the city
    nightfall brings an added cold.

終南望餘雪

祖 詠

終南陰嶺秀，積雪浮雲端，
林表明霽色，城中增暮寒。

MOORING ON THE RIVER AT JIANDE

Meng Haoran

My boat is moored
    beside an island of mists;
In the twilight
    a stranger grows melancholy.
Beyond the desolate fields
    the sky rests on the tree-tops;
In the clear river
    the moon seems very near to man.

宿　建　德　江

孟　浩　然

移舟泊煙渚，日暮客愁新；
野曠天低樹，江清月近人。

SPRING DAWN

Meng Haoran

Asleep in spring I did not heed the dawn
Till the birds broke out singing everywhere.
Last night, in the clamour of wind and rain,
How many flowers have fallen
    do you suppose?

春　曉

孟　浩　然

春眠不覺曉，處處聞啼鳥，
夜來風雨聲，花落知多少？

NIGHT THOUGHTS

Li Bai

The bright moon shone
    before my bed,
I wondered —
    was it frost upon the ground?
I raised my head
    to gaze at the clear moon,
Bowed my head
    remembering my old home.

夜　　思

李　白

牀前明月光，疑是地上霜；
舉頭望明月，低頭思故鄉。

PINING

Li Bai

A lovely woman
    draws her beaded blind
And sits within
    knitting her moth-like brows.
I only see
    wet traces of her tears
But cannot tell
    for whom her heart is grieving.

怨　情

李　白

美人捲珠簾，深坐顰蛾眉；
但見淚痕溼，不知心恨誰。

THE EIGHT BATTLE-FRONTS

Du Fu

His exploits surpassed all in the Three Kingdoms,
His strategy of 'the eight battle-fronts'
    made him immortal.
The stream flows on, but the stones he laid
    haven't shifted;
His lasting regret, the failure to take
    Eastern Wu.

Zhuge Liang, a famous general of the Three Kingdoms period, in the
service of the King of Shu, led the campaigns against Wei and Wu
kingdoms. He had advised his ruler to attack Wei first, but the King
turned instead against Wu and was defeated.

八　陣　圖

杜　甫

功蓋三分國，名成八陣圖；
江流石不轉，遺恨失吞吳。

CLIMBING THE CRANE PAGODA

Wang Zhihuan

White sunlight disappears
 from the hillside,
Yellow river flows on
 into the sea.
Desiring to scan
 the thousand-mile vista
I climb another storey
 of the pagoda.

登 鸛 雀 樓

王 之 渙

白日依山盡，黃河入海流；
欲窮千里目，更上一層樓。

FAREWELL TO THE MONK LING CHE

Liu Changqing

From Bamboo Wood monastery, dim and grey,
Faintly, faintly sounds the evening bell.
Sunlight falls obliquely
                    on your bamboo-leaf hat
As you turn back alone
                    towards the far blue hills.

送 靈 澈

劉 長 卿

蒼蒼竹林寺，杳杳鐘聲晚，
荷笠帶斜陽，青山獨歸遠。

THE LUTE PLAYER

Liu Changqing

Emotionless the mood of your 'Seven-string'[1];
In the quiet
   I sense the cool of 'Wind through the pines'.
I am one who loves the antique tunes,
There are few now who can play them.

1. Seven-string: the ancient Chinese lute. The seven strings were called *gong, shang, jue, zhi, yu, wen* and *wu*.

彈　琴

劉　長　卿

泠泠七弦上，靜聽松風寒；
古調雖自愛，今人多不彈。

TAKING LEAVE OF A BUDDHIST MONK
Liu Changqing

O wild crane,
    you are leaving with your lonely cloud —
How could you live
    among common men?
But do not settle
    on Wozhou mountain:
People know the way there too well!

送 上 人

劉 長 卿

孤雲將野鶴，豈向人間住？
莫買沃洲山，時人已知處。

FOR MR. SECRETARY QIU ON AN AUTUMN EVENING
Wei Yingwu

I hold you in my thoughts
    this autumn night
While I stroll in the cool air
    and chant poetry.
Pine cones will be falling
    on the empty mountain
And my solitary friend
    not asleep yet.

秋夜寄邱員外

韋應物

懷君屬秋夜，散步詠涼天，
空山松子落，幽人應未眠。

LISTENING TO A HARPSICHORD

Li Duan

She sounds her harpsichord
      with the gold chasing;
Her silk-soft hands are poised
      over the jade frame.
Desiring to attract Master Zhou's[1] attention,
From time to time she touches a false note.

1. Master Zhou was Zhou Yu, a lover of classical music, who is said to have looked up if anyone played or sang a false note.

聽　箏

李　端

鳴箏金粟柱，素手玉房前；
欲得周郎顧，時時誤拂絃。

THE YOUNG BRIDE

Wang Jian

On the third day
　　she goes into the kitchen,
Washes her hands
　　and makes a good soup.
Not knowing
　　mother-in-law's taste yet,
She asks her husband's little sister
　　to try it first.

新 嫁 娘

王 建

三日入廚下，洗手作羹湯；
未諳姑食性，先遣小姑嚐。

SONG OF THE JADE TOWER
Quan Deyu

Last night, my girdle fell loose,
This morning a luck-beetle flew over.
Powder and rouge I dare not neglect —
It must be that my husband is returning!

玉　臺　體

權　德　輿

昨夜裙帶解，今朝蟢子飛；
鉛華不可棄，莫是藁砧歸。

RIVER SNOW
Liu Zongyuan

In a thousand hills
    birds have ceased to fly;
On countless tracks
    footprints have disappeared.
A solitary boatman
    in bamboo cape and hat
Is fishing the icy river
    in the snow.

A solitary boatman
　in bamboo cape and hat
Is fishing the icy river
　in the snow.
孤舟蓑笠翁，獨釣寒江雪。

江　雪

柳　宗　元

千山鳥飛絕，萬徑人蹤滅；
孤舟簑笠翁，獨釣寒江雪。

THE IMPERIAL TRAVELLING LODGE
Yuan Zhen

How desolate
the old Travelling Lodge[1]!
Even its scarlet flowers
look forlorn.
The Court ladies
are all white-haired now —
Listless they sit
and talk about Xuanzong[2].

1. Travelling Lodge: one of the palaces where the Emperors used to stay when making journeys through the Empire.
2. Xuanzong: the Emperor whose abdication was brought about by the An Lushan rebellion.

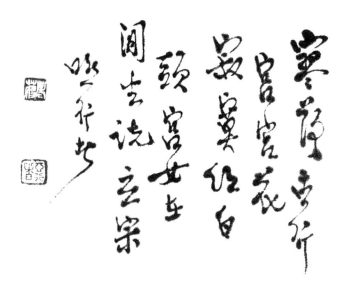

寥落古行宮
宮花寂寞紅
白頭宮女在
閒坐說玄宗

How desolate
  the old Travelling Lodge!
Even its scarlet flowers
  look forlorn.
The Court ladies
  are all white-haired now —
Listless they sit
  and talk about Xuanzong.

寥落古行宮，宮花寂寞紅；
白頭宮女在，閒坐說玄宗。

行　宮

元　稹

寥落古行宮，宮花寂寞紅；
白頭宮女在，閒坐說玄宗。

INVITATION TO LIU THE NINETEENTH
Bai Juyi

I have freshly-brewed Lüyi wine
On a little stove of red clay, warming:
Evening has come
    and the sky looks like snow —
Can you not drink a cup of wine with me?

問 劉 十 九

白 居 易

綠螘新醅酒，紅泥小火爐，
晚來天欲雪，能飲一杯無？

"HE MAN ZI"

Zhang Hu

Her native land
    a thousand miles away,
Shut in the Palace
    twenty years ago,
If she hears the tune of "He Man Zi"
Two tears roll down
    even in her Lord's presence.

"He Man Zi": in the Kaiyuan period of Tang, a singer from Cang-zhou, while awaiting punishment, composed this song in the hope of escaping the death sentence, but without success. Here it is sung by a Palace lady, longing for her freedom.

何 滿 子

張 祜

故國三千里，深宮二十年，
一聲何滿子，雙淚落君前。

CLIMBING LEYOU PLATEAU[1]
Li Shangyin

Towards evening,
   my thoughts being troubled,
I drove my carriage
   up to this ancient plateau:
The evening light
   was immeasurably sweet,
Only the yellow dusk
   was too near!

---

1. Leyou plateau was to the south of Chang'an. Emperor Xuan of Han had built a temple there.

登 樂 遊 原

李 商 隱

向晚意不適，驅車登古原；
夕陽無限好，祇是近黃昏。

ON LOOKING FOR A HERMIT AND NOT FINDING HIM
Jia Dao

I questioned a boy under the pine trees.
"My Master went herb-gathering"
    he says:
"He is still somewhere on the mountain-side,
So deep in the clouds I can't tell where."

尋 隱 者 不 遇

賈 島

松下問童子，言師採藥去；
只在此山中，雲深不知處。

ON CROSSING THE RIVER HAN
Li Pin

On the far side of the mountains
    no news came;
Winter went by, another spring is here.
Nearing home, my heart grows fearful —
I dare not question
    those who come to meet me.

渡　漢　江

李　頻

嶺外音書絕，經冬復立春；
近鄉情更怯，不敢問來人。

PINING IN SPRING

Jin Changxu

O drive away the golden orioles!
Do not let them warble on my trees,
For their song
    startles me from dreams
And I shall never reach Liaoxi[1].

---

1. Liaoxi: a north-east border region under the Great Wall, evidently
where her husband is stationed.

打起黄
莺儿
莫教枝
上啼
啼时惊妾
梦
不得到
辽西

O drive away the golden orioles!
Do not let them warble on my trees,
For their song
   startles me from dreams
And I shall never reach Liaoxi.

打起黃鶯兒，莫教枝上啼，
啼時驚妾夢，不得到遼西。

春　怨

金　昌　緒

打起黃鶯兒，莫教枝上啼，
啼時驚妾夢，不得到遼西。

SONG OF GE SHU[1]

Xi Biren

The seven stars of the Wain
    ride high,
Ge Shu brandishes his sword
    in the night.
Even now those prying nomad horsemen
Dare not venture past Lin Tao[2].

1. Ge Shu was a Tang commander of Tartar origin, under Emperor
   Xuanzong, who was victorious in Tibet.
2. Lin Tao is on the Chinese western border with Tibet.

哥　舒　歌

西　鄙　人

北斗七星高，哥舒夜帶刀；
至今窺牧馬，不敢過臨洮。

WRITTEN FOR MUSIC

SONG OF CHANGGAN
Cui Hao

"Your home, Sir — where do you come from?
I am a girl from Hengtang."
She stayed the boat a moment to put the question —
"Could it be we're from the same village?"

"My home was near the Nine River waters;
To and fro you went by the Nine River shores:
Both of us are Changgan people —
We were young then and didn't know each other!"

停船暫借問
或恐是同鄉
御筍筆

She stayed the boat a moment to
   put the question —
"Could it be we're from the same village?"
   停舟暫借問，或恐是同鄉。

樂　府
長　干　曲
崔　顥

「君家何處住？妾住在橫塘。」
　停舟暫借問，或恐是同鄉。
「家臨九江水，來去九江側。」
　同是長干人，生小不相識。

PINING BY THE JADE STEPS
Li Bai

The jade steps are grown white with dew —
In the long night
    it soaks her gauze stockings.
She has just lowered the curtain of crystal beads
And is gazing at
    the round bright autumn moon.

玉 階 怨

李 白

玉階生白露，夜久侵羅襪；
卻下水精簾，玲瓏望秋月。

TO THE AIR 'LEAVING THE FRONTIER'

Lu Lun

(I)

His arrows are tufted with the hawk's feathers,
His embroidered banners shaped like swallows' tails.
When he stands alone to issue a new edict
A thousand Companies roar with one voice.

塞 下 曲

盧 綸

鷲翎金僕姑，燕尾繡蝥弧，
獨立揚新令，千營共一呼。

(II)

In the dark forest grasses shudder with wind;
The General draws his bow in the night.
At dawn he searches for the white arrow-feather —
It was held fast in the crevice of a rock.

Li Guang of Han dynasty was out hunting when he mistook some
rocks half hidden in grasses for a tiger. He shot and pierced one of
the rocks with his arrow.

其 二

林暗草驚風，將軍夜引弓；
平明尋白羽，沒在石稜中。

(Ⅲ)

Moon blotted out, geese flying high,
Barbarian chief slinking away in the night:
Our General needs a sprightly horse for the chase;
Heavy snow has coated his bow and sword.

其　　三

月黑雁飛高，單于夜遁逃；
欲將輕騎逐，大雪滿弓刀。

(IV)

A rich feast is spread in our rude encampment
To celebrate victory over the Western tribes.
Drunken, we dance in coats of golden armour —
The drum's roll troubles hill and stream.

其　　四

野幕敝瓊筵，羌戎賀勞旋；
醉和金甲舞，雷鼓動山川。

TO THE AIR 'SOUTH OF THE RIVER'

Li Yi

I married a merchant from Qutang
But day after day he breaks his tryst.
Had I known how faithful were the tides
I would have married a river-side boy.

江 南 曲

李 益

嫁得瞿塘賈，朝朝誤妾期；
早知潮有信，嫁與弄潮兒。

RETURNING HOME UNEXPECTEDLY

He Zhizhang

I left home a youngster,
    return an old man;
My local accent's the same
    but the hair on my temples is thinner.
The children peep at me —
    they do not know me:
"Where do you come from, stranger?"
    they ask with a giggle.

兒童相見不相識笑問客從何處來

The children peep at me —
  they do not know me:
"Where do you come from, stranger?"
  they ask with a giggle.
  兒童相見不相識，笑問客從何處來？

回 鄉 偶 書

賀 知 章

少小離家老大回，鄉音無改鬢毛衰；
兒童相見不相識，笑問「客從何處來？」

PEACH FLOWER STREAM
Zhang Xu

Dim, vague the hanging bridge
    veiled in moorland mist.
By the landing-rock on the west bank
    I hail a fisher boat:
"All day long the peach petals
    are floating by with the current —
On which side of this clear stream
    could the cave be?"

See Wang Wei's "The source of the peach flower stream", p.240.

桃　花　谿

張　旭

隱隱飛橋隔野烟，石磯西畔問漁船；
桃花盡日隨流水，洞在清溪何處邊？

THINKING OF MY BROTHERS IN SHANDONG ON THE NINTH DAY OF THE NINTH MOON
Wang Wei

Alone now in a strange country,
    feeling myself a stranger,
On this bright festival day
    I doubly pine for my kinsfolk.
Far away, I know my brothers
    will be climbing the heights
With dogwood[1] sprays in their jackets,
    and one man missing!

1. Dogwood was supposed to drive away evil spirits.

九月九日憶山東兄弟

王 維

獨在異鄉為異客，每逢佳節倍思親。
遙知兄弟登高處，徧插茱萸少一人。

FAREWELL TO XIN JIAN AT HIBISCUS PAVILION
Wang Changling

A cold rain mingled with the river
    at evening, when I entered Wu;
In the clear dawn I bid you farewell,
    lonely as Chu mountain.
My kinsfolk in Luoyang,
    should they ask about me,
Tell them: "My heart is a piece of ice
    in a jade cup!"

芙蓉樓送辛漸

王　昌　齡

寒雨連江夜入吳，平明送客楚山孤；
洛陽親友如相問，一片冰心在玉壺。

LOVE-SICKNESS
Wang Changling

In her boudoir is a young bride
    who hasn't yet known sorrow;
One spring day she makes her toilet
    and climbs the kingfisher tower.
With a pang she notices the tender green
    of the roadside willows
And regrets having urged her husband away
    to seek official appointment.

With a pang she notices the tender green
  of the roadside willows
And regrets having urged her husband away
  to seek official appointment.
忽見陌頭楊柳色，悔教夫婿覓封侯。

閨　怨

王　昌　齡

閨中少婦不知愁，春日凝妝上翠樓；
忽見陌頭楊柳色，悔教夫婿覓封侯。

COURT SONG IN SPRINGTIME

Wang Changling

Last night a wind scattered
    the peach flowers at Lujing;
Above the Palace of Weiyang
    the moon spins high.
The lady from Pingyang, for her dancing and singing,
    has just been favoured by the Emperor —
A brocade gown for the cool spring air
    outside the door-screen.

春 宮 曲

王 昌 齡

昨夜風開露井桃，未央前殿月輪高；
平陽歌舞新承寵，簾外春寒賜錦袍。

SONG OF LIANGZHOU
Wang Han

Wine of the grape from cups that glow in the night —
We long to drink but the *pipa*¹ urgently summons.
If we lie drunk on the battlefield, don't mock us friend:
Since the old days, how many fighters ever got back?

1. The pipa was a kind of guitar. In the army it was used like a
   bugle, as a summons to battle.

涼 州 詞

王 翰

葡萄美酒夜光杯，欲飲琵琶馬上催；
醉臥沙場君莫笑，古來征戰幾人回？

FAREWELL TO MENG HAORAN, LEAVING FOR YANGZHOU

Li Bai

At Yellow Crane pavilion in the west
    you parted from me,
Sailing down to Yangzhou through a mist
    of April flowers.
The faint shape of your lonely sail
    melts into the vacant blue —
I can only see the Long River
    streaming to the edge of the sky.

I can only see the Long River
streaming to the edge of the sky.
惟見長江天際流

黃鶴樓送孟浩然之廣陵

李 白

故人西辭黃鶴樓，煙花三月下揚州；
孤帆遠影碧空盡，惟見長江天際流。

GOING DOWN TO JIANGLING
Li Bai

Baidi I left at dawn
    in the morning-glow of the clouds;
The thousand *li* to Jiangling
    we sailed in a single day.
On either shore the gibbons' chatter
    sounded without pause
While my light boat skimmed past
    a thousand sombre crags.

下　江　陵

李　白

朝辭白帝彩雲間，千里江陵一日還；
兩岸猿聲啼不住，輕舟已過萬重山。

ON MEETING A MESSENGER GOING TO THE CAPITAL
Cen Shen

I look east to the home fields —
　　the way seems unending;
My old arms tremble and my sleeves
　　are wet with tears.
Meeting you on horseback
　　with no brush or paper,
I beg you, convey my message — tell them
　　"I am safe!"

馬上相逢無紙筆
憑君傳語報平安

Meeting you on horseback
   with no brush or paper,
I beg you, convey my message — tell them
   "I am safe!"
   馬上相逢無紙筆，憑君傳語報平安。

逢　入　京　使

岑　參

故園東望路漫漫，雙袖龍鍾淚不乾；
馬上相逢無紙筆，憑君傳語報平安。

MEETING LI GUINIAN[1] IN JIANGNAN

Du Fu

I often saw you in the mansion of Prince Qi,
And many times I heard you play
    in the hall of Cui the ninth.
Just now in Jiangnan, the scene is so lovely,
But the flowers are falling
    now that I meet you again.

1. Li Guinian had been a Court musician to the Emperor Xuanzong.

江南逢李龜年

杜 甫

岐王宅裡尋常見，崔九堂前幾度聞；
正是江南好風景，落花時節又逢君。

BY WEST BROOK IN CHUZHOU

Wei Yingwu

Alone, I love the dark grasses
    growing beside the brook;
Above a golden oriole
    flutes in the thick of a tree.
The spring tide swollen with rain
    comes rushing in at dusk:
No one at the ferry — just the boat
    that swings to and fro.

野渡無人舟自横

No one at the ferry — just the boat
that swings to and fro.
野渡無人舟自橫

滁 州 西 澗

韋 應 物

獨憐幽草澗邊生，上有黃鸝深樹鳴，
春潮帶雨晚來急，野渡無人舟自橫。

ANCHORED AT NIGHT BY MAPLE BRIDGE

Zhang Ji

Moon sets, crows caw, sky is full of frost;
River maples, fishing-boat lights
    break through my troubled sleep.
Beyond the city of Suzhou lies Han Shan monastery.
At midnight the clang of the bell
    reaches the traveller's boat.

楓 橋 夜 泊

張 繼

月落烏啼霜滿天，江楓漁火對愁眠，
姑蘇城外寒山寺，夜半鐘聲到客船。

THE FESTIVAL OF 'COLD FOOD'

Han Hong

Spring in the city and not a corner
    where petals are not tumbling;
'Cold Food' day; an east wind
    strains the Imperial willows.
At sunset in the Han palace
    wax candles are prepared —
Their light smoke drifts into the mansions
    of the Five Dukes.

On 'Cold Food' day, fire of any sort was forbidden, and no smoke
would appear from the chimneys of ordinary people. The poem is a
veiled criticism of the Imperial House which was under the control of
powerful eunuchs. See also Wang Wei's 'Taking leave of Qiwu Qian',
p.30.

寒　食

韓　翃

春城無處不飛花，寒食東風御柳斜；
日暮漢宮傳蠟燭，輕煙散入五侯家。

MOONLIT NIGHT

Liu Fangping

Night deepens — the moon has painted
  half the houses,
The Great Bear hangs aslant,
  the Dipper slopes away.
This night I specially sense
  the softness of the spring air —
Insects' chirping begins to penetrate
  the green silk window-gauze.

月　夜

劉　方　平

更深月色半人家，北斗闌干南斗斜；
今夜偏知春氣暖，蟲聲新透綠窗紗。

SPRING BITTERNESS

Liu Fangping

Beyond the window gauze, sun sets
  and twilight deepens;
There is no one in the painted chamber
  to see the traces of her tears.
From the silent empty courtyard
  spring is about to depart;
Pear-blossom lies thick on the ground,
  nobody opens the gate.

春 怨

劉 方 平

紗窗日落漸黃昏，金屋無人見淚痕；
寂寞空庭春欲晚，梨花滿地不開門。

A SOLDIER'S COMPLAINT

Liu Zhongyong

Year after year at Jin river,
    then Yumen pass;
Day after day horse whip
    and sword hilt in our grasp.
Even at spring's end white snow
    returns to green graves
Where the endless waters of the Yellow River
    coil through Black mountain.

征 人 怨

柳 中 庸

歲歲金河復玉關，朝朝馬策與刀環；
三春白雪歸青塚，萬里黃河繞黑山。

A PALACE TRIFLE

Gu Kuang

From a Jade pavilion, half in the clouds,
    pipe music and singing —
Wind carries it down with the laughing chatter
    of the Court ladies.
Moonlight pours from the sky,
    they can hear the drips of the water-clock;
Rolling up their crystal blinds
    they sense the nearness of the Milky Way[1].

1. i.e. the Emperor's presence.

宮　詞

顧　況

玉樓天半起笙歌，風送宮嬪笑語和；
月殿影開聞夜漏，水精簾捲近秋河。

MARCHING TO SHOUXIANG AT NIGHT AND HEARING A PIPE

Li Yi

Below the peak Huile
    the sands are like snow;
Beyond the walls of Shouxiang
    moonlight glitters like frost.
Where someone was blowing a shepherd's pipe[1]
    I cannot tell,
But the whole night we soldiers lay
    longing for home.

1. A crude pipe cut from a wayside reed by Mongolian shepherds. It made these soldiers realise they were far from home.

夜上受降城聞笛

李 益

迴樂峯前沙似雪，受降城外月如霜；
不知何處吹蘆管，一夜征人盡望鄉。

BLACK GOWN LANE

Liu Yuxi

Flowers and grasses run wild
    by Red Bird bridge;
Evening sunlight feebly pierces
    Black Gown lane.
In years gone by, swallows would nest
    in the Wang and Xie mansions[1] —
Now they fly into the humbler eaves
    of ordinary people.

1. Wang Dao and Xie An were two great noblemen of Jin dynasty. Their sons were distinguished by wearing black gowns, hence the name of the lane.

舊時王謝
堂前燕
飛入尋常
百姓家

薛平南

In years gone by, swallows would
    nest in the Wang and Xie mansions —
Now they fly into the humbler eaves
    of ordinary people.
舊時王謝堂前燕，飛入尋常百姓家。

烏　衣　巷

劉　禹　錫

朱雀橋邊野草花，烏衣巷口夕陽斜，
舊時王謝堂前燕，飛入尋常百姓家。

SPRING FRAGMENT

Liu Yuxi

In new raiment lovely as her face
    she leaves the Red pavilion,
Frowns awhile at the spring light
    deeply locked in the garden,
Strolls to the centre of the courtyard
    idly counting the flower-heads;
A dragon-fly darts
    and alights on her jade hairpin.

行到中庭數花朵

蜻蜓飛上玉搔頭

辛亥夏 蔣青

Strolls to the centre of the courtyard
  idly counting the flower-heads;
A dragon-fly darts
  and alights on her jade hairpin.
行到中庭數花朵，蜻蜓飛上玉搔頭。

春　詞

劉禹錫

新妝宜面下朱樓，深鎖春光一院愁，
行到中庭數花朵，蜻蜓飛上玉搔頭。

PALACE PLAINT

Bai Juyi

Tears have soaked her gauze handkerchief
    but no dreams come;
Deep in the night, from the front of the Palace
    she can hear the beat of music.
Her rosy cheeks are still fresh
    but she lost the Emperor's favour —
She sits there, leaning on the clothes-airer,
    waiting for daybreak.

後 宮 詞

白 居 易

淚溼羅巾夢不成，夜深前殿按歌聲；
紅顏未老恩先斷，斜倚熏籠坐到明。

TO A COURT LADY

Zhang Hu

Traces of moonlight glide over the trees
    by the Palace gate,
Bewitching eyes just glimpse an egret
    perched in its nest.
She bends under the lamp's glow
    and drawing a jade hairpin,
Brushes aside the red flame
    to save a fluttering moth.

贈　內　人

張　祜

禁門宮樹月痕過，媚眼微看宿鷺窠，
斜拔玉釵燈影畔，剔開紅燄救飛蛾。

JILING TERRACE

Zhang Hu

(I)

Slanting sunlight falls across Jiling terrace,
The red-flowered tree blossoms, glad of the morning dew.
Last night the Emperor bestowed his favour
    on a new beauty —
Lady Yang, who smiled on her way
    to go behind the curtain.

集 靈 臺

張 祜

日光斜照集靈台，紅樹花迎曉露開，
昨夜上皇新授籙，太真含笑入簾來。

(Ⅱ)

The Duchess of Guo State
    has been honoured by the Emperor's summons;
At daybreak, she rides through the Palace gate.
Scorning powder and rouge that could mar her complexion
She lightly touches up her moth-like eyebrows
    before the audience.

其　二

張　祜

虢國夫人承主恩，平明騎馬入宮門，
卻嫌脂粉污顏色，淡掃蛾眉朝至尊。

WRITTEN ON THE WALL OF JINLING
FERRY-HOUSE
Zhang Hu

At Jinling ferry-head, a little hill hut,
For the lonely traveller an apt place for grieving!
The ebb-tide on the darkening river
    carries a setting moon;
Those two or three star-like flickers
    are Guazhou.

題 金 陵 渡

張 祜

金陵津渡小山樓，一宿行人自可愁，
潮落夜江斜月裡，兩三星火是瓜州。

WITHIN THE PALACE

Zhu Qingyu

Dull, dull the flowering time
    behind closed Palace gates;
Court beauties stroll together
    on a balcony of precious marble.
With much in their hearts, they long to talk
    of Inner Palace affairs,
But with the parrot beside them
    they dare not speak a word!

含情欲說宮中事
鸚鵡前頭不敢言

With much in their hearts, they long to
  talk of Inner Palace affairs,
But with the parrot beside them they dare
  not speak a word!
含情欲說宮中事，鸚鵡前頭不敢言。

宮 中 詞

朱 慶 餘

寂寂花時閉院門，美人相並立瓊軒；
含情欲説宮中事，鸚鵡前頭不敢言。

THE APPROACHING EXAMINATION: FOR
ZHANG JI
Zhu Qingyu

Last night in the bridal chamber
    red candles burned low;
At dawn she goes to pay respect
    to her new parents.
Having touched up her face,
    in a whisper she asks her husband
"Have I painted my eyebrows right
    for the present fashion? "

The poet asks his friend, also a poet, whether his work is up to the standard of the Civil Service examination. At this period, verse writing was one of the requirements.

近試上張籍水部

朱 慶 餘

洞房昨夜停紅燭，待曉堂前拜舅姑。
妝罷低聲問夫婿：「畫眉深淺入時無？」

CLIMBING LEYOU HILL BEFORE LEAVING
FOR WUXING

Du Mu

Calm times give interesting appointments,
    but I lack talent.
An idler, I love the lonely clouds;
    a dreamer, I love to be with monks.
Now I must carry my standard over river and sea,
But first I climbed Leyou hill
    to gaze at the tomb of Taizong[1].

1. The second and greatest Tang Emperor.

將赴吳興登樂遊原

杜 牧

清時有味是無能，閒愛孤雲靜愛僧；
欲把一麾江海去，樂遊原上望昭陵。

RED CLIFF

Du Mu

A broken lance buried in sand,
 the metal still unrusted —
I wash and burnish it to find
 the mark of an ancient dynasty.
I imagine if the east wind
 hadn't helped Zhou Yu,
The two Qiao beauties would have been shut
 in Bronze-bird pavilion in the full glory of spring.

赤　壁

杜　牧

折戟沈沙鐵未消，自將磨洗認前朝；
東風不與周郎便，銅雀春深鎖二喬。

MOORING ON THE QINHUAI RIVER
Du Mu

Mist shrouds the cold water,
    moonlight floods the shore;
We moored tonight on the Qinhuai,
    not far from a wine shop.
The sing-song girls don't understand
    the bitterness of losing a kingdom —
Across the river they are still singing
    the 'Backyard flowers'.[1]

1. See Li Shangyin's 'A Palace of the Sui Dynasty', p.530

泊　秦　淮

杜　牧

煙籠寒水月籠沙，夜泊秦淮近酒家；
商女不知亡國恨，隔江猶唱後庭花。

FOR ASSISTANT-PREFECT HAN CHUO OF YANGZHOU

Du Mu

Blue hills are fading, fading;
    the stream winds far...
In Jiangnan at autumn's end
    grass not yet withered.
Tonight, while the moon sparkles
    on the twenty-four bridges,
Where are the jade-like beauties
    who taught me to play the flute?

寄揚州韓綽判官

杜 牧

青山隱隱水迢迢，秋盡江南草未凋；
二十四橋明月夜，玉人何處敎吹簫？

CONFESSION

Du Mu

Out of luck, I roamed the lakes and rivers
    with my wine.
O the waists of Chu, so slender,
    the fairy-light dancers!
Now that I wake from ten years
    of Yangzhou dreams,
All I have earned is the name of a drifter
    even in the blue pavilions[1].

1. The blue pavilions were the houses of courtesans.

遣　懷

杜　牧

落魄江湖載酒行，楚腰纖細掌中輕；
十年一覺揚州夢，贏得青樓薄倖名。

AUTUMN EVENING

Du Mu

Autumn, and silver candlelight
    cold on a painted screen.
A small fan of filmy gauze
    flaps at the darting fireflies.
On the Heavenly Steps the colours of evening
    are cool like water:
She just sits and watches
    the Herdboy and Weaving-girl stars.

秋　夕

杜　牧

銀燭秋光冷畫屏，輕羅小扇撲流螢；
天階夜色涼如水，坐看牽牛織女星。

GIVEN IN FAREWELL

Du Mu

(I)

So slender, so supple,
    little more than thirteen,
A nutmeg bud on a twig tip
    when March begins.
On the three miles of Yangzhou road
    with a spring breeze blowing,
And they draw up their bead blinds,
    she is lovelier than all.

贈　別

杜　牧

娉娉嫋嫋十三餘，豆蔻梢頭二月初，
春風十里揚州路，捲上珠簾總不如。

(Ⅱ)

Deeply in love, but tonight
　　we seem to be passionless;
I just feel, before our last cup of wine
　　a smile will not come.
The wax candle has sympathy —
　　weeps at our separation;
Its tears for us keep rolling down
　　till day breaks.

蠟燭有心還惜別

淚到天明

替人垂

The wax candle has sympathy —
    weeps at our separation;
Its tears for us keep rolling down
    till day breaks.
    蠟燭有心還惜別，替人垂淚到天明。

其　二

杜　牧

多情卻似總無情，惟覺樽前笑不成。
蠟燭有心還惜別，替人垂淚到天明。

IN GOLDEN-VALLEY GARDEN

Du Mu

The old glories are gone
    with the fragrant dust;
Stream flows unfeeling,
    grass spreads unconcerned.
In the east wind at sunset
    birds call angrily;
Fallen petals remind me of 'Green Pearl[1]'
    tumbling from a high pavilion.

1. Lü Zhu (Green Pearl) was a favourite of Shi Chong (249-300). She killed herself here as the result of a Court intrigue.

金 谷 園

杜 牧

繁華事散逐香塵，流水無情草自春，
日暮東風怨啼鳥，落花猶似墜樓人。

FOR SOMEONE IN THE NORTH ON A RAINY NIGHT

Li Shangyin

You ask me, when I shall return —
    there's no date set.
Here at Bashan the evening rain
    has brimmed the autumn pools.
When shall we trim our lamp-wicks
    by the west window
While I tell you how the evening rain
    came down at Bashan?

While I tell you how the evening rain
  came down at Bashan?
卻話巴山夜雨時。

夜 雨 寄 北

李 商 隱

君問歸期未有期，巴山夜雨漲秋池，
何當共剪西窗燭，卻話巴山夜雨時。

FOR THE OFFICIAL LING HU

Li Shangyin

I have long left the clouds of Mount Song
    and the trees by Qin river.
Two carp shall swim far, far to you
    with my message[1].
Ask no more about the guest in Prince Liang's garden
    long ago;
In the wind and rain of Maoling
    is the ailing Xiangru.

1. Carp as well as geese appear in Chinese poetry as messengers. See also Notes p.805.

寄令狐郎中

李 商 隱

嵩雲秦樹久離居，雙鯉迢迢一紙書，
休問梁園舊賓客，茂陵風雨病相如。

BECAUSE...

Li Shangyin

Because in the cloud-painted screen
    she has seen her matchless beauty,
She dreads the shortness of spring nights
    now winter has left Phoenix city.
Unthinkingly she had married a high official
    of the Golden Tortoise
Who slips out of the scented coverlet
    to attend the early morning Audience.

為　有

李　商　隱

為有雲屏無限嬌，鳳城寒盡怕春宵，
無端嫁與金龜婿，辜負香衾事早朝。

A SUI DYNASTY PALACE

Li Shangyin

On an impulse the Emperor[1] left for the south
    and a carefree sojourn.
Deep in the palace, who was to heed a warning petition?
In the spring breezes the whole Empire
    was busy cutting out silks:
Half for the Imperial saddle-flaps, and half
    for the royal sails.

1. Emperor Yangdi of Sui dynasty was one of the most extravagant and depraved of all Chinese rulers, who exhausted the country's wealth for his indulgences; for instance, having leaves and flowers of silk fastened to the palace trees in winter.

隋　宮

李　商　隱

乘興南游不戒嚴，九重誰省諫書函？
春風舉國裁宮錦；半作障泥半作帆。

JASPER POOL

Li Shangyin

By Jasper Pool, Xi Wang Mu
    opens her silken casement;
Notes of the song "Yellow Bamboos"
    move the earth with their sadness.
In a single day his eight horses
    galloped ten thousand miles —
King Mu — why does he return here no more?

The palace of Xi Wang Mu — the Queen Mother of the west — was
thought to lie far to the west of China. Emperor Mu of Zhou was
supposed to have reached it with his eight magnificent horses, but he
never returned. The "Yellow Bamboos" song was a song of mourning
for him.

瑤　池

李　商　隱

瑤池阿母綺窗開，黃竹歌聲動地哀；
八駿日行三萬里，穆王何事不重來？

CHANG'E

Li Shangyin

Candles burn low behind a mother-of-pearl screen,
The Milky Way is sinking, the morning stars drown.
Chang'e must regret having stolen the mystic drug
As she broods night after night
       between the emerald sea and the blue sky.

Chang'e, according to legend, stole the drug of immortality and fled
with it to the moon where she became the moon goddess.

嫦　娥

李　商　隱

雲母屏風燭影深，長河漸落曉星沉，
嫦娥應悔偷靈藥；碧海青天夜夜心。

MR. JIA

Li Shangyin

Looking for talent,
    His Majesty questioned former courtiers —
Mr. Jia's gifts were quite incomparable!
What a pity — the Emperor entertained him half the night
But never consulted him on human affairs,
    only gods and deities.

Jia Yi is a statesman under Emperor Wen of Han. See Liu Chang-qing's poems 'Written at New Year', p.378 and 'On passing Jia Yi's house at Changsha, p.500.

賈　生

李　商　隱

宣室求賢訪逐臣，賈生才調更無倫。
可憐夜半虛前席，不問蒼生問鬼神。

COMPLAINT OF A JADE LUTE

Wen Tingyun

On the cool bamboo mat of a silver bed
    the dreams won't come...
The deep green of the sky is like water
    afloat with night mist.
The honking of geese fades into the distance
    as they make for the Xiao and Xiang;
The moon shines full
    on the twelve-storey pagoda.

瑤 瑟 怨

溫 庭 筠

冰簟銀牀夢不成，碧天如水夜雲輕。
雁聲遠過瀟湘去，十二樓中月自明。

AT MA WEI HILL

Zheng Tian

Xuanzong turned his horse back
    but the Lady Yang was slain.
The joy of possessing her was hard to forget
    as months followed days.
It was a wise decision, after all,
    of a sage Emperor.
Why should he cast himself and her
    into the well of Jingyang palace?

See Bai Juyi's 'Everlasting Regret', p.198. Also Li Shangyin's 'A Palace of the Sui dynasty', p.530.

馬　嵬　坡

鄭　畋

玄宗回馬楊妃死，雲雨難忘日月新，
終是聖明天子事，景陽宮井又何人？

ALREADY COOL

Han Wo

Beyond the jade green railings
    an embroidered curtain is drawn,
And there's a scarlet screen
    painted over with flowers.
A brocaded quilt is spread
    on her long mat of 'dragons' beards'[1].
The days are growing chill,
    though not quite cold yet.

1. The mat of 'dragons' beards' was one woven of coarse grass.

已　涼

韓　偓

碧闌干外繡簾垂，猩色屏風畫折枝；
八尺龍鬚方錦褥，已涼天氣未寒時。

IMPRESSION OF JINLING

Wei Zhuang

The Six Dynasties are gone like a dream
    leaving birds vainly crying;
Rain falls drizzling on the river
    and on the level sedges.
Most heartless are the willows
    by Jinling palace walls —
A green veil as of old
    along the three-mile dyke.

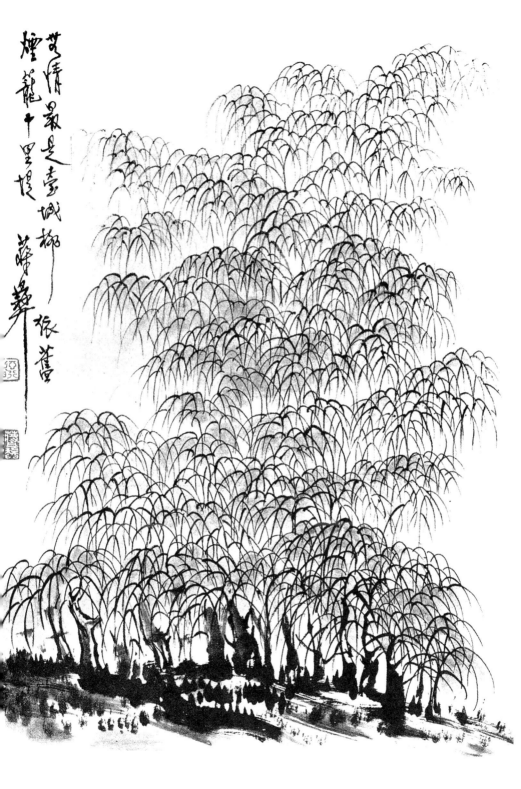

Most heartless are the willows
    by Jinling palace walls —
A green veil as of old
    along the three-mile dyke.
    無情最是臺城柳，依舊烟籠十里隄。

金　陵　圖

韋　莊

江雨霏霏江草齊，六朝如夢鳥空啼，
無情最是臺城柳，依舊烟籠十里隄。

SONG OF LONGXI

Chen Tao

They vowed to crush the Xiongnu,
     holding their lives light:
Five thousand in sable battle-dress
     died in the foreign dust.
How pitiful that the bones lying
     by Wuding riverside
Are still the lovers of
     many a woman's dream!

隴　西　行

陳　陶

誓掃匈奴不顧身，五千貂錦喪胡塵，
可憐無定河邊骨，猶是春閨夢裡人。

FOR SOMEONE

Zhang Bi

Parted, but my dream still lingers
    at the House of Xie,
On a little porch
    bordered with zig-zag railings.
Only the spring moon on that courtyard
    is full of passion,
Still shining on the fallen petals
    when I am gone.

寄　人

張　泌

別夢依依到謝家，小廊迴合曲闌斜，
多情只有春庭月，猶為離人照落花。

LINES

Anon

Near the Cold Food festival
    grasses grow lush in the rain,
Wind brushes the young wheat,
    willows shimmer on the dyke.
All men have a home
    but I cannot go back —
O cuckoo, stop shouting in my ears!

雜　詩

無　名　氏

近寒食雨草萋萋，著麥苗風柳映隄。
等是有家歸未得，杜鵑休向耳邊啼。

WRITTEN FOR MUSIC

SONG OF WEI CITY

Wang Wei

In Wei city morning rain
    has drenched the light dust;
Green, green the young leaves of the willows
    beside the inn.
Let me persuade you — empty one more wine-cup:
There are no friends where you are going
    west of Yang pass!

樂　府

渭　城　曲

王　維

渭城朝雨浥輕塵，客舍青青柳色新；
勸君更盡一杯酒，西出陽關無故人。

AUTUMN NIGHT

Wang Wei

The moon's orb just rising, a sprinkling of autumn dew,
The light silk dress too thin, but she will not change it.
All night long she plays diligently
    on her silver-chased harpsichord:
Afraid of the empty room, she cannot bear to go in.

秋 夜 曲

王 維

桂魄初生秋露微，輕羅已薄未更衣。
銀箏夜久殷勤弄，心怯空房不忍歸。

COMPLAINT IN THE PALACE OF LOYALTY

Wang Changling

She takes her broom at dawn to await
    the opening of Golden Palace;
To pass the time she strolls about
    dandling a round fan.
A jade-like face is not so fortunate
    as a wintry crow's
That can catch the sunlight
    in the Court of the Bright sun!

A court lady has lost the Emperor's favour to an uglier one.

長 信 怨

王 昌 齡

奉帚平明金殿開，暫將團扇共徘徊。
玉顏不及寒鴉色，猶帶昭陽日影來。

PASSING THE FRONTIER

Wang Changling

Under the Qin moonlight
    and through the Han passes
Mile after mile to battle they marched
    and never returned...
If only the 'Flying General[1]' of Long Cheng
    were still among us,
Never would the Tartar horsemen
    cross Yin mountain!

1. The 'Flying General' was General Li Guang of Han (died 125), much dreaded by the Xiongnu tribesmen, who gave him this nickname.

出　塞

王　昌　齡

秦時明月漢時關，萬里長征人未還；
但使龍城飛將在，不教胡馬渡陰山。

SONG OF QINGPING
Li Bai
(I)

From the clouds we remember her garments,
    in the flowers see her face;
A spring wind sweeps the balustrade,
    pearls of dew lie thick.
If you find her not on the mountain of Many Jewels,
You will meet her by moonlight
    in the Palace of Jasper.

清 平 調

李 白

雲想衣裳花想容，春風拂檻露華濃；
若非群玉山頭見，會向瑤臺月下逢。

(II)

She was a rosy peony, made more fragrant by dew;
The Emperor vainly yearns for their love-rapture
    on the Hills of Wu.
Can you tell of any in the Han Palace to compare with her?
There is only one so fit for loving —
    'Flying Swallow' newly dressed in her finery.

'Flying Swallow' or Zhao Feiyan, the daughter of a musician, was trained as a dancing girl. She won the love of Emperor Chengdi of Han (lst. Century B.C.), who made her an Imperial concubine of the highest rank. She was said to be so frail that she could dance on the palm of one's hand. See Du Mu's 'Confession', p.722

其　　二

一枝紅艷露凝香，雲雨巫山枉斷腸；
借問漢宮誰得似？可憐飛燕倚新粧。

(Ⅲ)

Lady Yang — ruin of an Empire — spread joy
    like a rare flower;
When she came to her lord the Emperor
    he would gaze on her laughingly.
With her he would dispel the endless longings
    brought by the spring wind,
Dallying by the balustrade, north of Perfumed Pavilion.

其 三

名花傾國兩相歡，常得君王帶笑看。
解釋春風無限恨；沉香亭北倚闌干。

PASSING THE FRONTIER

Wang Zhihuan

In the far distance the Yellow river
    climbs to the white clouds;
A lone town is perched in the mountains,
    many thousand feet high.
Why should a Tartar pipe
    mourn for willow trees?
Spring wind seldom crosses
    Yumen pass.

出　塞

王　之　渙

黃河遠上白雲間，一片孤城萬仞山。
羌笛何須怨楊柳；春風不度玉門關。

THE COAT WITH THE GOLD THREADS

Du Qiuniang

I warn you — cherish not your gold-threaded coat;
I warn you — cherish rather the days of your youth!
When the flower blooms, ready for picking,
    pick it you must:
Don't wait till the flower falls
    and pick a bare twig!

金　縷　衣

杜　秋　娘

勸君莫惜金縷衣，勸君惜取少年時，
花開堪折直須折，莫待無花空折枝。

NOTES

Page

2 *Zhongnan mountain*, or South mountain was some miles south of the Tang Capital, Chang'an, a favourite retreat of artists and men of letters. See also Wang Wei's 'Farewell', p.28, and 'The Zhongnan range' p.338; also Meng Haoran's 'On retiring to South mountain,' p.358.

10 *Yan* and *Qin* are the names of ancient States, corresponding roughly to present-day Hebei and Shanxi. The husband was evidently fighting on the N. E. Border, the wife living far to the West.

12 *Mount Tai*, the most revered of the Five Sacred Peaks, the other four being Hua in the West (Shanxi), Song in the centre (Henan), Heng in the South (Hunan) and another Heng in the North (borders of Hebei and Shanxi).
Qi and *Lu*, two ancient States lying North and South of Mount Tai, composing together the modern province of Shandong.

16 *Morning and Evening stars*: literally, Shen and Shang, the names of two constellations (3 stars in Orion and 3 in Scorpio). One rises when the other sets so that the two are never visible together in the sky.

18 *Mandarin ducks* sleep with their heads on each other's necks and symbolise the fidelity of man and wife (cf. Meng Jiao's 'Chaste Wife', p.112). *Cypress* is also a symbol for faithfulness, being evergreen and staunch in all weathers. The Chinese character for 'a section of bamboo stem' has the secondary meaning 'chastity, fidelity', hence the *tall bamboos* in the last line is another allusion to her faithfulness.

22 During the disorders following the An Lushan Rebellion (755), Li Bai had become involved with a Prince Lin, a relation of the Emperor's, who had attempted to set up an

independent administration at Nanjing. Although he soon defected, Li Bai was arrested and imprisoned for several months (*the net*). Later he was exiled to Yelang in Guizhou, part of the large area then known as Jiangnan or '*South of the Yangtze*', and sufficiently far from the Capital to be considered a place of exile. In this and the following poem, Du Fu expresses his uncertainty about the fate of his friend.

24 *Heaven's net*: an allusion to a saying in the 'Tao Te Ching', the Taoist classic: "Heaven's net has wide meshes yet nothing escapes from it."

30 *Guest of East mountain*: Xie An (320-385), a prominent statesman of E. Jin dynasty, retired to East mountain and was nicknamed 'The guest of East mountain'. After him, the term was commonly used for a recluse.
Gold Horse gate: one of the city gates of Chang'an, the Capital, where Qiwu Qian had sat his examination for the Civil Service.

40 *Autumn festival*: the Double Ninth (ninth day of the ninth moon). It was celebrated by climbing heights with one's friends, to drink wine and compose poems. See also Wang Wei's 'Thinking of my brothers on the Double Ninth', p. 648.

50 *Deputy-governor of Shanyin* modern Shaoxing in Zhejiang, the old State of Yue, thus very far from the metropolitan area.

60 *Phoenix and crane* are both magic birds in Chinese stories, though the phoenix has no myth of resurrection as with us. The last couplet implies that the poet would like to join his friend and become a recluse.

62 *Five Imperial Tombs*: the tombs of the five early Han Emperors, Gaodi, Huidi, Jingdi, Wudi and Zhaodi.

68 *Wu State*: this indicates Suzhou, which in the time of Confucius was the Capital of Wu State. In Wei Yingwu's day, it was known as a centre for poets and literati.

88   *Official girdle and hatpin*: the insignia of government office. The character translated as 'girdle' may mean the strings by which the official seal was attached. Men's hair was worn long and in a knot on top of the head; the broad-brimmed official hat was fastened to this with the hatpin.

90   *Pearl trees*: a rare species of tree with pearl-like excrescences on the leaves. *Kingfishers* with their gaudy plumage are symbolic of people in high positions. The poet indicates the danger of associating with them (kingfishers were snared for the sake of their feathers, which were used for elaborate headdresses etc.)

100   *Xiaoguan*, one of the important passes for the defence of the Chinese border to the north-west.
      You and *Bing*, ancient states corresponding to modern Hubei and Shanxi.

104   *Tian Shan*, a high mountain range in the extreme north-west. *Yumen* was a key pass on the north-west border between China and Turkestan. It figures in many poems of this period as the scene of battles against the Tartars, e.g. 'Ziye's autumn song', p. 106.

106   *The sound of beating clothes*: an indication of autumn. With the approach of cold weather it was time to prepare the *Hanyi* or winter clothes. These were often made of heavy material, double-lined and filled with floss, and thus required more washing and beating. In this particular poem, winter clothes were being made ready for sending to the soldiers on the cold north-west frontier.

108   *The yellow butterflies of October*: it is a common Chinese belief that the small white butterflies turn yellow in autumn — a symbol for 'growing old'.

112   *Wutong tree*: the only tree on which, it is said, the phoenix will nest.

122   *You and Yan*: the names of feudal States, corresponding to

present-day Liaoning and Hebei. *Liaodong*: an area east of Liao river in east Hebei.

130 *Lady Cai*: Cai Wenji of Later Han who was captured by Tartar horsemen and made the wife of their chieftain. Dong Tinglan is playing a Chinese lute, the ancient form of which had five strings, later seven.

132 *Phoenix pool* was an artificial pool in the Palace grounds, near the Imperial Secretariat; the *Gate of Blue Carvings* was one of the Palace gates. Mr. Fang to whom the poem is addressed (the 'scholar' of the final couplet) apparently had his office here.

134 *Liangzhou*: part of modern Gansu. In Tang times it was inhabited by Tartars.

136 *Pang Gong* was a recluse who lived on Lumen mountain in the East Han period; Meng is probably speaking here of his own mountain retreat.

138 *A madman of Chu*. This was the hermit Jie Yu of Chu State, a great drinker and eccentric. (See also Wang Wei's 'From my retreat on the river Wang', p.332). He is said to have stopped Confucius on the road and warned him against politics in a song.

Five Peaks: the five Sacred Mountains. *Lu* is a mountain south of Jiujiang, famous for its magnificent scenery; a nearby peak was the *Stone Mirror*.

Golden Gate appears in Taoist books as the dwelling of the Heavenly Emperor. Li Bai had been initiated into the Taoist faith and images from Taoist iconography appear in some of his greatest poems, as here in the last five lines, and in the following poem: 'A dream of wandering on Tian Mu'.

150 *Xie Tiao*: a former prefect of Xuan Zhou, a writer and poet of the 'Northern and Southern dynasties' period (420-588), and nephew of the still more illustrious writer

Xie Lingyun of Jin dynasty, hence 'the younger Xie', line 12.

Peng Lai was a legendary island where the Immortals were said to live.

152 *Luntai* is in present-day Xinjiang, a district where the Xiongnu tribes had harassed the Chinese border since Han times.

158 *General Cao*. This was Cao Ba, a descendant of the famous General Cao Cao, founder of Wei dynasty (220-265). The 'General' is an 'honorific': he was not a military man but a Court painter to Emperor Xuanzong. He achieved special distinction as a horse painter: his painting of 'Nine horses' which is the subject of this poem, is also described in a poem by the Song writer Su Dongpo (1036-1101), in which the Emperor's 'Curly-mane' and Guo Ziyi's 'Lion' are specially mentioned.

Evidently this painting was still in existence three centuries later. *The Prince of Jiangdu* was Li Xu, a nephew of Tai Zong, the second and greatest Tang Emperor. He was also an accomplished horse painter.

The story goes that his painting of 'Six horses' on the walls of one of the palace pavilions was so realistic that when, one day, only five horses were to be seen there, it was believed that a spirit had transformed the sixth into a living animal.

The late Emperor's grey. A painting of this horse by Han Gan, a pupil of Cao Ba, and an even more distinguished horse painter, still exists in the collection of Sir Percival and Lady David, entitled 'The Night-shining White Steed'. Du Fu speaks of Xuanzong as 'the late Emperor' as he had already abdicated when this poem was written.

Dragon Pool was in the Palace grounds at Chang'an, north of the Hall of Southern Fragrance (see the next poem: 'Inscription for a painting').

General Guo: Guo Ziyi, a wealthy General of this period.

160   *Wei Feng*, a native of Chengdu, was Recorder of Lanzhou. *Zhi Dun*: a Buddhist monk (314-366) of Jin dynasty who kept a stable of fine horses.

162   *King Wu of Wei*: Wu ('the Martial') was another name for Cao Cao, founder of Wei dynasty, who besides being a shrewd and brilliant general was also a considerable poet, contributing much to the development of the 5-character *Gushi. Lady Wei*: a calligraphist of East Jin dynasty. Wang Xizhi (321-379) is perhaps the most highly regarded of all Chinese calligraphists. His writing has been described as "light as floating clouds; vigorous as a startled dragon."

Riches and honour are like floating clouds: this is a reference to a saying of Confucius: The Master said, "With coarse rice to eat, with water to drink, and my bended arm for a pillow, I still have joy in the midst of these things. Riches and honour acquired by unrighteousness are to me as a floating cloud."

Kaiyuan was the reign title assumed by Emperor Xuanzong at his accession in 713 and maintained until 742 when it was changed to Tianbao.

In the Hall of Rising Mists... The portraits of twenty-four meritorious ministers and military men had been painted in this Hall by Imperial command in 644. The *Duke of Bao* was Duan Zhixuan, and the *Duke of O* Weichi Jingde, both rulers of States who had helped to establish the Tang dynasty.

164   *Han Gan*: see note to p. 158 above.

166   *Yueyang* was the home town of Du Fu's friend Han Chu, where he had retired after his demotion. It is on the borders of Lake Dongting in Hunan. In his commentary on this poem, David Hawkes (A Little Primer of Du Fu, Oxford

1968) suggests that the extravagant terms of line 3, and the imagery in general, may be an echo of Qu Yuan's language in his famous poem 'Encountering sorrow'. There the poet addresses his Sovereign as 'the Fair One', in a poem rich in allegory and Taoist images. Professor Hawkes further points out that this poem of Du Fu's is set "in Qu Yuan country" the Dongting lake, the rivers Xiao and Xiang, and this may have started the train of associations.

Jade city This second stanza presents an allegory of the Court: Jade city stands for Chang'an, the Pole star for the Emperor, and the host of gods for the courtiers. The winged Immortals are the truly lofty souls, among whom the poet numbers his friend Han the Censor.

Zhi Song a true Immortal, of whom the clever *Zhang Liang* became a disciple. The latter came from Han State, which in the 4th and 3rd centuries B.C. occupied what is now central Henan and South Shanxi. He became the trusted adviser of *Liu Bang*, the founder of the Han dynasty, who ruled as Emperor Gao Zu. In his old age, Zhang Liang retired to follow the teaching of the Taoist Chi Songzi. Du Fu probably intends an allusion to Han the Censor here, who has retired to study the Tao after being dismissed from office. There is an allusion in "the fragrant maple tastes better than stale meats" to the vegetarian diet of Taoist believers.

The old historian in Zhounan was Sima Tan of Han. When Emperor Wu went to offer sacrifices on the sacred Tai mountain, Sima Tan felt chagrined at being left behind in Zhounan, although he was specially interested in those proceedings.

168 *Zhuge Liang* (181-234) is one of the most revered characters in Chinese history, and appears to have been a special hero of Du Fu's. A statesman, general and scholar who

was was also regarded as a mechanical and mathematical genius, and an inventor of military tactics, he served Liu Bei, the founder of Shu kingdom in the Three Kingdoms period. These are the two referred to as 'Prince and Minister' in the first stanza and 'The First Ruler and his Marshal' in the second.

170 The *luan* is a mythical bird.

172 In a Preface to this poem, Du Fu explains how in 767 (only three years before his death) he saw a dancer from Linying performing the Sword Dance at the house of Yuan Qi, then Governor of Guizhou (also known as Bai Di — 'White Emperor City'), who turned out to have been a pupil of Lady Gongsun. He then remembered having seen Gongsun dance when he was a boy of five (717) (hence, line 17, 'Fifty years have passed...'). The thoughts aroused by this discovery prompted him to write the poem.
Yi the archer is the mythical archer who when ten suns appeared together in the sky, shot down nine of them.

174 *Pear Garden*: a School of Music founded by Xuanzong in 714 for the training of women entertainers for the Court.
The mound at Jinsu: Xuanzong's burial mound in Shanxi.

180 *Zhang the clerk* was Zhang Shu who together with Han Yu, the author of the poem, and Li Fangshu, had been degraded to be District Magistrates in the South (Hunan), which in Tang times was considered uncivilised.

182 *The road to Heaven*, i.e. to the Court.

184 *Heng mountain* was the Southern Sacred Mountain, near Hengzhou in Hunan. See note to Du Fu's 'Gazing at Mount Tai', p.12. *'Purple Canopy'*, *'Heaven's Pillar'*, *'Stone Granary'* and *'Fire God'* are the names of four peaks belonging to the Heng mountain range.

186 *Divination box*: a small box of jade or wood is thrown on the ground and the fate of the applicant is interpreted

according to its position.

188 Ten *stone drums* were engraved with poems by the orders of Emperor Xuan of Zhou dynasty (reigned 827-781 B.C.). Three are still preserved in the temple of Confucius at Fengxiang, together with replicas of the remaining seven. They are among the most precious ancient engravings of the Chinese.

Mr. Zhang is the poet Zhang Ji (represented in this anthology by the poem on p.406, 'On an old friend lost in Tibet').

The two books of Solemn Songs: the 'Da Ya' and 'Xiao Ya', two sections of the classic Book of Songs — those containing the formal odes for Court ceremonies.

190 *Sun and moon*: literally Xi and E, for Xi He the god of the sun, and Chang'e the goddess of the moon.

The reign title changed to Yuanhe: this was in 806 at the accession of Xianzong. Han Yu was then recalled from Jiangling to take up office at the Capital.

You Fufeng is Fengxiang in Shanxi.

192 *The Tripod of Gao*: Gao was one of the minor Zhou feudal States. The ruler of Lu State acquired a large tripod from Gao and enshrined it in the Ancestral Temple.

Wang Xizhi, the famous calligraphist of East Jin, had once copied the Dao De Jing for a Taoist priest, and received a flock of geese in return. (See also note to p.162, Du Fu's 'Inscription for a painting').

198 *Ming Huang*: another title of the Emperor Xuanzong (reigned 713-756).

Huaqing pool: a natural spring of warm water in the grounds of Huaqing Palace, in present day Lintong, Shanxi. Li Palace (p.200) was another name for this building.

200 *The war drums of Yuyang*: this alludes to the rebellion led by An Lushan in 755, which forced the Emperor to flee from the Capital. He escaped towards Sichuan with Yang

Guifei and others of his entourage, but on the way his body-guard revolted and refused to proceed, demanding the life of Yang Guifei, whom they regarded as the cause of the weakened government. She was strangled before the Emperor's eyes, and the cavalcade proceeded into Sichuan. *'The song of the rainbow skirt'* was a ballet with music said to have been composed by the Emperor himself.

202 *The Dragon Chariot came back.* On reaching Sichuan, the Emperor abdicated in favour of his son, Suzong. After the Rebellion had been put down, he was allowed to return to the Capital.

204 *The players of the Pear Garden* see note to p.172, Du Fu's 'On seeing a pupil of Lady Gongsun perform the Sword Dance.'

206 *Yellow Springs*: the land of the dead.

208 *Penglai*: the home of the Immortals.

212 *The Guitar song.* In 815, Bai Juyi fell into disfavour at Court and was relegated to the office of Assistant Prefect of Jiangzhou (modern Jiujiang), also referred to here as Xunyang and Pencheng. From the poet's Preface to this poem we learn that the encounter had actually taken place. He concludes: "Since my departure from the Capital I had not felt sad, but that night I began to realise my banishment, and I wrote this long poem."

218 *Qiuniang* is the poetess Du Qiuniang, a contemporary of Bai Juyi's (See 'The coat with the gold threads', p.782, and the biographical notes).

222 *Yuanhe times*, i.e. 806-821, the reign of Emperor Xuanzong. *Xuan and Xi*: these were two legendary Emperors, Fuxi, whose dates are traditionally given as 2852-2738 B.C., and Xuanyuan, the 'Yellow Emperor', 2698-2598 B.C.
Huaixi was an area west of the Huai, a large river draining Henan and northern Anhui.

The minister called Du: this was the Premier Pei Du who in 817 was put in general command of the armies, Han Yu, the high official and poet, being appointed his aide-de-camp, while retaining his civil post in the Secretariat. It was due to the energy of Pei Du that his General, Li Su, was able to suppress the troubles in Huaixi and capture the bandit chief Wu yuanji, who was brought for display in the Capital. For this, Pei was created a Duke. This campaign, known as 'the pacification of Huaixi', was commemorated on a memorial stone, engraved by Han Yu. Afterwards, due to personal jealousy, the monument was pulled down and replaced by an inferior one. On the death of Emperor Muzong in 826, Pei Du retired from public life and built a country retreat, where he enjoyed the friendship of Bai Juyi and Liu Yuxi. He died in 838.

Su, Wu, Gu and *Tong* were four leading generals under Pei Du. Their names were Li Su, Han Gongwu, Li Daogu and Li Wentong.

224   *Yao and Shun*, i. e. Yao Dian and Shun Dian, two Books in the Classic of History, Yao and Shun being the names of two Sage Kings reigning over two thousand years B. C. *Qingmiao and Shengmin:* the titles of two poems in the Classic of Poetry (the 'Book of Songs').

226   *The Tang dish and the Confucian tripod*: This Tang was the name of the founder of the ancient Shang dynasty, 1766 B.C. The tripod was an ancient engraved bronze, handed down from the time of Confucius.

The Three Emperors and Five Rulers were the rulers in the legendary period of ancient Chinese history.

228   *The Yan Song* was a song current on the northern border. In a Preface to his poem, Gao Shi wrote: "In the sixth year of Kaiyuan (718), a friend came back from the border and showed me the Yan Song. Moved by his tale of the

campaign, I wrote this poem, using the same rhymes."
Elm Pass: now Shanhai Pass.

230   *Northern Ji*: modern Hebei.

232   *Beacon fires*: detachments on Border guard communicated with one another by lighting beacons on the hill tops.

The boom of watches: the night watches were sounded by banging on a soldier's cooking pot.

A princess sang to a guitar: a Han princess who for political reasons was to marry a barbarian chieftain, had also travelled this road. She is usually represented in paintings carrying a guitar.

Light Chariots: there is an allusion here to the Han officer Li Cai, cousin of the famous general Li Guang. Li Cai was Commander of the Light Chariots, and also took part in the campaign against the Xiongnu.

Barbarian grapes. The Xiongnu beyond the western border of China brought grapes and other rarities to the Emperor as tribute after being subdued by the Han armies.

236   *He chased a Tartar horse...* General Li Guang of Han, who distinguished himself in driving back the Xiongnu, was once captured in battle by an enemy horseman. He pretended to be dead till seeing an enemy soldier on a lively horse, he fell upon the rider, seized his mount and galloped to safety.

A white-faced mountain tiger: a certain Zhou Chu of East Jin dynasty heard his village Elders say there was a white-faced tiger on South Mountain and a dragon in the river below Long Bridge, both of which were molesting the villagers. Zhou went into the mountain and shot the tiger, then dived into the river and killed the dragon.

Wei Ching died 106 B.C. He served in high military commands under Emperor Wu of Han and gained distinction in seven campaigns against the Xiongnu. He had originally come to the Emperor's notice through the beauty of his sister, who became one of the Emperor's favourites. Wang Wei ascribes his success more to luck than merit.

Li Guang, died 125 B.C. A cavalry commander of outstanding character and military ability, a contemporary of Wei Qing's, but whose career was marred by intermittent failures in the campaigns. He finally committed suicide. Emperor Wu said of him: "He is simple and sincere, as though one of the people, yet all the Empire looks up to him."

His arrow could hit a bird's eye: literally 'would not miss a bird's left eye'. A story is told of the famous archer Yi that when walking one day in the country he was asked by a friend who accompanied him to shoot a sparrow through the left eye. Yi took aim but hit the right eye. Yi was ashamed and never forgot this failure.

He will sell melons by the roadside: an allusion to the Marquis of Tongling, a person of eminence under the Qin dynasty (221-205 B. C.). At the overthrow of the dynasty, he lost his position and took to growing melons on some waste ground outside the Green Gate at Chang'an.

Or...plant willows: an allusion to the poet Tao Yuanming (372-427) whose nickname was 'Mr. Five-Willows', after the trees he had planted beside his country house (See also Wang Wei's 'From my retreat on the river Wang', p.332).

The Three River Provinces: Hebei, Henan and Hedong.

238 *A Yan bow*: Yan is the present Hebei, and was famous for its bows and arrows.

The Yue armies: an allusion to an occasion when the army of Yue state was threatening Qi state. The mere presence of the Yue army was such a source of shame to the Qi minister, Yongmen Zidi, that he committed suicide. The Yue army then retreated.

244 *Can Cong and Yu Fu* were rulers of Shu (Sichuan) in the

legendary period: Can Cong is said to have been the First Ruler.

The Sichuan road was a winding and precipitous path leading from Shanxi into Sichuan through the Emei ranges. It was along this path that the Emperor Xuanzong with his entourage escaped from the rebel armies of An Lu-shan in 756; many commentators have assumed that Li Bai wrote this poem to dissuade the Emperor, when Chang'an was threatened, from leaving the Capital, but Waley has shown ('The poetry and career of Li Bai', p.814) that this cannot be upheld since the poem was included in an anthology collected in 753. Li Bai was a Sichuan man; the scenery was familiar to him, and the theme — an old song-theme of which the original words are lost — provided him with the opportunity for creating passages of amazing beauty, power and splendour. This seems sufficient raison-d'etre.

248   *Cuckoo*: King Wang of Shu lost his kingdom and was said to have been changed into a cuckoo at his death. The call of the cuckoo is thought to sound like the Chinese for 'O to go back again!"

256   *Yanran mountain* was in Inner Mongolia, the scene of battles against the Xiongnu.

258   *The difficulties of the Journey.* In these three poems, the journey stands for the way through life, or in a narrower sense, the way to the Court and official promotion. In the first, the poet expresses discontent with his idle self-indulgent existence and wants to strike a blow for his country, but is frustrated on all sides. The second begins on the same note of self-accusation, but goes on to recall many figures from past history who had tried to serve but met with indignity or rejection: "Put not your trust in Princes!" — and the Princes themselves, like the great Zhao Wang of

Yan are subject to the common fate. The third is still more pessimistic: an enumeration of great men of the past who won their 'lonely eminence' but came to a violent end. Perhaps it is better to keep away from the dangers of high position, he says, and rather enjoy a cup of wine and one's independence. The occasion for these poems was Li Bai's having been expelled from Court through the jealousy of a powerful eunuch, Gao Lishi.

268   *Ballad of the Army Wagons*. This poem evidently describes a recruiting campaign to raise troops for defence against the Tibetans. During the years when Du Fu was writing, the borders of the Chinese Empire, which had been immensely extended under Taizong, the second Tang Emperor, were constantly under threat. The Khitan were pressing in Manchuria, Mongolia was in the hands of the Uigurs after 745, the Arabs were challenging China's sovereignty west of Turkestan, and the Tibetans, though beaten in several campaigns, were a continual menace on China's western flank. The regular soldiers and reservists were evidently not enough to contain so many pressures, and men were often forcibly conscripted.

The River, i.e. the Yellow River, the upper reaches of which were threatened by the Tibetans.

The farms: at this period, the frontier districts, which had to be permanently garrisoned, had their own agricultural settlements, maintained by the military, to avoid the necessity of bringing up supplies through difficult terrain, and from great distances.

272   *The third day of the third moon* was the day of the Spring Festival, when everybody put on their best clothes and picnicked in the open air. This poem is the description of an extravagant Imperial picnic held in tents by the lakeside in Chang'an's principal park.

The Empress here is the notorious beauty, Yang Guifei, whose sisters had been ennobled as the *duchess of Guo* and the *duchess of Qin*.

Tinkling knives: carving knives had little bells attached to the handles.

The horseman was evidently Yang Guozhong, cousin of Yang Guifei, who had been appointed Premier, was much feared and highly unpopular. His approach, 'measured and slow', was that demanded by Court etiquette. A hint of his identity is given by the mention of 'willow-fluff' in the following line, the character for 'willow' being the same 'Yang'. The whole line hints at his adulterous intentions: he was thought to be carrying on an illicit love affair with his cousin the Duchess of Guo.

272 *Bluebirds* carried messages from goddesses to their lovers, and red silk veils or handkerchiefs were dandled like a fan by fashionable ladies. Thus this line hints at a secret assignation.

274 *Old fellow of Shaoling*: Du Fu speaks of himself in the third person. He had some property at Shaoling, a village near Chang'an.

Winding river: a river and artificial lake in the south-east corner of Chang'an, the scene of the revels in the previous poem, 'A ballad of lovely women'.

The First Lady, i.e. Yang Guifei

274 *The clear Wei... the Sword Cliffs*: the river Wei flows east below Mawei slope where Yang Guifei was killed. The Emperor escaped into Sichuan by a mountain pass through Sword Cliffs. See Bai Juyi's "Everlasting Regret", p.198.

The Tartar horsemen: this poem was written after Chang'an had been captured by the rebel followers of An Lushan. Du Fu had been caught while trying to join the new Emperor at Lingwu and was detained in Chang'an.

276 *Lament for a Prince.* This poem was probably written in occupied Chang'an. The young prince had evidently been abandoned by the Court when the Emperor escaped with his favourites and officials.

White-headed crows were birds of ill omen; here they are also a symbol of the invading rebels.

Nine horses died: the Emperor in his escape rode horses to death.

Emperor Gao: the first Tang Emperor.

Stench of blood: the families of princes and others who had fled were massacred by the rebels. Du Fu may well have been a witness to this.

Camel bands were sent to carry off loot from the Palace and the houses of noblemen. Chang'an is called '*The old Capital*' since the Emperor was no longer there: the new Emperor, Suzong, was at Lingwu.

The northerners, literally 'the Shuofang soldiers', were the troops under the famous Chinese general Geshu Han, who had been defending the Tongguan pass north of Chang'an, and had been overpowered by the rebels before the Capital fell.

276 *Our Uigur allies*: the Uigur Turks had made a treaty of friendship with the Chinese.

The Five Tombs: the tombs of the five previous Tang Emperors.

280 *Master Kong*: i.e. Confucius; in Chinese, Kongfuzi.

284 *Shu*, the old name for Sichuan.

286 *Exile from the south*: Luo Binwang's home was in Zhejiang. See biographical notes.

306 *Luqi lute*: synonym for a precious lute. Sima Xiangru, a famous musician of Han dynasty who won his wife by his singing had such a lute. *Emei peak* is a mountain in Sichuan (ancient Shu).

314 *The kingdom is ruined*: this poem was written at the time

of the An Lushan rebellion. The *partings* refer to the general breakup of families.

322 *At the world's end*: this poem was probably written at Qinzhou, Gansu, one of the north-west frontier towns and thus very far from the Capital. It would be subject to fierce winds from the Gebi desert. Li Bai at that time may have been in the south, in the area of lake Dongting. The Miluo river was also in that region.

324 *General Yan*: Yan Wu, a friend of Du Fu's, a Governor of Sichuan.

Three reigns: he had served under Xuanzong and Suzong (both of whom died in 762) and was then in the service of Taizong whose summons to Court was the occasion of this farewell poem.

336 *Mount Song*: in Henan; one of the five Sacred Mountains.

338 *Taiyi*: a mountain south-west of Chang'an ('the Imperial city').

344 *Tong*: a tree which grows particularly in Yunnan, from the flowers of which a cloth is made. *Taro*: an edible tuber, similar to a yam.

346 *Three Xiangs*: Xiangtan, Xiangxiang, and Xiangyin. *Chu* is modern Hubei. *Jing Gate*: a mountain in that province.

362 *East Wood*: the name of a Buddhist monastery.

366 *On the public road*: Meng means, 'who will help me to advance in the government service?'

404 *Zhuge Liang*: a brilliant general and statesman of the Three Kingdoms period (221-277), who helped Liu Bei to establish the kingdom of Shu. He is celebrated in many of Du Fu's poems, e.g. 'Night at the pavilion', p.486, 'Remembering the past' (IV), p.494.

432 *Liangzhou*: on the western border of Sichuan.

436 *Wild geese*: the traditional bearers of messages.

456 *Double Ninth*: see note to p.40.

458 *Phoenix tower*: a Song dynasty tower in Jiangsu.

468 *Morning glory*: blossoms which open in the morning and fade in a day, symbolizing the transience of human life.
Seagulls: a reference to a story in the philosopher Liezi. A man living by the seashore had made friends with some seagulls. His father asked him to bring him some gulls too, but when he went to the shore the next day to entice them back to his father, they flew away.

472 *Brocade City*: this was Chengdu, the capital of Sichuan (ancient Shu). It was once a centre of the brocade industry.

476 *West Mountain*: also called Snow Mountain, west of Chengdu in Sichuan.
The Three Towns: Songzhou, Weizhou and Paozhou on the Turfan boundary. North-west Sichuan at that time was being harassed by Turfan tribes.
Myriad mile bridge: in the south of Chengdu.

478 *The recovery of Henan and Hebei*: the final collapse of the rebel forces under An Lushan which followed the fall of Luoyang to the Imperial armies in November 762.
Jianko: a pass into Sichuan. *Ba and Wu*: two of the gorges on the Yangtze river. Du Fu's home was near Luoyang.

482 *Brocade River* flowed south of Chengdu. The weavers were said to have washed their brocade in it. *Jade Rampart*: a mountain north-west of Chengdu. *The Imperial court*: this refers to a brief period when Chang'an had been taken by the Tibetans, who had set up a puppet ruler. Emperor Taizong had then been restored, though 'the brigands', i.e. the Tibetans, still held parts of Sichuan.

486 *Drums and bugles*: watches were sounded in camp or barracks by 333 drum beats and 12 bugle notes. *The Three Gorges*: Qutang, Wu and Xiling on the Yangtze. See also Du Fu's "Remembering the past" (I), p.488.

490 *Chu palaces*, of the ancient feudal State of Chu which existed 740-330 B.C.

528   *The morning drum*: Court officials were summoned at dawn.
      Orchid Tower was the name of a Secretariat at the palace.
538   *Helpful bluebird*: bluebirds were said to carry messages
      between lovers.
558   *The deer enclosure*: this and the following two poems are
      part of a series of 5-character cut-shorts, written from Wang
      Wei's retreat on the river Wang, together with his poet
      friend, Pei Di. The whole series has been translated by
      Jerome Chen and Michael Bullock in 'Poems of Solitude'
      (Abelard-Schumann, 1960).
566   *Red berry*: the berry of the *Abrus precatorius*, known to
      the Chinese as 'love beans'. Presumably they were thought
      to be an aphrodisiac.
648   *The ninth day of the ninth moon* (the Double Ninth) was
      the autumn festival of 'Deng Gao' (climbing heights).
      Family and friends would join in a picnic on some high
      spot, to drink wine, enjoy the scenery and compose poems.
      Cf. Meng Haoran's 'On climbing Orchid mountain in
      autumn', p.40.
656   *Lujing and Weiyang* were the names of two Han dynasty
      palaces.
664   *Baidi*, literally 'White Emperor' city, was another name for
      Guizhou in Sichuan. In the 1st century, a war-lord called
      Gungsun Shu ruled a large area of western China, with
      Guizhou as his capital, and was known as the 'White
      Emperor'. The *Jiangling* of this poem was in Hubei: to
      sail from Guizhou to Jiangling in a single day indicates
      the speed of the current in this part of the Yangtze river.
670   *Prince Qi* was a younger brother of Emperor Xuanzong.
      Cui the ninth was Cui Di, a palace chamberlain.
686   *Jade pavilion*: This is a general term for a brightly painted
      and beautifully ornamented building where the ladies of
      the palace would live. Cf. 'Red pavilion in Liu Yuxi's

'Spring fragment', p.694.

688   *Shouxiang* and *the peak Huile* were far to the north-west; Shouxiang was a district north of the Yellow River and Huile a mountain in Shanxi, about 160 miles west of Datong.

704   *The Duchess of Guo* was an elder sister of Yang Guifei. Cf. Du Fu's 'Ballad of Lovely Women' p.272

716   *Red Cliff* is a historical spot on the Yangtze river, east of Hankou. In the Three Kingdoms period, the Wei fleet sailed down river to attack the fleets of Wu and Shu, Wu's being under the command of General Zhou Yu. Fire ships were sent among the Wei fleet and, helped by a change in the wind, destroyed it.
The two Qiao beauties were the wives of the King of Wu and of General Zhou Yu. If the King of Wei had won the river battle, he could have carried them off to his Bronze Bird pavilion.

720   *The twenty-four bridges.* This was a district of Yangzhou, built in the Sui dynasty. In Du Mu's time, Yangzhou was a rich and luxurious city, famous for the beauty of its singing girls.

722   *The waists of Chu.* Duke Zhuang of Chu was specially attracted by girls with tiny waists. Thereafter, tiny waists were often called 'Chu waists'. *The fairy-light dancers.* Literally, 'light enough to dance on the palm of one's hand'. This is a reference to Zhao Feiyan ('Flying Swallow'), a singing girl of great beauty and slenderness who became a favourite of Emperor Ceng of Han, 1st. century B.C. She was said to be light enough to dance on his hand.

732   *Golden-valley garden* was the name of a country retreat near Luoyang, belonging to the wealthy Shi Chong of Jin dynasty (249-300). The story alluded to in this poem is

about one of his favourites, Lü Zhu ('Green Pearl') who was coveted by General Sun Xiu. Since Shi Chong would not give her up, Sun Xiu came to arrest him on a trumped-up charge. He found the two feasting in an upper room. In remorse for having caused her lover's downfall, Lü Zhu threw herself from the window and was killed.

738 *Xiangru*: Sima Xiangru, a noted scholar and poet of Han dynasty, was a member of Prince Liang's household, but retired and died at Maoling. Li Shangyin is here alluding to his own misfortunes.

740 *Golden tortoise*: an insignia worn by officials above the third rank.

746 *Chang'e*. There is possibly an allusion here to an illicit love for a Taoist nun. The Taoists were concerned with finding the elixir of immortality.

756 *Jinling*. The Six Dynasties: Wu, E. Jin, Song, Qi, Liang and Chen (317-589) ruled in the southern half of China during the Period of Division between north and south. The capital was at Jinling — the modern Nanjing.

764 *Cuckoo*. The cry of the cuckoo is said to sound like the Chinese for "O to go back!" Cf. Li Shangyin's 'Inlaid zither', p.526.

766 *Yangguan* is a Pass in Gansu, south of the important Yumen pass on the north-west border, which appears in so many Tang poems.

BIOGRAPHICAL NOTES

Bai Juyi 772-846

Born at Xincheng, Henan. After graduating in 800 he rose to high rank under Emperor Xianzong, being appointed Omissioner in 808, and a member of the Hanlin Academy. In 815 he was transferred to Jiangzhou (modern Jiujiang) as Governor; this was the scene of his famous poem 'Song of the Guitar', which he wrote the following year. Later he became Provincial Governor of Hangzhou, then the greatest city of East China, and subsequently governor of Suzhou, but this office he resigned owing to ill health. He lived to a good age, 74, and his poems won immense popularity, even in his lifetime. He came to be regarded as one of the greatest Chinese Poets, and is certainly one of the best loved: humorous, ironic, genuine in feeling and direct in expression. His 'Song of Everlasting Regret' is one of the most famous poems in Chinese.

Cen Shen 8th century

A native of Nanyang, graduating about 744. On the recommendation of Du Fu he was appointed Censor by Emperor Suzong, and later Governor of Jiazhou. On his retirement he went to live among the Duling mountains, and died while on a visit to Sichuan. He once took part in a military expedition, and many of his poems are on war themes, especially the privations of soldiers on the North-west frontier, forceful and passionate in mood.

Chang Jien Early 8th century

Very little is known of this poet. He graduated about 727 and held a secretarial post at Shuyi in Anhui. Later he became a hermit, retiring to a mountain and devoting himself to the cult of Tao.

Chen Tao Late 9th and early 10th centuries
A native of Poyang in Jiangxi, he repeatedly failed the civil service examinations and retired to West mountain in Hongzhou, where he spent his life as a recluse. Besides being an outstanding poet, he was interested in the study of Buddhism and Taoism, styling himself 'the Countryman of the Three Faiths' (Confucianism, Buddhism and Taoism). He also experimented in alchemy. In his old age, he began to wander about the country on foot, and it is not known where he died; the legend arose that he had become an Immortal and disappeared into Heaven.

Chen Zi'ang 656-698
He was born at Shehong in Sichuan. He studied hard despite difficult circumstances and became an accomplished writer. He graduated at 28, and held office under the Empress Wu (who in 684 usurped the throne for 20 years). In later life, ill health and the attacks of his political enemies drove him into retirement. Finally he was arrested on a trumped-up charge and died in prison. His poetry ranks among the most beautiful of the early Tang; he was held in high esteem by Li Bai, Du Fu and their followers.

Cui Hao Died 754
A native of Bianzhou. After graduating in the Kaiyuan period (713-42) he held the post of Assistant Director in the Bureau of Official Rank. It is said that the great Li Bai, when visiting Yellow Crane pavilion near Wuchang on the Yangtze, found Cui Hao's poem inscribed on the wall and praised it highly. Cui was romantic by nature, loved wine and beautiful girls.

Cui Shu Early 8th century
He was born in Dingzhou of a poor family and was early left an orphan. Clever and persistent, he studied hard and succeeded

in graduating in 738. Many of his poems are tinged with sadness.

Cui Tu Later 9th century
He was born somewhere in the large area south of the Yangtze, known in Tang times as Jiangnan, and graduated between 885 and 888. Nothing else is recorded of him.

Dai Shulun 732-789
A native of Jintan. An essayist as well as poet, with a successful administrative career. As provincial governor of Fuzhou, he improved the irrigation methods so that the agriculture yielded larger returns every year; the people were contented and respected him deeply. Later he became a Defence Commander of a Border district where he was equally admired.

Du Fu 712-770
Born at Duling in Shanxi. He was unsuccessful at the official examinations, but was appointed, fairly late in life, to some minor posts through the recommendation of influential friends. He held a small appointment under Emperor Xuanzong at the time of the An Lushan rebellion; on the Emperor's abdication, and while trying to join his successor, Suzong, Du Fu was captured by the rebels and detained for some time in the old Capital of Chang'an. He escaped and reached the Court of Suzong at Fengxiang, where he was rewarded with the post of Recorder in the Imperial Chancellery, 758. He was demoted the following year to the post of Education Officer at Huazhou, probably because his patron, the Minister Fang Guan, had fallen into disgrace. Du Fu resigned in 760 and spent the rest of his life wandering, his 'thatched hut' at a river village outside Chengdu in Sichuan being one of his more permanent resting places. In 766 he settled in Guizhou, where he wrote many of his most famous poems, describing the bitterness of exile and failure,

and the ruin of the Empire. He died while travelling alone by boat on a journey back to the Capital. His greatness of heart as well as his brilliant technique make him one of the most appealing of Chinese poets, he and Li Bai ranking together as the two greatest poets of China. William Hung has made an admirable study of this poet in his work 'Du Fu: China's Greatest Poet', and David Hawkes in his 'Little Primer of Du Fu' has examined with great critical insight those poems of Du Fu's which are included in this anthology.

Du Mu 803-852
Born in Chang'an. He graduated about 830 and rose to be Secretary in the Grand Council. He had a sterling character: broad-minded and bold in promoting what he believed to be right. This is also reflected in his poetry which is vigorous and daring in expression, warm-hearted and human in feeling. He was a master of the 7-character 'cut-short' (*jueju*). These are both vivid and effortless within their strict form.

Du Qiuniang Early 9th century
She was born at Jinling and at 15 married the poet Li Chi. At his death, she entered the Court of Emperor Muzong (reigned 821-825) as Lady-in-waiting and governess to the Heir Apparent, Prince Zhang. When the Prince was removed as Heir, she was allowed to return to her home town. She is the only woman poet represented in this anthology.

Du Shenyan 7th century
Born at Xiangyang, Hubei. He was an excellent calligraphist as well as poet. After graduating he had a small post as Clerk, and during the reign of Emperor Zhongzong (reigned 684-710) he was appointed Archivist in the Academy of Letters. He was the grandfather of the poet Du Fu.

Du Xunhe 846-904

He was born in Chizhou, a son of the poet Du Mu. He graduated in 891 and subsequently was made a member of the Hanlin Academy, which was open only to the most eminent scholars. On retiring from office, he went to live on Jiu Hua mountain as a recluse, styling himself 'The Man of Jiu Hua'. As a poet, he had specialised in 'Palace poetry', which became a distinct 'genre' in Tang times.

Emperor Xuanzong 685-761

The sixth Emperor of Tang dynasty, reigning 713-755. He was a great patron of the arts, a lover of music, poetry and dance, and himself a not inconsiderable poet. He surrounded himself with a brilliant Court and Chang'an became the centre of a glittering assembly of poets and painters. But his adventures in expanding the Tang empire, and the growing extravagance of the Court led to crippling taxation, and the administration was weakened by the appointment of eunuchs to official posts. This culminated in the rebellion of An Lushan in 755. Xuanzong fled from the Capital to Sichuan and abdicated in favour of his son, Suzong. The story of his love for the beautiful Yang Guifei, their escape from the rebels and her death are told in Bai Juyi's 'Everlasting regret' (p. 198).

Gao Shi Died 765

He came from Bo Hai in Cangzhou, Shandong, of a very poor family; as a youngster, he lived by begging. In the Tianbao period (742-756), when the composition of good poems was often the passport to a successful career at Court, Gao Shi, then over 50 started to study poetry. With his determined and steadfast character, he mastered the art and became a widely appreciated poet, winning the approval and friendship of Li Bai and Du Fu, especially for his ballad-type verse (*Yuefu*). His style is sometimes compared with that of Cen Shen; both wrote on the bitterness of fighting on the Chinese borders. He won the admiration of Geshu Han, an army Commander under Emperor Xuanzong, and became his secretary. In later life he was appointed Minister of Justice and Minister-in-Waiting, and was ennobled as Duke of Bo Hai.

Gu Kuang c.725-c.814
Born in Suzhou. He excelled in balled-type poetry (*Yuefu*), and was also a good painter and calligraphist. After graduating in 757 he became Assistant to the Commander Han Guang. Under Emperor Dezong (reigned 780-805) he was appointed Collator of Books in the Grand Secretariat, and a member of the Writers' Bureau. He was a great joker and showed scant respect for people in high position. In later life he went into retirement and became a recluse. He styled himself "The spiritual idler of Huayang" (the name of his mountain retreat).

Han Hong 8th century
A native of Nanyang in Henan. He graduated about 750 and rose to high position in later life, under Emperor Dezong (reigned 780-805), being appointed a Director in the Board of Prefectures and finally Secretary in the Grand Secretariat. He had a high reputation as a poet and belonged to the group known as the 'Ten Men of Genius of Dali period' (766-780)

Han Wo Died 905
Born in the Capital, Chang'an. He was a precocious scholar, able to write poetry at the age of 10. He graduated in 889, and under the last Tang Emperor, Zhaozong (reigned 889-905), he became Vice-Minister of War, and by Imperial decree was made a member of the Hanlin Academy, the highest reward of scholarship. His direction of military policy was so effective that

the Emperor wished to make him Prime Minister, but he repeatedly declined. He made a bitter enemy of Zu Quanzhong, a powerful General, who eventually forced the young Emperor to abdicate in his favour, and was for a time degraded to be Sub-Prefect of Dengzhou. In 904, Han Wo was restored to his former position, but with the continued enmity of Zhu Quanzhong, and his awareness of the impending fall of the dynasty, he dared not appear at Court. He took his family to Fujian and went into retirement under the protection of Wang Shenzhi (862-925), the able Governor of Fujian province.

Han Yu 768-824
Born at Nanyang in Henan. He was an assiduous scholar and enjoyed, on the whole, a successful career, holding many offices and rising to be President of the Board of Rites. As a writer and thinker, he was one of the most influential figures of the mid-Tang. Better known as essayist than as poet, he was leader of the 'Old Prose' movement which advocated a return to the simple, direct prose of Confucius and Mencius in place of the ornate style of his contemporaries. Much of his poetry is in the 'Old Style' (*Gu shi*) and displays considerable originality in diction and imagery. He initiated a revival of Confucianism which led to the decline of Buddhism in China and to the Neo-Confucianism of the Song philosophers. In both character and writings, he was a person of the utmost sincerity and breadth of outlook.

He Zizhang 659-745
A great drinker, talker and calligraphist as well as poet, who had a long and varied official career under Emperor Xuanzong (reigned 713-756). He befriended the young Li Bai when the latter first arrived at Court, and gave him the nickname of 'Banished Immortal'. They both belonged to the group of poets

who called themselves 'the Eight Immortals of the Wine-cup', and He's own name for himself was 'the Madman of Siming' (the district in Zhejiang from which his family came). In 743 he became ill and was unconscious for some days. When he recovered, he said he had been in the Taoist Heaven and asked to be allowed to resign his office and become a Taoist monk. At his departure for the Monastery of a Thousand Autumns, the Emperor himself, as well as many other leading poets of the day, composed poems of farewell.

Huangfu Ran 714-767

A native of Danyang. He was a precocious boy, able to compose a good essay at the age of 10. Zhang Jiuling, a prominent statesman and poet of early Tang, called him his "little friend." He graduated in 756 and was appointed as Chief Police Commissioner to the Magistrate of Wuxi. Not long after, he resigned and retired to the mountains of Yang Xian to escape the disorders of the An Lushan Rebellion. In later years he held good positions at Court, including that of Imperial Omissioner, and finally became envoy to Jiangnan — a huge area South of the Yangtze River.

Jia Dao 793-865

A native of Fanyang in Zhili. Having failed the official examinations repeatedly, he became a Buddhist monk at Luoyang. Later he went to live in Blue Dragon monastery at Chang'an. The story is told that he was once riding through the streets of the Capital on a donkey, searching for poetic inspiration, when he accidentally collided with the carriage of the prominent statesman and poet Han Yu. This led to a friendship between the two men; Han Yu, a Confucianist, persuaded the monk to give up the religious life and helped him to obtain a small official post. Much of his life was a struggle, and like Meng Jiao's, his poetry gives

evidence of the distress he suffered. He left ten volumes of poetry.
Jin Changxu 10th century
Hardly anything is recorded of this poet except that he came from Yuhang.

Li Bai 701-762
His birthplace is uncertain; possibly he was born in what is now Soviet Turkestan. He grew up in Sichuan, but left about 725 for a long period of wandering in Eastern China. He never seems to have set up his own home, did not sit the official examinations, and was not given any official appointment, though he was summoned to Court about 743 and remained for some time a Court Poet. His failure to obtain advancement was partly due to the jealousy of the powerful eunuch Gao Lishi, and partly no doubt to his own irresponsible nature and addiction to wine. He was implicated in the rising of Prince Lin, sixteenth son of Emperor Xuanzong, who in 757 attempted to set up an independent regime in Central China. For his part in this, Li Bai was imprisoned for some months, but then pardoned. As a young man, he was interested in Taoism and studied under the Taoist Master, Sima Changzheng. His extraordinary personality and poetic gifts won him the nickname of the 'Banished Immortal'. Li Bai is regarded by many Chinese as their greatest poet, especially for the splendour of his language and imagery and the originality of his thought. Arthur Waley has written a useful short biography of him.

Li Duan Later 8th century
Born in Zhaozhou, he lived as a boy on Lu mountain and studied under the monk-poet Jiaoran. In 770 he graduated and was appointed Collator of Books in the Grand Secretariat, though he was obliged to resign later owing to ill health. A subsequent appointment as Assistant Prefect of Hanzhou he also gave up and went into retirement on Heng mountain in Hunan. There he

devoted himself to poetry, to studying the Book of Changes, and to practising the 7-stringed lute. He is named among the 'Ten men of Genius of Dali period' (766-780).

Li Pin 9th century
He came from Luzhou in Shouchang. As a youngster he gave evidence of a quick intelligence and keen memory and appeared to be a promising poet. He graduated about 854. He was appointed Magistrate of Wukong and rose to be Censor-in-Waiting at Court. In later life he was made Prefect of Jianzhou where he set up an excellent administration, bringing peace and order to a region which had formerly been lawless and disturbed. In all his public life he worked conscientiously and without flattery. He died in office.

Li Qi Early 8th century
Born at Yingchuan. He graduated about 725 and rose to be Military Governor of Xinxiang district. His 'regulated verse' *(lü shi)*, which shows considerable originality, has been compared with Gao Shi's.

Li Shangyin c. 812-858
A native of Henei in Honan. He graduated about 836 and rose to be a Reader in the Hanlin Academy. He was an outstanding man of letters, as well reputed among his contemporaries as the poet Wen Tingyun, with whom his name is sometimes coupled, though Li is regarded as the more original. In 838 he married a daughter of his political patron, Wang Maoyuan. It is thought that his many untitled love poems were addressed to a concubine of Wang's, or possibly to a Taoist nun. His poems are full of suggestion and allusion, and he is one of the very few writers of *shi* to express the love of women. He uses the ornate, sumptuous imagery characteristic of late Tang poetry.

Li Yi c.749-c.827

Born in Longxi. He graduated about 769 but little is known of his career. As a writer, he has been compared with Li Bai, another very gifted poet of the mid-Tang. He enjoyed a wide popularity; it is said that musicians competed to buy a sheet of his ballads as soon as he had composed them. In later life he became a sub-Librarian in the Imperial Library, and finally retired as President of the Board of Rites.

Liu Changching Early 8th century

A native of Hejian. He graduated in the Kaiyuan period (713-742) and rose to be Governor of Suizhou. He was known for his firmness of character and the bold, downright expression of his thoughts. His poetry won high praise: a later poet, Quan Deyu (759-818), called him 'The Stalwart of 5-character verse'.

Liu Fangping 8th century

A native of Henan. He lived as a hermit on the Yingyang mountainside and never held any official appointment. He often exchanged verses with his poet friends, Huangfu Ran and Li Qi. He was also a good friend of Yuan Dexiu, also of Henan (died 754), at one time magistrate at Lushan, much beloved for his simplicity of life and compassion. Liu spent some time with the Duke of Xingguo, who wanted to recommend him to the Emperor for an appointment at Court, but he declined and returned to his mountain retreat. He excelled in describing scenery and his poems have a great appeal to the human heart.

Liu Shenxu 8th century

A native of Xinwu. He was a good friend of the poets Meng Haoran and Wang Changling. Critics have described his poetry as 'restrained in feeling, the passion controlled, the thoughts deep and the expression strikingly original.' He was a prolific writer and held various official posts, including Collator of Texts in the Academy of Letters.

Liu Yuxi 772-842
A native of Pengcheng. After graduating, he was appointed Censor, and in later life was successively Secretary and President of the Board of Rites. He was a scholar of considerable learning, an excellent essayist, and as a poet considered the equal of his two distinguished contemporaries, Han Yu and Liu Zongyuan. The two Lius served at Court together and exercised a strong influence upon the direction of policy. Many of his verses were satirical, which brought him into trouble and resulted in dismissal to provincial posts on several occasions during his career. The great poet Bai Juyi recognised his worth and praised him as a 'hero of song'.

Liu Zhongyong late 8th and early 9th centuries
Born in Hedong. Both he and his brother, Liu Zhongxing, enjoyed a high reputation in the literary world of their time. He held a small post as Chief Clerk in the Department of Taxes at Hongfu.

Liu Zongyuan 773-819
A native of Hedong. A good scholar, calligraphist and essayist as well as poet, He rose to be Secretary to the Board of Rites, but in 815 was demoted to be Governor of Liuzhou in Guangxi. He was a friend of the statesman and poet, Han Yu, who wrote a memorial of him, describing his work as 'virile, deep, refined, vigorous'.

Lu Lun Later 8th century
A native of Pu. He graduated about 766. A literary patron, Wei Chumou, recommended his talents to Emperor Dezong who sum-

moned him to Court. He held the post of Executive Assistant to a Military Command, and later that of Acting Director in the Ministry of Revenue. He won a high reputation as a writer and poet — he was one of the 'Ten Men of Genius of Dali period' (766-780).

Luo Binwang Early 7th century
Born at Yiwu, Zhejiang. He could read and write poetry at the age of 7, and in time became a prominent essayist and poet — he was known as one of the 'Four Heroes of Early Tang', the other three being Wang Bo, Yang Jiong and Lu Zhaolin. At the death of Emperor Gaozong in 684, the throne was usurped by Empress Wu. Luo accepted a small post as clerk at Linhai, but later resigned and joined the party of Xu Jinye who led a rebellion against the Empress in favour of the legitimate successor. The movement failed, Luo Binwang escaped with his life, but his ultimate fate is not known. Some say he retired to a monastery and became a Buddhist.

Ma Dai Mid 9th century
He graduated about 844 and was given a small post as a clerk. He rose later to be Collator of Texts, but fell into disfavour and was given some posts with the army at Lunyang and Datong. Finally his scholarly merits were recognised and he received a Doctorate.

Meng Haoran 689-740
Born at Xiangyang in Hubei. He failed to pass the official examinations and retired to the mountains (Lumen shan) to lead the life of a recluse. Wang Wei once introduced him to Emperor Xuanzong, but he caused offence and was dismissed. He became a poet of the first rank and won the approbation of Li Bai and Zhang Jiuling among others. Li Bai's poem 'For Meng Haoran'

(p. 300) gives a good picture of his character. He was predominantly a nature poet, like his friend Wang Wei, and his simple, unforced style had much in common with Wang's too.

Meng Jiao 751-814
Born in Wukang. He did not pass the official examinations till he was 50 and obtained only minor official posts. The bitterness of poverty shows in his work. He belonged to the circle of poets led by Han Yu, and used the bold imagery and rough, direct diction of that group.

Pei Di Mid 8th century
Born in Guanzhong. Sometime after the Tianbao period (742-756) he became Military Governor of Shuzhou, but little is known about his career. He was a good friend of the poets Du Fu, Li Qi, and especially Wang Wei, with whom he lived in retirement for some time at Wang's mountain retreat. Here they wrote a series of poems together, 'Poems of the River Wang' (translated in 'Poems of Solitude' by Jerome Chen and Michael Bullock), but not much of his other work has been preserved.

Qian Qi 8th century
Born at Wuxing. He graduated about 750 and held the post of Collator of Books. Later he became a Director in the official Examining Board. He was an admirer of the poet Wang Wei, to whom he addresses one of these poems, and formed one of the group known as 'The Ten Men of Genius of Dali period' (766-780).

Qin Taoyu Late 9th century
A native of Chang'an. He was fortunate in enjoying the friendship of the influencial eunuch Tian Lingzi, who helped him into several good appointments. Under this patronage, he rose to be Director of the Bureau of Salt and Iron. In 882 he graduated

with the highest rank and became Secretary in the Ministry of Works. He left three volumes of poems.

Qiu Wei 8th century

Born at Jiaxing. He held high position as Assistant Tutor to the Heir Apparent. He had a long official career and did not retire from office till over 80. He is known for his filial devotion to his stepmother whom he continued to support all her life, giving her half his salary. He was a good friend of Wang Wei and Liu Changqing.

Qiwu Qian Early 8th century

He was born at Jingnan and graduated during the Kaiyuan period (713-42). He held the appointments of Minister-in-Waiting at Jixian Palace, and Assistant Minister to the Board of Works. He was recognised as a talented man of letters, with a high reputation as a poet.

Quan Deyu 759-818

Born in Luoyang. It was said that he could understand poetry at 4 years of age, and by 15 had written a large volume of essays. His father died when he was a young boy, and though he was not able to sit for the official examinations, Emperor Dezong (reigned 780-805) heard of his talent and appointed him as Secretary in the Grand Secretariat. Under Emperor Xianzong (reigned 806-821) he rose to be President of the Board of Rites with the right to attend Cabinet meetings and make administrative decisions; later he presided over the Ministry of Justice. He was a highly cultured person of outstanding intellect and admirable moral character. In spite of his high position, he lived without ostentation, greatly loved and admired by friends and colleagues. He left 50 volumes of poetry and essays.

Shen Quanqi Died 713
Born in Neihuang, Henan. He graduated about 680 and held a post in the Bureau of Literature. He and Song Zhiwen (660-710) were regarded as the two leading poets of that period. Both contributed much to the development of the characteristic Tang poetry with its rich language and complicated verse forms. On one occasion, the Emperor was so delighted with a poem of Shen Quanqi that he presented him with gifts of ivory and silk. He was eventually appointed Adviser to the Heir-Apparent, and died in that office.

Sikong Shu 8th century
A native of Guangping, Hebei. A distinguished poet and official, known as one of the 'Ten Men of Genius of Dali period' (766-780). He served as Magistrate of Zhanglin, was promoted to the office of Remembrancer of the Left, and finally became a Director in the Ministry of Works. His style is described as limpid but colourful. He left two volumes of poetry.

Song Zhiwen c. 660-710
Born in Fenzhou, Shanxi. During the reign of Empress Wu (reigned 684-705), he served as Minister-in-Waiting at Court. When one of the Empress' favourites, Zhang Yizhi, was discovered to have treasonable designs against her, Song Zhiwen, who belonged to Zhang's party, was banished. After the Empress' abdication in 705 he was recalled and appointed Archivist in the Court of State Ceremonial. He was one of the most delightful poets of his time, and his name is coupled with that of Shen Quanqi as having helped to perfect the 'new style' poetry, evolved during the Tang period.

The monk Jiaoran Died 754
He came from North China, from a family of the surname Xie,

and was a descendant in the tenth generation of Xie Lingyun, a well-known poet of the 4th century. In middle age he became a Buddhist and lived as a recluse on Chu mountain, Huzhou. The poet Wei Yingwu thought highly of his writings; he was also a good friend of Yan Zhenqing, an eminent general and a good calligraphist.

Wang Bo 648-675
Born at Longmen, Jiangzhou, in Shanxi. A grandson of Wang Tong of Sui dynasty. He was a precocious scholar, starting to write at the age of six and graduating before he was twenty. He was employed by the Emperor in preparing the dynastic histories. When only twenty-nine, he was drowned while crossing the sea to visit his father who was Governor of Jiaozhi (modern Indo-china). Together with the poets Yang Jiong, Luo Binwang and Lu Zhaolin, he was known as one of the 'Four Heroes of Early Tang.'

Wang Changling 8th century
Born at Jiangning. He graduated during the Kaiyuan period (713-742) and was appointed Keeper of the Imperial Archives. Later he fell into disfavour and was demoted to a minor post at Longbiao. During the Rebellion, he was killed by the Censor Lu Qiuxiao. His poetry is noted for its clarity of thought and metrical accomplishment; his 7-character 'cut-shorts' (*jueju*) were considered among the best in the period.

Wang Han Early 8th century
A native of Jinyang. He graduated about 710 and held a number of official posts, including Assistant Director in the Ministry of Public Works and Vice-Prefect of Xianzhou. As a youth he was adventurous and somewhat overbearing, loved to drink and gamble. Later in life he had a passion for hunting and for engaging in

dangerous adventures. He left 10 volumes of his works.

Wang Jian Late 8th and early 9th centuries
Born at Yingchuan, Anhui. He graduated in 775 and served as Assistant to the Magistrate of Weinan. Later he was made Censor-in-waiting at Court, and in 831 Assistant Prefect of Xiazhou. He was a distinguished poet, specially praised for his ballad-type poetry (*yuefu*). His collection of 'One hundred Palace poems' (*Gong Ci Bai Shou*) became famous. A good friend of the poets Han Yu and Zhang Ji (Wenchang).

Wang Wan Early 8th century
A native of Luoyang. He graduated about 712 and after holding a small post in the Yingyang district, he entered the Department for the Collating of Classical texts. In later life, he held an administrative office as Chief of Police at Luoyang.

Wang Wei 699-759
A native of Taiyuan, Shanxi. He was successful in the Imperial examinations at the age of twenty, and held the appointments of Court Musician, Censor and Court Secretary. During the An Lushan rebellion, he fell into the hands of the rebels, but Emperor Suzong pardoned him and made him Vice-Premier in 757. His wife died young, but he never re-married. In later life he became a devout Buddhist and lived in extreme simplicity at his country retreat at Lantian by the river Wang, a little south of the Capital, Chang'an, where he died in 759. He was an accomplished painter, as well as poet and musician, and was described as the founder of the Southern School of landscape painting by the Ming art critic, Dong Qichang. His poetry is largely 'word-painting', very pure and limpid in diction.

Wang Zhihuan 8th century

A native of Bingzhou. He had an enterprising, chivalrous nature and as a young man enjoyed making heroic exploits with his friends. In middle age he began to study seriously and won fame as a writer, together with his two brothers, Wang Zhixian and Wang Zhifeng. His poems were much sought after by musicians for setting to music. The story is told of his visiting an inn to drink with two friends, Gao Shi and Wang Changling, also distinguished poets. A number of actors were entertaining the company with songs, and without having recognised the newcomers they sang a poem of Gao Shi's, two of Wang Changling's and finally the handsomest actor sang three of Wang Zhihuan's. The story indicates the value set on Wang Zhihuan's poetry by his contemporaries.

Wei Yingwu 735-830

A native of Chang'an. As a young man he was a member of Emperor Xuanzong's bodyguard, but he later studied and obtained official appointments, becoming Governor of Suzhou about 785. Suzhou was then a cultural centre, and Wei belonged to a circle of well-known poets there. He was a benevolent administrator of great personal integrity. His poetry is relaxed and direct, and is compared by some with the pastoral poetry of Tao Yuanming (375-427) for its simple, lucid utterance.

Wei Zhuang Early 10th century

Born in Duling. He graduated in 902 and served as Secretary to Wang Jian, a somewhat unscrupulous politician who won the favour of Emperor Xizong and was made Prince of Shu (Sichuan). Wang threw off his allegiance to the Emperor and set himself up as ruler in Shu, Wei Zhuang serving as his First Minister. Wei was of an easy-going, carefree nature; as a poet, his lyrics (*ci*) were rated as highly as his *shi*. While living in Sichuan he searched for the great Du Fu's original 'thatched hut' and had it repaired.

Wen Tingyun Mid 9th century
A native of Taiyuan. He failed to pass the official examinations, though he held a few posts in the government. He was skillful at lyric poetry (*ci*) and essays as well as 'regulated verse', and had a reputation in poetry equal to that of his great contemporary Li Shangyin.

Xu Hun Early 9th century
A native of Danyang. He graduated about 832 and rose to be an Examining Censor and Assistant Director in the Ministry of Finance, having formerly held administrative posts in Anhui and Yunzhou. He won praise both for his administration and his poetry which was immaculate in composition and powerful in feeling.

Xue Feng 9th century
A native of Hedong in Puzhou. He graduated in 841 and held some small official posts until, under the patronage of Cui Xuan, a Prime Minister, he was invited to become a member of the Academy of Letters. He finally rose to be Secretary of State. He was a prolific poet, leaving 10 volumes of poems.

Yuan Jie 719-772
He graduated in his early twenties. At the accession of Suzong in 756, he was summoned to Court and served for a time but later went to live at Fanshang in Hubei and wrote for his own pleasure. Later in life, he became Governor of Daozhou and was highly respected in that office. He abolished forced labour on government service, provided for refugees, and kept bandits under control. He restored peace to many districts; the people praised his administration and set up a memorial to him commending

his virtues. He spent his last days at the Capital, dying at fifty.

Yuan Zhen 779-831
He came from Henan and was a descendant of the Imperial family of Wei Tartars who ruled North China in the 5th and 6th centuries. He passed the Imperial examinations at the same time as the poet Bai Juyi, and with him was given the post of Collator of Texts in the Imperial Library. In 802 he married a girl of nineteen called Wei Huicong, who died seven years later. He wrote a long series of poems about his bereavement, of which three are included in this collection. In 806 he was appointed Omissioner, but fell into disfavour and was banished to Jiangling in Hubei. In 814 he became Marshal of Tongzhou, and was even promoted to Chief Minister for a short while in 822. Finally he became President of the Board of Rites. As a poet he cultivated a plain style, as did Bai Juyi, his life-long friend. Abandoning the elaborate imagery and formality of expression found in much Tang poetry, he wrote with natural feeling and humanity. Bai Juyi said of him: "Your strong point as a writer is that even when hampered by the rules and restrictions of cramping literary forms, you always manage to say exactly what you want to say."

Zhang Bi 10th century
He came from Huainan and served as an official under the Southern Tang, one of the Five Dynasties which ruled after the breakup of the Tang. Not much is known of his life: he appears to have served as Chief of Police to the Magistrate of Jurong, and to have been promoted to the post of secretary in the Grand Secretariat.

Zhang Hu Early 9th century
He came from Nanyang but lived at first in Suzhou. In the mid-Zhangqing period (821-825) he enjoyed the patronage of the

statesman Linghu Chu who recommended him to the Emperor, but he was maliciously attacked by the poet Yuan Zhen and lost the Emperor's favour. Later he became a good friend of the poets Du Mu and Bai Juyi. He ended his days as a hermit. He is specially known for his 'Palace poetry', examples of which are included in this collection.

Zhang Ji (Zhang Yisun) Died 780

He was born in Xiangzhou, Hubei, and graduated in 753. He held the post of Executive Assistant in the Ministry of Finance, and later Assistant Director of the Bureau of Temples in the Ministry of Rites. The feeling in his poetry is pure and rather remote — a Taoist flavour. The example included in this collection: 'Anchored at night by Maple bridge' was widely cited and became his most famous poem.

Zhang Ji (Zhang Wenchang) c.765-c.830

He came from Wujiang in N. Anhui, graduating about 799. The great writer and statesman Han Yu praised his scholarship and recommended him to the Emperor. He rose to be Tutor in the Imperial Academy. Familiar with all the outstanding scholars and poets of his day, he was specially noted for his ballad-type verse (*Yuefu*) and for his originality of expression.

Zhang Jiuling 673-740

He was a native of Qujiang in Guangdong, an outstanding scholar with great integrity of character, who rose to the highest office in the earlier part of Emperor Xuanzong's reign. After graduating high on the list of candidates for *Jinshi*, he became Omissioner and later, in 736, Chief Minister. He ventured to remonstrate against the licentiousness of the Court and the misrule brought about by the influence of powerful eunuchs. He also tried, though without success, to warn the Emperor against the treasonable designs of An Lushan. In 737 he was forced out of office by Li Linfu, who made himself a virtual dictator in the period 737-52, and banished to Jingzhou. His poems are among the most brilliant of the early Tang.

Zhang Qiao Second half of the 9th century
He came from Chizhou and graduated during the Xiantong period (860-74). Little is known of his career but he seems to have enjoyed a considerable reputation as a poet, being known as one of the 'Ten Men of Genius' of the time. During a political rebellion, he retired to Jiu Hua and lived as a hermit.

Zhang Xu 8th century
He was a native of Suzhou in Jiangsu. He belonged to the group of poets, which included Li Bai and He Zhizhang, who called themselves the 'Eight Immortals of the Wine-cup', and also appears in the poems of Du Fu and Gao Shi. A brilliant calligraphist, especially in the 'grass' style, and an unconventional, bohemian character who came to be known as 'Crazy Zhang', he also has the nickname, 'The Divine Grass-writer'. There was a saying that Li Bai's poetry, Pei Min's performance of the Sword Dance and Zhang Xu's 'grass' writing were the Three Wonders of the age.

Zheng Tian c.823-c.885
He came from Yingyang and graduated about 841. He was then so young that the Emperor Wuzong doubted his ability and tested him personally. His official career was a distinguished one. He became a Counsellor under the Prime Minister Liu Zhan, who recommended him for the Hanlin Academy, an institution for scholars of the highest learning. After serving in the Grand Secretariat, he was promoted by Emperor Xizong to be Vice-minister of War, sharing responsibility in the making of policies. He took

an active part in the suppression of the Huangchao rebellion, as Military Commander at Fengjiang, and later, as a Minister without portfolio, he helped shape the policies which restored order to the whole country. He left 65 volumes of writings.

Zhu Qingyu Early 9th century
A native of Yuezhou. He graduated about 825 but nothing is recorded of his subsequent career. A friend of the poet Zhang Ji (Wenchang).

Zu Yong Early 8th century
Born in Luoyang. He graduated about 724. Under the patronage of the poet and statesman Zhang Yue (667-730) he became Secretary in the Board of Rites. He was also a good friend of the poet Wang Wei. His style is graceful and precise, meticulous in the choice of words.

國家圖書館出版品預行編目資料

英譯唐詩三百首 / Innes Herdan 英譯；蔣彝繪畫,
　-- 初版. -- 臺北市：遠東, 2000 [民 89]
　　　面；　　公分
　　中英對照
　　ISBN　978-957-612-471-6（精裝）
831.4　　　　　　　　　　　　　　　　89015983

THE 300 TANG POEMS
英 譯 唐 詩 三 百 首

25 K精裝本定價 550 元 (外埠酌加運匯費)

英　譯　者 /	Innes　Herdan
繪　畫　者 /	蔣　　　　　　　　　彝
出　版　者 /	遠　東　圖　書　股　份　有　限　公　司
印　刷　者 /	遠　東　圖　書　股　份　有　限　公　司
發　行　所 /	遠　東　圖　書　股　份　有　限　公　司
地　　　址 /	台 北 市 重 慶 南 路 一 段 6 6 - 1 號

www.fareast.com.tw

電　　　話 / (02) 23118740　　傳真 / (02) 23114184
郵 政 劃 撥 / 00056691
登　記　證 / 局版台業字第 0820 號